Combating Computer Crime

Prevention, Detection, Investigation

Combating Computer Crime

Prevention, Detection, Investigation

Chantico Publishing Company, Inc.

McGraw-Hill, Inc.

New York St. Louis San Francisco Auckland Bogotá Caracas
Lisbon London Madrid Mexico City Milan Montreal New Delhi
Paris San Juan São Paulo Singapore Sydney Tokyo Toronto

FIRST EDITION
FIRST PRINTING

© 1992 by **Chantico Publishing Company, Inc.**
Published by **McGraw-Hill, Inc.**

Library of Congress Cataloging-in-Publication Data

Combating computer crime : prevention, detection, investigation / by
    Chantico Publishing Company.
p.   cm.
Includes index.
    ISBN 0-8306-7664-3
    1. Computer crimes—Investigation.   2. Computer crimes-
-Prevention.   I. Chantico Publishing Co.
HV8079.C65C65   1990
363.2'5968—dc20   90-44600
                                                       CIP

For information about other McGraw-Hill materials,
call 1-800-2-MCGRAW in the U.S. In other countries
call your nearest McGraw-Hill office.

Senior Editor: Jerry Papke
Technical Editor: Laura Bader
Production: Katherine G. Brown
Book Design: Jaclyn J. Boone
Cover Design: Lori E. Schlosser

Contents

1

How to use this book

THIS BOOK EXPLAINS WHY A MANAGEMENT PLAN OF ACTION IS VITAL TO the establishment of an effective computer crime prevention program that guards against unacceptable risk while surfacing those risks that are acceptable from a cost/payback view. It describes the options available to senior management in preventing and detecting computer crime. It explains the categories of computer crime threats and examines the strategies available to management to reduce computer crime. Strategies are identified in terms of effectiveness against threats. The end-product of this part is twofold:

- A recommended organizational computer crime policy
- A management level plan of action for implementing that policy

It is designed to identify **computer crime risks**. Procedures are then presented to help organizations identify threats to which the organization is most vulnerable. Several techniques are presented for identifying computer crime vulnerability profiles to illustrate the threats requiring the most attention.

It describes how to **prevent computer crime**. Two options are available for addressing computer crime. The first is to install measures aimed at preventing the computer crime, and the second is using measures that **detect computer crime**. In actual practice, both approaches are necessary. "How to" information is presented for supporting the prevention strategies adopted during the management computer crime plan of action.

The fourth thrust of this book is how to detect computer crime. The standard management and audit functions are not designed to specifically detect computer fraud, but if properly executed, they should detect such frauds over a period of time. Large computer crimes should be easily detected, while smaller ones can be detected through management oversight and audit tests over an extended period. Some computer crime detection methods are introduced, in addition to the emphasis placed on the value of many regular management and audit practices that are beneficial in detecting computer crime. Detection involves investigation, which plays an important part in the uncovering of computer crime.

The science of preventing and detecting computer crime is maturing. Unfortunately, at the same time the enforcement mechanisms improve, criminals are learning new and better ways to defraud organizations. In order to keep the users of this manual current in the new methods of conducting, preventing, and detecting computer crime, this manual will be periodically updated.

Senior management

Computer crime is a responsibility of senior management. While they personally need not be involved in the prevention and detection of computer crime, it is important that they establish an appropriate environment to encourage the prevention and detection of computer crime.

Chapter 2 explains how to establish a computer crime policy and a management plan of action to implement that policy. The material in chapters 3, 4, and 5 provide the necessary background information needed to develop an effective computer crime policy and plan of action.

Senior management should take personal responsibility for developing the computer crime policy and plan of action. This does not exclude assistance by staff personnel. Rather, it implies strong management support for such a policy and plan of action and a personal involvement by one or more members of senior management in the development of that policy and plan.

Operating management

The primary responsibility for the prevention of computer crime resides with operating management. Operating management should also be involved in the detection of computer crime, even though it may not be one of their prime responsibilities. Because operating management is so closely involved with day-to-day events, they are frequently one of the first parties to detect irregularities in computer processing.

Because responsibility for the correctness of computer systems is shared between user and data processing management, there is a shared responsibility for the prevention of computer crime.

Auditors and investigators

The internal and external auditors, investigators, and other assessment-oriented individuals have a primary responsibility for detecting computer crime. Although their investigations may result in recommendations to prevent computer crime, this is a by-product of their investigative work. This does not imply that all auditors and investigatory individuals have a computer crime prevention responsibility but, rather, if the responsibility exists in an organization, it most likely exists with review-type individuals.

Information services department

Information services/data processing personnel implement the controls in automated applications. They are responsible for assisting users in protecting their applications and for creating a computer environment in which it is difficult to commit a crime. In some organizations, the data processing organization may perform much of the computer crime analyses for the users, in which case they will assume some of the user management responsibilities.

Legal implications

According to the *Computer Crime Investigation Manual* by Timothy A. Shaebeck, the legal implications of computer crime are as follows:

> Elements of computer crime: The Battelle study for the Law Enforcement Assistance Administration entitled *The Investigation of White-Collar Crime: A Manual for Law Enforcement Agencies*, defines the five elements of white-collar crime. In general, these five elements can also apply to computer crime. It is important to recognize at the outset that the elements discussed below apply more to the white-collar types of computer crime and not to types of "common" crime, such as arson or burglary.

As stated in the white-collar crime manual, it is important that the investigator and prosecutor of white-collar crime, vis-à-vis computer crime, recognize that these crimes invariably display certain characteristics. It is possible to analyze the execution of these schemes and note that the offenders have certain common objectives. Familiarity with these five elements can serve as a general framework for planning and undertaking action to combat computer crime.

Before reviewing the individual elements, consideration must be given to the possible cycle or recidivist nature of computer crime (see Fig. 1-1). The majority of the computer crimes that are responsible for large monetary losses take place over a period of time and usually require the repeated commission and covering up of an illegal act. Usually, only small amounts of money are embezzled from an organization at one time. However, over a period of time, the amount usually grows (as in the financial industry where computer-related embezzlements average $1.5 million).

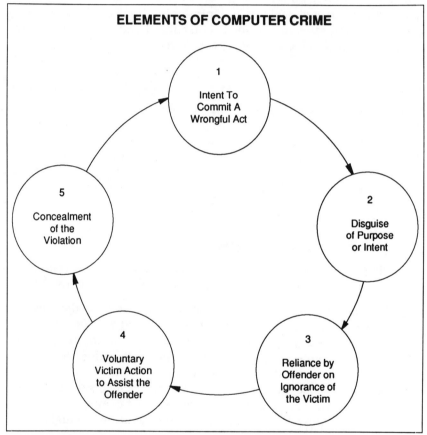

Fig. 1-1. Elements of computer crime.

Elements of computer crime

Intent to commit a wrongful act   As mentioned earlier, many of the computer abuse incidents border on the line between unethical and illegal acts. However, most electronic data processing (EDP) personnel know the essence of the laws that apply to their conduct in their work environment and can be held responsible for their acts. These people usually know when they are involved in a wrongful act, although they may not have an awareness that a particular statute is being violated. Intent involves the presence of some wrongful purpose or objective.

Disguise of purpose or intent   Disguise of purpose involves the character of the offender's conduct or activity in the implementation of his plan. He uses disguise to cover up the actions he undertakes to implement his scheme. Disguises can take the form of forged source documents, altered computer input or output, or hidden program routines. Verbal disguise is also usually employed in combination with these items.

Reliance by the offender on ignorance or carelessness of the victim   *The Investigation of White-Collar Crime* manual states, "While intent and disguise, the first two elements, are clearly elements which originate with and are controlled by the white-collar offender—involving the offender's own objective and chosen method of execution—reliance . . . on ignorance and carelessness of the victim is a victim-related element, since it is based upon the offender's perception of victim susceptibility. The offender will not go forward unless he feels he can depend upon the inability of the victim to perceive deception."

One of the biggest fears that a computer criminal has is the fear of being caught. In order to avoid this situation, he carefully plans and executes the crime, taking great care to cover his trail to avoid being apprehended.

Voluntary victim action to assist the offender   The offender must usually induce the victim to voluntarily undertake some act for his illegal scheme to be successfully completed. In computer crime instances, this may include the following:

- Obtaining management approval to run a test on the organization's accounts receivable system. The "test" is really a disguise for the offender to produce a list of the organization's customers which will then be sold to a competitor.

- Creating fictitious medical claims so that payment checks are generated by the computer, signed by the authorizing personnel, and mailed to the offender.

- One of the early classical cases of computer crime involved MICR encoded bank deposit slips. The offender ordered extra slips from the bank that were MICR encoded with his account number. Upon receipt of these slips, he went to several of the bank's branches and put his deposit slips with blank deposit slips at the counters. Although the bank's customers wrote their own account number on the deposit slip, the MICR scanner only read the MICR code provided on the bottom of the slip. The perpetrator accumulated $250,000 in 4 days from other people's deposits. He then withdrew $100,000 from his account. He has never been apprehended.

Concealment of the violation   It is important for the computer criminal to conceal his illegal acts in order to be able to continuously repeat his crime and, of course, to avoid being caught. It is a well-known fact that the best computer fraud schemes will probably never be detected. In fact, about 95 percent of the computer crimes that have been uncovered to date have been uncovered purely by accident, not through investigation.

Concealment is important to the computer criminal because he usually works in the open as an employee of the organization. Due to the nature of the computer and its processes, concealment can be quite easy, especially in the remote terminal teleprocessing environment. Manipulation of accounts via a remote terminal aids in concealing the identity of the offender.

In addition to the assault from the outside, computer professionals must take into account the violations of law that can occur within their own company and cause them to become computer criminals. Several large corporations have been successfully sued for copyright violations. For example, Lotus Development Corporation sued Rixon, Inc., for $10 million because Rixon copied and distributed Lotus 1-2-3 to its branch offices. Since then, Lotus has also sued The Health Group in Nashville, Tennessee, for over $1 million. With this kind of precedent, it is important for managers to ensure that their employees do not violate copyright laws.

Most of the examples of computer crime presented deal with large computer systems. However, the proliferation of micro- or personal computers has accelerated the incidence of computer crime, both because the number of computers available to attack has increased, and because there are more computer-literate people capable of committing these crimes. Therefore, it is incumbent upon all levels of computer professionals within an organization to support the computer security effort. In this book we will explore the methods of support that have worked in other companies in hopes that they will provide additional ideas for the computer professionals of today.

2

Developing a plan of action

THE PREVENTION AND DETECTION OF COMPUTER CRIME ARE IMPORTANT responsibilities. The fulfillment of these responsibilities involves the development of a computer crime policy and a plan of action to implement that policy. The growing threat of computer crime makes it difficult for any computer owner to avoid addressing this potential threat.

This chapter describes the magnitude of the threat of computer crime. It also describes the need for a computer crime prevention policy, how to develop such a policy, and the process of developing a plan of action for implementing that policy.

Classes of computer crime

Computer crime is crime against an organization or individual in which a computer is involved. The Equity Funding Insurance Company fraud in the late 1970s was the first highly publicized example of a crime involving a computer.

The commonly accepted definition of computer crime is a **"crime against an organization in which the perpetrator of that crime uses a computer for all or part of the crime."** This is a very general definition, but we know that the computer can be used as a tool to help commit a crime, or the data within the computer can be manipulated to result in a loss to the organization. The two classes of computer crime are fraud and abuse.

Of the two terms (fraud and abuse), *fraud* is the only term with a precise, legal definition. It is defined as "obtaining something of value unlawfully, through willful misrepresentation." It is an intentional perversion of truth designed to induce another to part with something of value. The key aspects of fraud are that it is intentional, it is unlawful, and there is an element of misrepresentation. An example of fraud is a physician who submits a claim for reimbursement under medical insurance for a service he/she knows was never performed.

The following are definitions of computer fraud and computer crime:

> "*Computer fraud* is any defalcation or embezzlement accomplished by tampering with computer programs, data files, operations, equipment or media, and resulting in losses sustained by the organization whose computer system was manipulated. In most instances, this would encompass all activities in the computer department, as well as those departments that directly enter or prepare computer input." Brandt Allen, "The Biggest Computer Frauds." *Journal of Accountancy*.

> "We define *computer-related crimes* as acts of intentionally caused losses to the government or personal gains to individuals related to the design, use, or operation of the systems in which they are committed. Computer-based data processing systems are comprised of more than the computer hardware and the programs (software) on which they are run. The systems include the organizations and procedures (some manual) for preparing input to the computer and using output from it. Computer-related crimes may result from preparing false input to systems and misuse of output, as well as more technically sophisticated crimes, such as altering computer programs." *U.S. General Accounting Office*.

Abuse is the improper use of resources provided by an organization to the individual who misuses those resources. The key aspects of abuse are that it is intentional and improper, but it does not necessarily imply the violation of a specific law or the presence of misrepresentation. In theory, any conduct or activity that is fraudulent will also be abusive. When an individual commits fraud against an organization, the individual is abusing the organization's programs. Examples of abuses that are not fraudulent are an employee who makes excessive telephone calls from his office phone, or a computer user who uses a company computer for personal business or financial gain.

Computer fraud and abuse both involve the intentional and improper use of the computer, but fraud also implies the violation of a law or the presence of misrepresentation. Obviously, abuse is much harder to diagnose and prove than fraud; but in actual practice, computer abuse may be much more costly to organizations than computer fraud. Fortunately, the same measures that prevent and detect computer fraud are also effective against computer abuse.

The true definition of computer abuse is more difficult to pin down. In general, any abuse will involve the unauthorized use or manipulation of computer equipment and often the data contained within that equipment. Some additional examples of specific types of abuse will clarify the definition.

Storing personal data on a company machine can be considered abuse, for it consumes valuable storage resources. On the other hand, a much more serious type of abuse can involve the theft or destruction of data. In the case of Donald Gene Burleson of Fort Worth, Texas, the abuse took the form of a logic bomb left in the company's computer after his employment had been terminated. When the bomb went off, it destroyed 168,000 sales commission records. The loss of this data was unrecoverable and Burleson was convicted of "harmful access." This represented the first time a computer user was convicted in an abuse case.

Another widely publicized example of massive computer abuse was the virus released over many networks by Robert Morris, Jr. It has been determined that this virus cost many millions of dollars to clean up, and it was designed as a harmless virus! Like Burleson, Morris was convicted of misuse of a computer.

There is a third class of computer crime which is spreading like an epidemic across the computer community and does not fall neatly into either the fraud or the abuse category. This is the theft of computer software through illegal copying. Software piracy is considered the most common and most expensive type of computer crime. Although many people feel that stealing software is a personal matter, the liability of both the individual and the company whose employees are stealing copyrighted software must be examined.

Examples of computer crime

In the preceding chapter we looked at some specific examples of particular computer crimes which illustrated class distinctions. However, the spread of computer crime has touched nearly every form of occupation. It is estimated that within 10 years all crimes will involve the computer in some way. Currently computer crime breaks down into six major areas. Listed below are each of those areas and their related percentages:

- Trespass, 2%
- Theft of services, 10%
- Alteration of data, 12%
- Damage to software, 16%

- Theft of information or programs, 16%
- Theft of money, 44%

(Source: National Center for Computer Crime Data.)

Looking at this list, it is obvious that no one is safe from some form of computer attack. The attack may take the form of simple trespass, or it may be a more insidious invasion via some sort of destruction software such as a virus or Trojan horse.

It would be foolish to assume that the computer user is always the target of the crime and not, at times, the perpetrator. Software piracy has reached epidemic proportions across the computer community. Looking at the numbers, it seems safe to say that most personal computers in homes and businesses today have at least one "hot" program in residence. It may be a shareware program for which the user has yet to pay, or it may be a more blatant "borrowed" copy of a game or utility. Software developers have determined that for each copy of a software package sold, between one and three illegal copies exist. Sometimes this form of crime takes on almost laughable proportions. Studies of college students have found some with hundreds of stolen programs amounting to millions of dollars.

It is also common for a company to buy one copy of a business program and then copy it across all the machines in the company. This form of computer theft has recently been the target of extensive litigation. The personal computer software publisher Ashton-Tate, in the person of Geoffrey A. Berkin, is suing several major corporations who have illegal copies of some popular business programs such as dBase III.

Other examples of major computer crimes include:

- Rebecca Doyle, who owned a title company in St. Petersburg, Florida, and was once named American Businesswoman of the Year, was charged with embezzling $2 million using a computer.

- In 1985, American Brands Co. paid an undisclosed amount to Micropro International Corporation and Association of Data Processing Service Organizations Inc. through an out-of-court settlement of a software piracy claim. American Brands admitted some of its employees had stolen copies of programs such as WordStar, a Micropro program.

- For over a year an intruder had free access to the data files of over 36 U.S. military research computers. This intruder was working from his home in West Germany, picking out data on the Strategic Defense Initiative and other defense-related topics. If it had not been for the curiosity of Clifford Stoll, a manager of computer systems at the Lawrence Berkeley Labs in California, this hacker might still have free reign of those computers.

- Robert Morris's computer worm, mentioned above, was released on November 2, 1988, and in a matter of hours had infected some 2,000 to 5,000 computers across the country. It took between $2 and $60 million to recover from this worm, which was not destructive by design. The excessive cost was merely to remove the worm from the infected systems and recover lost time and productivity.

No listing of computer crimes is complete without at least considering the virus issue. Much has been printed about this class of computer software which attacks computers and then replicates (or copies) itself across many programs within the computer under attack. The Scores virus is an excellent example of this type of program. It spread across many Macintosh computers including those owned by the FBI (Federal Bureau of Investigation) and NASA (National Aeronautics and Space Administration). This virus caused thousands of dollars of damage, and took untold hours to remove from systems that had been infected.

And then there are computer-related crimes that have a profoundly physical aspect. In 1988, in Manhattan, a disgruntled ex-employee walked into the main computer room of a major financial institution and shot the bank's computer six times with a .38. Thousands of files were destroyed and some were never recovered.

Many millions of dollars are lost each year to computer-related crime. Now we will examine just how great this threat is to the average computer user.

Magnitude of the computer crime threat

As a result of computer crime, U.S. organizations lose several billion dollars per year. There are many reasons why the amount is difficult to pinpoint.

Lack of definition of computer crime

Without a precise definition, crimes involving the computer may not be properly categorized.

Difficulty in detecting computer crime

Most experts believe that the magnitude of computer crimes is far greater than that reported by law enforcement agencies. This premise is based on the lack of good controls and detection measures against computer crime. Without appropriate detection and prevention measures, the practice of computer crime may go largely undetected. Many experts are convinced that the majority of computer crimes is yet to be detected.

Difficulty in estimating computer crime losses

Many computer crimes involve manipulation of electronic evidence. Electronic evidence is composed of transactions recorded on electronic media. Fraudulent checks and other paper documents can normally be detected and the magnitude of the crime identified. On the other hand, good electronic evidence looks identical to fraudulent electronic evidence. The ability to differentiate a good transaction from a bad electronic transaction is extremely difficult. Thus, while a computer crime may be detected, the magnitude of that crime might not be identifiable.

Failure of computer crime victims to report the crime

Many victims of computer crime refuse to report the attack for a variety of reasons. These include:

Fear of alarming their stockholders   Suppose a major corporation reported that it had lost several million dollars to a computer hacker. The stockholders of that company could justly feel less than secure with their investment and withdraw support, hurting the company.

Fear of opening the company up to further attacks   If the company admits that it was victim to a hacker, then other hackers may feel that this company is a prime target for attack.

Fear of loss of clients   This is especially true of financial institutions. If a bank or brokerage house admits that it has lost significant capital or assets, then its clients may justifiably feel that their investments are at an unacceptable level of risk.

Assessing the possibility of different threats

Different situations will require different responses to the changing face of computer crime. If a company has no phone lines into its computer facility, then an extensive system of software to prevent hacker intrusion is more than ludicrous, it is wasteful. On the other hand, if a company is in the business of supplying on-line processing to a variety of customers via phone lines or radio links, then the prospect of a hacker penetrating to the sanctum sanctorum is more probable. It is up to the MIS team to determine where the risk comes from for without an analysis of the risk factors, it is absurd to develop a computer crime response package. In the following paragraphs we will examine some of the most common sources of attack. Using these as a starting point, the MIS team must determine exactly where the threat to any specific installation is most likely to appear. It then becomes the responsibility of the security team to deal with the threats. It is important to remember that the world of computer crime is constantly changing, and today's safety zone could well be tomorrow's weakest link.

The first and most significant area of concern must be the employees themselves. They have access to the data, and they are aware of those few activities that will cause the maximum amount of harm. Donald Burleson is an excellent example of this type of threat. Former or terminated employees are not the only source of trouble, however. It could be the case that a competitor hires one of your employees, without that employee leaving your shop. Or a valued and respected employee may develop a grudge against the company. All in all, the current staff is the greatest of all security risks.

A second area of risk again comes from within the company. If the computer use rules allow employees to bring in software to use on company machines, then the possibility of infection with one of the various forms of snuffware exists. Snuffware is a word first used in *Personal Computing* magazine in 1986. It refers to software that is harmful to the computer or the data on the machine upon which it is run. Examples of snuffware include virus-infected code, Trojan horses, logic bombs, and time bombs. All these different threats will be discussed in detail later in this book.

A third hazard is significant only if your computer has direct access through phone lines. In this case, the modems on your computer can represent a significant possibility of danger. There are several different ways in which phones that directly interface with your computer can cause problems. These threats can be divided into two different classes: out-calls and in-calls.

Outward calling is more risky than opening up your computer to employee supplied software. You still run the risk of picking up a virus or other snuffware; but besides that, there exists a pathway for private company information to move from your computer to the outside world, either to other computers or to other storage media. If employees access bulletin boards, company data could rapidly be spread across the country or even the world. One major problem with this type of computer crime is that it is very difficult to identify or trace.

Inbound calls, where the computer answers the phone directly, are a more severe risk than the outward calls. In the case of inbound calling, more opportunities exist for crimes to occur. The obvious threats of hackers are not the greatest threats. More important is the possibility of fraud and misuse of the computer. The possibility of the import of snuffware is also of concern, as well as the availability of the data on your machine for some form of espionage.

Finally the computer security manager needs to be aware of the physical accesses granted to the computer. As we noted above, computers have been executed, gangland style, when physical access was sloppy. But damage is the least of the concerns where physical access is involved. Why should an industrial spy work for days and days to crack your computer security system, if he or she can simply walk into your computer center and steal a tape or disk pack? Too many people take physical access for granted. Usually terminals are not logged off during the day. A hacker or other computer criminal could walk in and use a viable account to perform criminal acts that may be impossible to perform from outside the data processing suite. Take for example Donald Burleson, the only way he was able to plant his bomb was to physically enter the code from a terminal inside the company.

All of these different types of threats must be evaluated on a site-by-site basis, and a rational approach developed to prevent or contain computer crime. It makes little sense to spend time and money protecting your dial-in access if you have no modems attached to your machines. By the same token, if access to your machine is controlled by a sufficient site security plan, then you need not spend time and money developing a plan to prevent attack from within the computer room.

In subsequent chapters we will examine these threats in greater detail, and discuss ways to prevent damage on a threat-by-threat basis. But before we continue, perhaps it would be a good idea to consider your computer configuration and make a list of possible hazards. In so doing, it is important to remember that there are many self-styled experts filling the media with horror stories to help themselves sell security plans. The incidence of hackers, for example, is very rare on a national level. Yet to hear the security-selling moguls talk, you would think that nearly every computer in the country is under daily attack.

These problems are typical of the computer-related crimes occurring in both the public and private sector. While many of the crimes are for very large amounts of money, the methods of conducting and detecting the crime are typical regardless of the amount of funds involved. However, as technology advances, so will the methods and techniques used for computer crime.

Developing a rational policy

A reduction in the possibility for computer crime does not just happen; it must be planned. A computer crime policy should be the cornerstone of that plan. The policy is management's statement on their intent and guidance regarding the prevention and detection of computer crime.

The reduction of computer crime begins when senior management defines their policy on computer crime for all employees in their organization. The policy states their definition of and expectations on computer crime, as well as their intention to enforce the policy. In order to ensure that all employees are aware of the policy, it must be made known.

A computer crime policy involves the following four criteria:

- Definition of computer crime: A clear, brief, and unambiguous definition of computer crime.
- Management intent: The position that management intends to take on computer crime.
- System: The method through which management intent will be achieved.
- Measurement: How management intends to measure and evaluate the methods and procedures used to reduce computer crime.

The result of a computer crime policy by senior management will be the development of procedures, standards, and guidelines to accomplish that policy. The policy will be the basis for expending the necessary time and effort to develop the appropriate computer crime countermeasures. Without the senior management policy, the prevention and detection of computer crime will be left to the discretion of the individual operating units. Some may do a reasonably good job, while others may not consider it their responsibility, and thus do nothing.

A sample computer crime policy for an organization is illustrated in Fig. 2-1. Note that this policy should be customized to meet the specific needs of the developing organization. Also, the sample policy identifies each of the policy criteria. In actual practice, it is not necessary to include these headings in the policy.

Management computer crime strategies

Management has many options available to implement strategies to reduce computer crime. The selection of these strategies is a management responsibility. The methods and procedures for implementing the strategies are included in later chapters of this book.

The two primary management computer crime strategies are the prevention and detection of computer crime. Both strategies are highly recommended. However, there are a number of options available to management for preventing and detecting computer crime. The individual strategies selected will depend on where management perceives their primary computer crime threat to be. The strategies and threats are listed in Fig. 2-2 and are described below.

Computer crime threat categories

People, not machines, perpetrate computer crime. However, the threat can be consummated by people or systems. For example, the threat that can exploit a vulnerability can be an individual in a certain position, such

---

COMPUTER CRIME POLICY

ABC Corporation

Computer Crime Definition

Fraud or abuse against the corporation involving the use of the computer or resources controlled by the computer.

Management's Computer Crime Intent

It is the intent of management to prevent computer crime, wherever economical, to instigate reasonable measures to detect computer crime, and to prosecute, through due course of law, any individual, employee or otherwise, involved in a crime against the corporation in which the computer is involved.

Computer Crime System

The prevention of computer crime is a responsibility of the data processing department for the involvement of computer resources, and the users of applications systems for the data contained within those systems. These same individuals have the primary responsibility for detecting computer fraud in their areas of responsibility. In addition, the internal audit department and security function have a secondary responsibility for the prevention and detection of computer fraud.

Fig. 2-1. Computer crime policy.

as a payroll clerk, or it can be a weakness in the system, such as the ability to change overtime hours immediately prior to processing the payroll without being subjected to the normal payroll controls.

The six threat categories are divided between people and systems as follows:

People threat—employees   Individuals who are on the payroll of an organization.

People threat—customers or vendors   Individuals or organizations who regularly conduct business with the organization, such as the customers who buy the services or products, and vendors who supply services or products.

Management Strategies	Threat Category					
	People			System		
					Automation	
	Employees	Customers	Non-Related	Manual	Batch	On-Line
Prevention						
System of Internal Controls	P	S	S	S	P	P
Internal/External Audit	P	S	S	P	P	P
Security Force	S	S	P	P	S	S
Supervisory Surveillance	S	P	S	P	S	S
Detection						
Network of Informants	P	P	S	P	S	S
Complaint Investigation	P	P	S	P	S	S
Computer Crime Investigations	P	P	P	P	P	P
Computer Crime Analysis	P	S	S	S	P	P

P = Primary Purpose of Strategy

S = Secondary Purpose of Strategy

Fig. 2-2. Management of computer crime strategies.

People threat—nonrelated parties   Individuals or organizations who have no direct day-to-day contact with the organization, but who intend to benefit from that organization through criminal action. Examples include college students attempting to defraud a bank, criminals desiring to rob an organization through computer manipulation, and individuals who are able to use some special knowledge to defraud an operation. In these days of *Perestroika*, Eastern Bloc countries are searching out Western technology more than ever. A wise manager must consider this risk as well.

System threat—manual system   The pre- or postprocessing part of an automated system. This might involve the manual preparation of input transactions or the documents produced by the system, such as bank checks.

System threat—automated batch systems   Computer systems that process and control transactions in batches.

System threat—on-line systems   Computer systems that receive and send information from computer terminals. Processing normally occurs on single transactions as opposed to batches of transactions.

Management strategy options

Strategies that management should select are those aimed directly at reducing their major computer crime threats. Strategies can be divided into both prevention and detection strategies. The more effective computer crime strategies that can be adopted by management are as follows.

Prevention strategy—system of internal controls   The totality of the methods and procedures used to reduce the risk of computer crime. (Note that the other prevention strategies could fall within this general definition of internal controls, but they are separated because they are more of a control on a control, as opposed to a primary control.)

Prevention strategy—internal/external auditing   The use of auditors serves two purposes. A major purpose is the prevention of wrongdoing through the existence of a function designed to detect those wrongdoings. Thus, the establishment of an internal audit department or the use of external auditors in assessing the adequacy of the system of controls provides a preventive force that, by its very existence, deters people from committing computer crimes and, at the same time, evaluates and strengthens the basic system of controls in order to prevent computer crime.

Prevention strategy—security force   The establishment of a function designed to provide physical and logical security over the organization becomes a prevention strategy. Like auditors, the security force is charged with evaluating and improving the prevention measures to stop computer crime. However, to be effective against computer crime, the security force must be assigned that responsibility and staffed with individuals having the appropriate skills to develop and evaluate computer security measures.

Prevention strategy—supervisory surveillance While supervisors are not normally considered to be police, they are the first line of defense against computer crime. Adding this responsibility to first-line supervision, coupled with appropriate training, tools, and techniques, provides a strong deterrent to computer crime.

Detection strategy—network of informants Many individuals desire to prevent crime against their organization, but are unfamiliar with how to fulfill that responsibility. A network of informants is not a formalized organizational structure but, rather, a conduit through which individuals are encouraged to report suspicious events. Personnel must be made aware of the methods for reporting suspicious events and the type of personal protection they will receive as a result of reporting that information.

Detection strategy—complaint investigations Complaints can be from both people and computer systems. Note that in computer systems, complaints are referred to as error or warning messages. The prompt investigation of these complaints can lead to the detection of wrongdoing.

Detection strategy—computer crime investigations The normal audit and security function is not charged with conducting special investigations, reviews, or audits directed at uncovering computer crime where there is no suspicion of computer crime. These investigations are conducted based on the identification of a threat to determine whether that threat has been exploited and, if so, the magnitude of that exploitation.

Detection strategy—computer crime analyses These are special analyses performed for the purpose of detecting irregularities. In many organizations, these analyses are performed by financial analysts who are looking for unusual variances. Once a variance has been uncovered, such as a reduced gross profit on a line of inventory, then a computer crime investigation can be undertaken to determine the cause of the variance. The difference between a computer crime investigation and computer crime analysis is that the analysis precedes the investigation and can focus the investigation on a specific area where a problem is suspected, as opposed to a broader investigation looking for potential problems.

Selecting a management computer crime strategy

While a computer crime strategy drives the computer crime reduction process, the strategy cannot be developed without some preliminary investigation. The following seven steps are recommended to management to assist them in the development of a computer crime strategy.

1. **Appoint a computer crime task force**   A task force made up of key individuals should be appointed to study the computer crime threat in the organization. The makeup of the task force should include key users, auditors, security personnel, and data processing personnel. The task force should be chaired by a member of senior management. The objective of the task force is to develop a computer crime strategy for the organization.

2. **Identify computer crime threats**   The task force should be provided with an inventory of computer applications, together with the resources controlled by each application. Using the threat identification process outlined in chapter 3, the task force should identify the most probable computer crime threats to the organization.

3. **Determine the magnitude of the identified threats**   The task force should determine the range or probable magnitude for each computer threat. This can be accomplished by using one of the magnitude estimation methods included in chapter 3. The threats should then be ranked according to their magnitude.

4. **Identify the threat category**   Identify the type of person or system vulnerability where the threat is most likely to occur. Divide the threats into the six threat categories previously described in this chapter.

5. **Prioritize threats by threat category**   A determination should be made as to which threat category is the most prevalent in the organization and then prioritize downward. For example, employees may be considered to be the greatest threat or the manual part of systems may be the greatest threat, etc.

6. **Allocate computer crime reduction resources**   Determine whether the organization wants to emphasize prevention, detection, or both in reducing computer crime. For example, an organization, such as a bank, may determine that it is best for them to put most of their computer crime reduction resources into preventing computer crime, as opposed to detecting it, because they feel computer crime to be a major threat. On the other hand, an organization that perceives computer crime to be rare, and perhaps not in very large amounts, may decide it would be better to periodically attempt to detect whether a problem has occurred before they spend large amounts in prevention.

7. **Select a management computer crime strategy**   Using the information provided in Fig. 2-2, pick which of the eight strategies appears to best meet the needs of the organization. These will be the strategies whose primary purpose is to reduce

the threats identified to be the major computer crime threats against the organization. For example, if a threat was considered to be employees manipulating the manual part of computer systems, and the organization wants to prevent that from occurring, internal or external audits have proven to be one of the better prevention strategies for that type of computer crime.

Once the strategies have been selected, an individual or function within the organization should be appointed the responsibility of implementing and operating the selected strategy.

3

Computer crime threats

THE KEY TO THE PREVENTION AND DETECTION OF COMPUTER CRIME
begins with identifying the types and locations of computer crime threats
facing your corporation. There are many computer crime schemes, but
most concentrate on the basic processing relating to major business con-
vertible assets, such as billing, loans, sales, payroll, etc. This tendency and
an understanding of the vulnerabilities leading to computer crime constitute the basic knowledge necessary to address this important topic.

This chapter describes computer crime characteristics as defined by
the American Institute of Certified Public Accountants (AICPA) Computer
Crime Task Force. In addition, the chapter describes the more common
computer vulnerabilities as defined by a task force assembled by the
National Bureau of Standards and subsequent research and experience.

The objective of this chapter is to provide sufficient background
information for development of effective countermeasures. Rapid technology advances (networked systems, etc.) and increased complexity of
systems are increasing the occurrence of and level of damage from computer crimes. The preparation of a computer crime threat list is described
and identified as a tool to help avoid the incidence of computer crime.

History of computer crime

Statistics on computer crime have been kept since 1958. This data was
compiled by the Stanford Research Institute (SRI). Rather than simply

recording crimes committed by computer, this group kept data on what they referred to as computer "abuses." These were divided into the following categories:

- Vandalism against computer hardware
- The theft of property or information
- Computer-based fraud or the theft of monies
- Unsanctioned use of the computer or theft and sale of computer time

The data recorded are not considered significant until 1968, the year when 10 or more of these abuses were recorded. In that year, 13 of these events were reported.

In 1966, a Minnesota bank was robbed using a computer as the tool to accomplish the theft. This was the first case of a computer being used to commit a theft. The advent of computers as tools of common criminals marked a major change in the world of crime. Since then, computer crime has grown and expanded into many areas which did not even exist in the 1960s. To begin with, computer criminals stole time on the computers. This time was used for such far reaching tasks as building betting pools for football games and playing games like Star Trek.

The SRI tracked computer crime until 1978. To give some insight into the magnitude of the problems of crime, the SRI recorded 10 computer crimes in 1969 and 85 in 1977. This shows the growth of computer abuse in the U.S. In 1978, the SRI stopped collecting and reporting these statistics because they were no longer reflecting the number of computer crimes which were taking place, nor was this collection of any help in determining causal factors leading to computer crime.

Since those days, the computer has become much more a part of everyday life. Therefore, computer crime has become more important in our society. One recent avenue of attack using the computer is the submission of fraudulent orders. Many examples of this have appeared in the news media. One of these schemes was perpetrated by an employee of a phone company in California. This individual placed orders for phone equipment to be delivered to a given address. The order was then entered as paid in the computer. The address was an abandoned warehouse, where the employee's cohorts would pick up the merchandise and later sell it back to the phone company.

There are many more examples of specific types of computer crimes which we will discuss throughout this book. In fact, we have a whole chapter devoted to the most recent and most popularized fad in computer crime, the virus. This form of computer crime can be included in the class of crimes called system infection programs. This includes programs like Trojan horses, worms, time bombs, and viruses. One of the most spectacular of these computer crimes, mainly because of the inadvertent damage it did, was the Internet worm released by Robert Morris on November 2,

1988. This virus invaded between 3,000 and 4,000 computers, doing a conservatively estimated $190 million in damage. This includes both the damaged data and time lost to clean up the systems after the virus attack.

As we examine the phenomenon of computer crime, we will explore more fully the different forms of attack possible on the various computer systems.

Computer crime definitions

A computer crime vocabulary is necessary to understand the literature and communicate prevention and detection concepts. All losses and controls are attributable to (some form of) risk. Thus, risk becomes the basis for understanding the threat of computer crime. The risk of computer crime is ever present. Computer-related crime is reduced by identifying the threats, controls, and vulnerabilities associated with a computer crime risk.

The definitions shown in Fig. 3-1 will be used in this book. The definitions were developed by the National Bureau of Standards in order to precisely define the terms and concepts used in the areas of computer crime, security, control, and audit. These definitions also help explain some of the concepts that are basic to both understanding and controlling computer crime threats.

Term	Definition
1. Computer Application	Data (including logically related computer programs) and associated manual activities designed to accomplish specific objectives or functions for the benefit of the computer user.
2. Computer Audit	An independent evaluation of the controls employed to ensure a. The appropriate protection of the organization's information assets (including hardware, software, firmware, and data) from all significant anticipated threats or hazards. b. The accuracy and reliability of the data maintained on, or generated by, an automated data processing system. c. The operational reliability and performance assurance for accuracy and timeliness of all components of the automated data processing system.
3. Computer Security	A state or condition that a computer system possesses. Computer security is never absolute. Rather, each system possesses security

Fig. 3-1. Computer crime definitions.

Fig. 3-1. Continued

Term	Definition
3. Computer Security Continued	at some level. Computer security is provided by internal safeguards (built into the hardware and software) and external safeguards (physical and procedural) against possible threats. The level of computer security is dependent on the degree to which: a. The computer system's components (including hardware, software, firmware, and data) are protected against all significant threats. b. Data maintained on, or generated by, its data processing systems are accurate and reliable. c. Its data processing systems are operationally reliable and satisfy criteria that assure the accurate and timely performance of the system. d. All systems operations are subject to review and audit.
4. Computer Security Flaw	An internal defect of a computer system or application, or an unstated capability which deviates from the published specifications of the computer system or application, that can cause unauthorized or inaccurate performance of that system or application.
5. Computer System	An interacting or interdependent group of components, consisting of hardware, software, firmware, data, and people functioning as an entity to accomplish a specific set of objectives.
6. Control	Anything that tends to cause the reduction of risks. A special advisory committee of the AICPA on internal accounting control listed, in their September 1978 report, the following definition: "Control comprises the plan of organization and all of the coordinate methods and measures adopted within a business to safeguard its assets, check the accuracy and reliability of its accounting data, promote operational efficiency, and encourage adherence to prescribed managerial policies."

Term	Definition
7. Exposure	The condition of being exposed to danger or loss.
8. Hazard	A chance event of a dangerous nature (natural or man-made) that occurs without design, forethought, or direction, and that can harm a computer system or facility (e.g., fire, flood, earthquake, accidental unauthorized access to data).
9. Risk	The potential loss or damage to an organization, for example, that loss which is a result from the use or misuse of its computer. This may involve unauthorized disclosure, unauthorized modification, and/or loss of information resources as well as the authorized but incorrect use of a computer. Risk can be measured to some extent by performing a risk analysis.
10. Risk Analysis	An analysis of an organization's information resources, its existing controls, and its remaining organization and computer system vulnerabilities. It combines the loss potential for each resource or combination of resources, with an estimated rate of occurrence to establish a potential level of damage in dollars or other assets.
11. Risk Assessment	A synonym for risk analysis.
12. Threat	A possible event that can exploit a vulnerability in the security of a computer system or application. Threats include both hazards and the triggering of flaws.
13. Vulnerability	A design, implementation, or operations flaw that may be exploited by a threat, to cause the

Fig. 3-1. Continued

Term	Definition
13. Vulnerability Continued	computer system or application to operate in a fashion different from its published specifications and to result in destruction or misuse of equipment or data.

Characteristics of the computer criminal

When we examine computer crime, it is wise to consider the perpetrator of the criminal act as well as the act itself. Probably the most significant characteristic of the computer criminal is that he or she has no previous criminal record. The offender cannot be readily identified by any set of special characteristics. Unlike the terrorist, who can often be identified by certain actions or behaviors, the computer criminal fits no stereotypical model. Some of the commonalities of computer criminals in the 1970s and early 1980s include:

- They tend to be males ranging in age from 19 to 30.
- They have no previous criminal record.
- They identify with their technological expertise far more than with their employer's business or their work group.
- They are usually employed in the data processing or accounting departments.
- They are considered to be bright, highly motivated, outwardly self-confident, and willing to accept challenges. They are also seen as very adventurous.
- In addition to the above attributes, most computer criminals work in areas where they are given a great deal of trust by their companies.

So far this sounds like the model employee. That is part of the problem; employers seek just this sort of individual to fill professional vacancies in their business. But there exists a dark side to these individuals, a set of additional characteristics separating them from the mainstream professional. These peculiarities include:

- These individuals often feel exploited by their employers and have a desire to get even.

- They usually have no desire to harm persons, rather they see themselves as hurting a cold, indifferent, impersonal, and exploitative employer or corporation.
- If they are taking software or data, they feel they are borrowing, rather than stealing.
- In addition to the above listed characteristics, they often feel desperate due to some economic problems resulting from high living, expensive tastes, family sickness, excessive drug use, or gambling.

Recently, the profile has begun a rather extreme change; the modern computer criminal is getting younger. For example, in August 1989, a 14-year-old boy broke into the computer of Citibank and used access codes to order more than $11,000 in merchandise, having it sent to a post office box he had set up. Two eighth-grade students from Sterling Heights, Michigan, admitted to hacking into a network of computers, helping defraud more than 20 companies of over $1.5 million in goods. Besides getting younger, as the current group of computer hackers ages, the upper limit of the range will increase. Therefore, the age of the computer criminal will no longer be of interest.

Gender is also no longer as significant. In the past, all computer criminals were male. However, beginning in 1988, some female hackers began to make their debut.

The motivation for a criminal to commit this type of crime is also changing. In the past, the single most important motivation was financial, and to a far lesser extent to prove finesse. Recent studies into the current motivation of computer criminals has brought to light these incitements:

- Resentment. The computer criminal feels that his/her employer has passed over him/her for a promotion or raise or other such recognition. The computer crime is his/her way to strike back at the employer and gain recognition as well.
- A sense of gaming. Playing against the security manager and the software in place to prevent access becomes a game. This sort of criminal is usually the least destructive by intent.
- Challenge. Much like the previous item, the criminal (usually a hacker) sees his/her position as me versus them and enjoys the mental effort required to crack a system.
- Last but surely not least is still financial motivation.

As we will see, the computer criminal of today is a more complex and sophisticated threat than in previous generations. This means that the computer security force in any corporation plays an increasingly important role in the defense of the system. An important point is that most of the computer criminals are trusted members of the staff, not outsiders and not strangers.

Even though we will consider the signs of computer crime in later chapters, it is worthwhile to now consider some serious signs that indicate an individual is engaged in some form of computer crime. Some of the more common signs are:

- A major change in the standard of living. Suddenly buying a boat, a fancy car, or a new home can indicate a new influx of money from some outside source.

- Intense dedication. Any employee who spends excessive time in the corporation may be doing things that require company equipment and a quiet environment. It is interesting to note that the current management philosophy toward overtime has shifted from viewing extensive overtime as good for the company, toward wondering if there is a problem with the employee who needs more than the allotted eight hours to finish his/her work.

- The aging process is also a factor. It is wise to closely watch those employees who seem to be in the midst of a crisis in their home life. A divorce or separation could be very stressful and lead a valued employee into activities not previously considered.

- Chronic lateness in production of reports may be a sign that the data requested needs to be massaged or created, and may signal that data can be recovered.

- A major change in relationships with others also frequently accompanies a change in feelings about oneself, which may telegraph a change in behavior as well. This change could be caused by many different things, but needs to be carefully evaluated nonetheless.

Since the characteristics of the computer criminal have become less clear, we have a greater need to protect our systems and data from unauthorized access and damage.

Characteristics of computer crime

The characteristics of computer crime are useful in describing the types of people that commit crimes, as well as the environment and situations in which computer crimes occur. The objective of understanding these characteristics is to put computer crime into the proper business perspective. Computer crime occurs most frequently in the mainline applications of an organization. The characteristics describe the situations relating to the current practice of computer crime. These characteristics describe the people, methods, processes, and detriments involved in computer crime.

The characteristics of financially motivated computer crime are those presented by Brandt Allen in the AICPA report on computer crime. These computer crime characteristics are

Control weaknesses lead to computer crime The primary source of computer crime opportunity is a weakness in the basic system of internal control in the major business applications.

Input manipulation is the major source of fraud A large percentage of crime occurs through the manipulation of input data to computer systems.

Perpetrators use their own accounts Frequently the perpetrator of a computer crime moves whatever assets are being confiscated into that individual's own personal account. For example, in a bank, funds might be moved into the perpetrator's savings or checking account.

Most people are honest The large majority of people are honest, want to remain honest, and want to keep other people honest. Not only is this a major deterrent to computer crime, but it can also be capitalized upon as a computer crime detection device.

Converting sums through the banking system Most people don't know how to convert large sums through the banking system. Thus, even if they were able to commit computer crimes for large sums of money they would have great difficulty depositing and using those funds through the banking system. This is a deterrent to committing big computer crime frauds.

Most computer crimes are small The average loss due to computer crime is in the $10,000 to $50,000 range. Although most cases are small, the potential for taking large amounts is great. Perhaps the difficulty with the banking system keeps computer crime amounts small.

Computer crime involves many transactions Many financially based computer crimes require hundreds of transactions, although it is possible for very large amounts of money to be taken with a single transaction. Many of the cases investigated by the AICPA showed that most frauds are committed with very large numbers of computer transactions.

Most perpetrators are clerks All types of people commit computer crime, but the most common perpetrators are clerks. Thus, the average computer crime perpetrator is not an individual highly skilled in computer concepts. This is an important fact to remember, for all too often we tend to look at the computer criminal as someone who has advanced computer skills. This is true for those crimes that are highly technological, such as logic bombs, virus attacks, Trojan horses, and hacking. However, the majority of the computer crimes committed are performed by manipulating the input data to an existing program. To perform this task all that is required is access to the computer and minimal skill.

Most perpetrators expect to repay funds   In a large number of financial cases involving employees, it was the intent of the perpetrator to repay the funds to the organization. Thus, another reason why most cases are small. Unfortunately, circumstances usually prevent the repayment of funds and, in fact, lead to the continuation of the fraud.

Few computer crime cases are sophisticated   In most of the cases investigated, the scheme used was an old one capitalizing on a weakness in the computer technology.

On-line systems are especially vulnerable   The more sophisticated the technology, the more vulnerable the system to computer fraud. Thus, on-line database systems are much more vulnerable than batch computer systems.

Management involvement increases the size of the loss   When management is involved in the computer crime, the scheme usually lasts longer and the losses are greater.

As we put these characteristics together, we see the following scenario developing as the most common type of computer crime:

The perpetrator of computer crime is a clerk knowledgeable about entering data into computer applications. The application in question is one of the major "bread and butter" applications of the organization. The clerk uses one of the more common defrauding schemes (such as in a bank, making a loan to oneself), and bases the scheme on a detected vulnerability in the computer system, such as the failure to investigate warning messages. The clerk intends to repay the funds and thus the computer crime is minimal in starting, but tends to build as the clerk is unable to repay the embezzled funds.

With the recent explosion of personal computers in the corporation, a new form of computer crime is also growing. This is crime using or against the smaller personal or microcomputers. It is common for a business to have a large number of microcomputers tied together in a network functioning as both electronic communications and access to a mainframe computer. In this environment the opportunities for computer crime increase tremendously. Both the microcomputer and the mainframe are independently available as targets and the network between the micros is another important and vulnerable avenue of attack. Besides these three areas, the interface between the micro network and the mainframe is a ripe target for attack.

When employees have personal computers at home, and use compatible machines at work, the chances of computer crime increases dramatically. One personal computer crime has become the most common, and will no doubt be the premier crime of the 1990s. It is software piracy. If an employee uses a particular software package at work, and wishes to use it at home as well, it is all too easy to make a copy of the software and carry it home on floppy diskette. By the same token, if an employee has obtained a software package for use at home, and wishes to use it at the office, and he/she can make a copy and bring it to work and load it into the office machine. This use of bootleg software opens up the business to litigation for copyright violation by the manufacturer of the software.

Besides this legal issue, which promises to become more common, the possibility of infection by some form of snuffware dramatically increases. If the employee obtained his software from a bulletin board or some other use, then the risk of infection becomes nearly intolerable. Therefore, the use of software for which no purchase order exists is an area of extreme risk and a frequent source for computer crime. Even though the software is commercial, the application could be contaminated and thus infect software in the work environment. If the employee's personal computer is part of a network, then the potential for risk becomes enormous.

Types of computer crime threats

Threats are the opportunities for perpetrators to capitalize on application system vulnerabilities. The vulnerabilities are grouped according to system function in order to aid in determining the applicability of individual threats to the organization.

The threats are divided into the following categories, which are indicative of categories of threats that must be addressed when evaluating the probability of computer crime:

- Erroneous or falsified input data
- Misuse by an authorized end-user
- Uncontrolled system access
- Ineffective security practices for the application
- Procedural errors within the EDP facility
- Program error
- Operating system flaw
- Communication system failure
- Litigation due to illegal practices and procedures

Note that the above threats are not intended to be all inclusive, but merely suggest the various kinds of vulnerabilities that may exist in any application system. However, it is believed that these represent the more common computer crime vulnerabilities.

Erroneous or falsified input data

Erroneous or falsified input data is the simplest and most common cause of computer crime in application systems. A vulnerability can occur whenever data is collected, manually processed, or prepared for entry to the computer. The specific computer threats are as follows.

Undetected, unreasonable, or inconsistent source data
Source data values can be changed within the limits of detection. If these limits are large, the ability to manipulate data is large.

Entry changes not detected Data can be changed during the entry process if detection procedures are not incorporated to uncover those changes. This means that if the computer accepts whatever is entered, data can easily be changed and accepted.

Misinterpretation of record formats The miscoding of one type of record (for example, an invoice) so that it is interpreted as another type of record (for example, a payment) allows data manipulation. People knowing how the system functions may know that there are very few controls over entering one type of transaction (for example, an invoice) or very stringent controls for another type of transaction (for example, a payment). If the invoice-type transaction can be modified so that it is interpreted as a payment, an unauthorized manipulation can occur.

Fraudulently adding, deleting, or modifying data Data within records can be added to, deleted, or modified unless controls exist to detect those occurrences. For example, extra items can be added to a shipping order or quantities can be changed or substituted to permit inventory to leave a distribution center in an unauthorized manner.

Inserting or deleting transactions Without document controls or other controls over source data or input transactions, additional transactions may be inserted or deleted without control. For example, payment records can be deleted so that the funds can be used for other purposes.

Modification of personal data Records about personnel may be modified, deleted, or added to during data entry unless controls exist to track and monitor such transactions.

Emergency entry of transactions Data that arrives at the last minute or changes that must be entered at the last minute may not go through the normal control procedures. This vulnerability may enable fraudulent changes or transactions to be made to the application system.

Improper use of error correction procedures Records in which errors have been detected may be corrected without verification of the full record. If this is the case, changes in the portion of the record that will be reentered but not reverified can be changed without the appropriate checks.

Misuse by authorized end-users

End-users are the people who are served by the computer system. The system is designed for their use, but they can also misuse it for undesirable purposes. It is often very difficult to determine whether their use of the system is in accordance with the legitimate performance of their job. Examples of these types of threats include the following.

Sale of privileged information   An individual having access to the information in a computer system may acquire privileged information from the system. That information can then be sold to outside parties (for example, amount of bids submitted, company statistics affecting stock market prices, etc.).

Acquisition and sale of a complete list of information   A user whose job requires access to individual records in a file may manage to compile a complete listing of the file and then make unauthorized use of it. For example, an accounts receivable clerk could over a period of time acquire a listing of all major customers of an organization, or a payroll clerk could acquire a list of all company personnel and their salaries. These lists could then be sold to a competing firm.

Theft of services   An authorized user may use the system for personal benefit by using the computer to run personal programs, or by processing personal data using the organization's programs.

Destruction or modification not for personal gain   A disgruntled or terminated employee may destroy or modify records to get even with a company for some act by organization management or for some policy disliked by that individual. In addition, the destruction or modification may be made in such a way that back-up records are also corrupted and useless.

Sale of information to an unauthorized individual   An authorized user may accept a bribe to modify or obtain information for another party. The bribe may be monetary or for personal benefit of the person accepting the bribe. In addition to selling this information to a competitor, with the current atmosphere of openness between the U.S. and the Soviet Union, an excellent opportunity exists for the Soviets to spy on U.S. businesses. The State Department has determined that the Soviet Union is currently training its own hackers to penetrate U.S. firms and extract industrial secrets. Therefore, the employee who is selling your firms secrets may be helping the Russians prosper and advance their technology. This is another serious consideration in this form of crime.

Uncontrolled system access

Organizations expose themselves to unnecessary computer crime threats if they fail to establish controls over access to the computer area, use of the computer system, and access to the information contained in the system. The computer crime threats that are prevalent through lack of control of system access include

Theft of data or programs   Data or programs may be stolen from the computer room or other storage areas. Both data and programs have sales value. Programs can be used to analyze processing methods so that unauthorized manipulation of data can be accomplished.

Destruction of EDP facilities   EDP facilities may be destroyed or damaged either by intruders or by access of unauthorized employees. Damage may be done to divert attention away from a crime, to destroy evidence, or to get even with the organization.

Unauthorized access to the EDP facility　Individuals may not be adequately identified before they are allowed to enter the EDP area, resulting in unauthorized use of the facilities.

Unauthorized access through remote terminals　Remote terminals may not be adequately protected from use by unauthorized persons. Unattended terminals, or ones without passwords or similar protection, provide ready access to computer resources.

Unauthorized access through dial-in lines　An unauthorized user may gain access to the system through a dial-in line. The threat is increased if the perpetrator has an authorized user's password.

Inadvertent revealing of passwords　Passwords may be inadvertently revealed to unauthorized individuals. The user may write his/her password in some convenient place, or the password may be obtained from card decks, discarded printouts, or by observing the user as he types it.

Piggybacking a terminal　A user may leave a logged-in terminal unattended, allowing an unauthorized person to gain access to computer resources. This occurs when the facility is opened by an individual who leaves the terminal without terminating usage.

Password not voided when employee is terminated　A terminated employee may retain access to computer systems because his/her name and password are not immediately deleted from authorization tables and control lists.

Unauthorized access　An unauthorized individual may gain access to the system for his/her own purposes even though that individual is not authorized to use the system. Access in this instance is intentional and for the purpose of unauthorized events.

Undetected repeated attempts at unauthorized entry to the system　Repeated attempts by the same user to gain unauthorized access to the system or to data may go undetected. Normal practice restricts the number of attempts an individual is given to access the system before the system resources are denied that individual.

Ineffective security practices

Inadequate manual checks and controls to ensure correct processing by the computer system, or negligence by those responsible for carrying out those checks, result in many vulnerabilities. The types of vulnerabilities associated with ineffective security practices include

Poorly defined criteria for access authorization　Poorly defined criteria for authorized access may result in employees not knowing what information they or others are permitted to access. Thus, unauthorized access occurs without it being noted by the individual performing the access or by those concerned with detecting and controlling unauthorized access.

Incomplete enforcement of security   The person responsible for security may fail to restrict user access to only those processes or data which are needed to accomplish assigned tasks. Thus, users can gain access to unauthorized resources.

No follow-up on unusual conditions   Large fund disbursements, unusual price changes, and unanticipated inventory usage may not be reviewed for accuracy. Thus, conditions that should initiate investigations do not.

Repeated processing of the same event   An authorized event may be entered many times. For example, repeated payments to the same party for the same invoice may go unnoticed because there is no review.

Careless handling of sensitive data   Sensitive data may be carelessly handled by the application staff, by the mail service, or by other personnel within the organization, resulting in unnecessary vulnerabilities.

Lack of follow-up on potential security violations   Security logs and other postprocessing reports analyzing system operations may not be reviewed to detect security violations.

Lack of management follow-up   Appropriate action by management may not be pursued when a potential security violation is reported to a member of management or a security officer. In practice, procedures governing how such occurrences should be handled may not exist. Thus, not knowing what to do, management may do nothing.

Procedural errors within the EDP facility

Both errors and unintentional acts committed by the EDP staff may result in improper operational procedures, which in turn may result in lax control or losses of storage media and output. Errors of this type are usually attributable to either lack of appropriate procedures or inadequate supervision. The type of vulnerabilities that may occur due to procedural error include

Ignoring operational procedures   Operators or shift supervisors may ignore operational procedures and permit improper processes to occur (for example, allowing programmers to operate computer equipment because it appears the easiest thing to do).

Operations manager or supervisor circumventing operational controls   Supervision and management may use their position to circumvent operational controls to obtain information.

Lapses in security during reorganization and recovery   Careless or incorrect reorganization and recovery procedures may allow unauthorized events to occur during periods in which normal control procedures may not be operational.

Failure to protect files during maintenance   Production data and program files may be on-line during hardware or software maintenance, thus making that information potentially available to the individuals performing the maintenance. Note that in some advanced systems, maintenance may be performed from remote areas using dial-in facilities.

Inadequate supervision during nonworking hours   Supervision of operations personnel may not be adequate during periods when office personnel are not working. This can include not only the operations performed during the day but, also, those performed during weekends and on holidays.

Control overrides   A console operator may override a control check without recording the action on a security log or obtaining approval to perform the procedure.

Inadvertently or intentionally mislabeling storage media Operators may put the wrong label or an incorrect label on storage media so that it can be used for unauthorized purposes. The labels may be internal or external.

Failure to erase sensitive information   Valuable information, such as passwords, may be readily available if storage media containing sensitive information is not erased before that media is made available for other uses. Information can also be made available through the improper destruction of carbon paper or unnecessary copies of reports. Remember, with all the concern over hackers breaking into computer systems, it is often much easier to obtain data by walking into a computer facility and physically stealing the media containing it.

Outputs routed to the wrong individual   Printed outputs may be sent to the wrong individual or left in an unattended mode. In addition, on-line systems may route messages to the wrong terminal.

Program threats   Application programs should be developed in an environment that requires and supports complete, correct, and consistent program design; good programming practices; adequate testing, review, and documentation; and proper maintenance procedures. This structured process ensures that programs perform the functions for which they were designed. Additionally, programs should not be subjected to unauthorized modification procedures. Program threats include:

- **Key data stored in programs**   Data that has important effects on the accuracy and completeness of information can be modified by the programmer or any other individual having access to the program. This enables both data and processing to be under the control of a single program.

- **Trojan horse routines**   Programmers may insert special provisions and programs that manipulate data concerning themselves or manipulate data to their own personal advantage. For example, a payroll programmer may alter his/her own payroll records or direct that funds to be sent to him/her through an accounts payable program.

- **Programs readily accessible** The application programs may be readily accessible for unauthorized change on either the source master or object master libraries.

- **Program theft** An employee may steal programs he/she is maintaining and use them for personal gain. For example, they may be sold to a commercial organization or may be used in a new organization where that individual is employed.

- **Program time bombs** Programs may contain routines not compatible with their intended purposes. This can disable or bypass the security protection mechanisms. For example, a programmer who anticipates being fired inserts a code into a program causing vital system files to be deleted as soon as his/her name no longer appears on the payroll file.

- **Ghost program versions** Special versions of the program may be cataloged for use at special times in lieu of the authorized version. When the ghost version is brought into a production status, it can perform unauthorized acts, but analysis of the authorized version will not show how the unauthorized processing occurred. These ghost versions may be cataloged as routines called in by the primary program under special situations or by operator intervention.

- **Back doors and trap doors** Programmers may intentionally insert special codes which enable entry into a program that is running for purposes of testing during design and development. If these devices are not removed, they may provide access while the programs are in production, severely compromising system security and integrity.

Operating system flaw

Design and implementation errors, system generation and maintenance problems, and deliberate penetrations resulting in modifications to the operating system can produce undesirable results on application systems. Computer crime, implemented through operating system vulnerabilities, is often difficult to prevent and detect. The types of vulnerabilities occurring with operating systems include

Operating system control weaknesses The failure of operating systems to control specific threats may permit individuals to access and manipulate data through those operating system control weaknesses.

Disabling of operating system controls An operating system design or implementation facility or error may allow a user to disable audit controls or access all system information without control detection.

Failure to correctly initialize controls Many of the controls included with operating systems are optional controls. For example, passwords are an optional control in many operating systems. If these control features are not generated in the operational system software, the control feature will not be active, and thus cannot prevent or detect the condition it was designed to control.

Poor protection of copies   The operating system may not protect a copy of information as thoroughly as it protects the original.

Unauthorized modification to the operating system   Procedures may allow an individual to make unauthorized and unrecorded modifications to the operating system, thus allowing that individual to circumvent normal system controls.

Unbroken audit trails   Operating systems can be started and stopped with the intervening processing not included within the audit trail. The audit trail created by the operating system during interim processing can be destroyed. Unless the unaccounted for processing time is noted, the events occurring during that interim processing will not be known.

On-line system crash protection   When restarting after an on-line system crash, the operating system may fail to ascertain that all terminal locations that were previously occupied are still occupied by the same individual. This may leave open terminals for access by unauthorized individuals.

Communication system failure

Information being routed from one location to another over communication lines is vulnerable to processing abuse and to interception and modification by unauthorized parties. The types of vulnerabilities associated with communication system failure include

Lack of positive identification   Communication protocol may fail to positively identify the transmitter or receiver of a message. Possible reasons for this include system errors or sequencing of actions by the user.

Unauthorized monitoring   Communication lines may be monitored by unauthorized individuals.

Unauthorized acts at remote terminals   Remote terminals may have data and programs of value. These data or programs may be stolen from a remote terminal without involvement or monitoring by the central processing site.

Unauthorized modification of communication software   Programs in the network switching computers may be modified to compromise security and, thus, gain unauthorized access to data.

Unauthorized takeover   An unauthorized user may "take over" a computer communication facility as an authorized user disconnects from it. Many systems cannot detect the change. This is particularly true with much of the currently available communication equipment and in many communication protocols.

Stealing encryption keys If encryption is used, the keys may be stolen.

Spoofing A terminal user may be "spoofed" into providing sensitive data. This concept makes the user believe that the security software is in control of the system, when in actual practice, a user program or procedure has "spoofed" the individual into believing he/she is interacting with the system.

Replaying messages Messages may be recorded and replayed into the system. For example, a message indicating that $100 has been deposited in an account may be replayed over and over to increase the account balance.

Estimating the magnitude of a threat

Threat identification is a two-part process. The first part identifies the threat. (The previous chapter provided guidance in threat identification.) The second part determines the magnitude of the identified threat.

The importance of knowing the magnitude of the threat is to determine whether resources should be expended to reduce the threat. If the threat is very small it does not make economic sense to spend large amounts of resources to reduce it. For example, there is the threat that boxes of printed paper may be stolen, but to spend money to hire a guard to protect a few hundred dollars' worth of paper is not economically viable. Moving the paper to a secure area would be more cost effective.

The following are the most common methods used for determining the magnitude of a threat.

Ranking

Ranking requires a listing of all of the threats in a descending order of magnitude. The actual dollar amount of the threat is not needed, but the relationship between the threats must be known. Ranking is normally done independently by several individuals who then compare their rankings. The differences in ranking are discussed and then the individuals rerank the threats. This process continues until one ranking can be agreed upon by the group. After ranking, the threat at the top of the list will receive the most control attention, while the threat at the bottom of the list will receive the least control attention.

Judgement

The individuals involved in the threat use their judgement and experience to determine the magnitude of the risk. This method is effective when the threats are in areas in which the group performing the threat analysis has had personal experience.

Formula

The formula method requires the threat analysis team to determine two risk variables. These are the frequency of occurrence and the average loss per occurrence. Each threat is then analyzed. For each threat the threat team must determine how frequently it is likely to occur and the average amount of loss that would occur. For example, if the threat is that an unauthorized transaction will be entered into the input stream, the threat team must determine the average value of that transaction and how frequently they believe the transaction will be entered. The two variables are multiplied together to give the annual loss expectation for the threat.

Historical analysis

The future threat value is based on historical analysis of information. This method is most effective when information has been collected on previous computer crimes. Using statistical inference, the information collected about historical events can be projected into the future based on known variables and volume of processing.

Qualitative assessment

The simplest method is to rank the magnitude of threats into qualitative categories such as high, medium, and low. This is done by judgement and experience or is based on available information. If a lot of information is available the historical method can be used; however, even with limited information there still may be enough data to make a qualitative assessment. This method is also a simplified version of the ranking method and, like ranking, can use the iterative approach involving many people assigning the qualitative category.

At the end of this process, the computer crime threats will have been identified and the magnitude for the threats determined. This threat list is used for two purposes. First, it becomes the basis for establishing a computer crime policy because it defines the potential magnitude of the threat. Second, the list of threats is used to develop countermeasures against those threats. The high-value threats require the more stringent countermeasures and the low-value threats require minimal countermeasures.

Documenting the threat list

At the completion of the threat analysis exercise, the threats should be documented. Figure 3-2 is provided for this purpose. Each threat should be numbered and named using easy-to-understand wording. The threat should then be described in the "description" column. For example, a threat may be "Add a fictitious employee to the payroll system" with a description such as "The payroll system could be defrauded if a fictitious individual could be added to the payroll system and then regular payroll checks issued to that individual."

No.	Computer Threat	Description	Magnitude Of Threat	Basis For Magnitude

Fig. 3-2. Computer crime threat list.

The magnitude of each threat should be determined and recorded in the "magnitude of threat" column. If the magnitude can be expressed in monetary terms, the dollar value should be listed. If the threat is described in other terms, such as ranking, qualitative category, etc., that should be listed. The final column on Fig. 3-2 is to indicate the criteria for determining the "basis for the magnitude" of the threat. For example, if it is a formula method the frequency of occurrence and average loss should be included in this column, together with any information that would support those two variables. For a ranking, the basis for ranking should be documented as a support for substantiating the determined magnitude of the threat.

This computer crime threat list will be used as the basis for all other fraud prevention and detection countermeasures. Unless the threat can be identified, it is difficult to focus attention on where to put computer crime countermeasure resources. A computer crime threat is the sole basis for taking management action against potential perpetrators.

4

Vulnerability self-assessment

AN ORGANIZATION'S VULNERABILITY TO COMPUTER CRIME CAN BE affected by many factors. Among these factors are liquidity of assets, the type of industry, the adequacy of the internal controls system, and senior management's direct involvement in the prevention and detection of computer crime. Some of the factors that make organizations susceptible to computer crime are within their direct ability to control, while others are not.

This chapter addresses both controllable and uncontrollable computer crime vulnerabilities. A self-assessment document is provided to help an organization determine the vulnerabilities that relate to their industry, environment, and organizational philosophy. As a second measure of vulnerability, a data collection tool is provided to gather information about the organization's history with computer crime. Combining these two instruments will help an organization assess its vulnerability to computer crime.

Assessing vulnerability to computer crime

An organization's computer crime vulnerability is dependent on both the environment in which it operates and the applications software that are run. The industry environment (for example, the banking industry environment) may provide a high susceptibility to computer crime. Most environmental factors are beyond the control of the organization. However, the type of applications and the level of control also affect vulnerability and these are within the control of the organization.

An integral part of the prevention and detection of computer crime is determination of the organization's vulnerability. Obviously, the more vulnerable the organization is to computer crime, the more resources are necessary to prevent and detect computer crime. On the other hand, if vulnerability is low, it may be uneconomical to devote many resources to the prevention of an event that is unlikely to occur.

The recommended vulnerability assessment process involves the following two steps:

1. Assess the vulnerability criteria. There are criteria that exhibit a high correlation with vulnerability to computer crime. These criteria involve both environmental and application risks. Conducting this evaluation provides an organization with an indication of their degree of vulnerability to computer crime.

2. Computer crime experience. Organizations can learn from their own previous experience. Being under attack is not usually a one-time process, but one in which the organization continues to gather experience. This experience database is built by collecting information on each reported computer crime. A sample data collection instrument is provided for this purpose later in this chapter (see Fig. 4-3).

The process outlined in the remainder of this chapter is a data-gathering process. This, coupled with a more detailed analysis of the controls, can be used to develop a computer crime vulnerability profile. The profile indicates the probability of a computer crime occurring, the area where it is most likely to occur, and the most likely perpetrator. This profile (described in chapter 7) can form the basis of a computer crime prevention and detection strategy. It is important to remember, however, that a vendor attack cannot be predicted, and as such will fall outside the scope of this strategy.

Vulnerability criteria

The science of statistical correlation is one that attempts to identify criteria that correlate to some special features. Performed properly, the science uses regression analysis to show the amount of positive or negative correlation between two variables. For example, the Surgeon General of the U.S. has shown that there is a high positive correlation between cigarette smoking and lung cancer. A high positive correlation means that when one of the attributes is present (smoking) the other attribute (lung cancer) is also likely to be present.

On the opposite side of the correlation coin, there is a strong negative correlation between wearing a seat belt and being thrown from your car during an accident. A strong negative correlation means that if one of the conditions exists (wearing the seat belt) then the likelihood of the other condition happening is very low. All of this statistical work is in the realm of inferential statistics which attempts to answer questions about the probability of some activity occurring given some set of related conditions.

A true statistical correlation requires large amounts of data and careful statistical analyses. Unfortunately, in the area of computer crime, the amount of data needed to show true correlation is not readily available. Therefore, the instrument that will be discussed in this chapter cannot be guaranteed to be statistically correct.

Experience in any field provides common knowledge. For example, data processing professionals know that large programs using complex source statements are more difficult to maintain than small programs using straightforward coding. The U.S. Air Force spent large amounts of money studying the performance of computer programs. As a result of this study, the Air Force has demonstrated statistically that large programs and complex code increase the cost of maintenance. Thus, while common sense is not as statistically valid as studies, there is much we can learn based on our personal experience. The combination of statistical analysis, modified or corroborated by experienced judgment, allows for a valid vulnerability assessment.

Completing the self-assessment checklist

Two self-assessment checklists are included for evaluating your organization's vulnerability to computer crime. One checklist is for environmental criteria (Fig. 4-1), and the other is for application criteria (Fig. 4-2). These checklists should be completed by a team of individuals knowledgeable about the organization's data processing functions and applications.

Please note that this book is written from the perspective of the large corporation, with a team of data processing professionals available to provide the services listed. However, these same criteria, albeit reduced in scope, need to be applied by the owner of a personal computer. It is important to realize that this collection of concerns is as important when securing a home computer as it is when developing the security for a large computer installation. The only difference is that the owner of a personal computer must wear many different hats and analyze the computer environment from varied perspectives.

No.	Criteria	Applicability				Comments
		High	Avg.	Low	None	
1.	Does your organization have a computer crime policy that defines senior management's philosophy regarding: a. The prevention and detection of computer crime? b. The method of prosecuting individuals convicted of perpetrating computer crime?					
2.	Does you organization have an internal audit department that is independent of the organizations that it evaluates?					
3.	Does your organization's internal audit department have a responsibility to conduct reviews designed to disclose computer crime?					
4.	Does the internal audit department have sufficient skills to fulfill that responsibility?					
5.	Is your organization a financial institution whose primary functions deal with the collection and disbursement of cash?					
6.	If your organization is in the private sector, is it currently losing money?					
7.	If your organization is in the public sector, has its budget been cut from last year?					
8.	If your organization is in the private sector, has it been losing money for over a two-year period?					
9.	If your organization is in the public sector, has your budget been cut for two or more consecutive years?					
10.	Has your organization been reducing staff during the past year?					
11.	Does your organization plan to reduce staff during the next year?					
12.	Has your organization: a. Suspended pay raises during the past year?					

Fig. 4-1. Environmental criteria.

No.	Criteria	Applicability				Comments
		High	**Avg.**	**Low**	**None**	
	b. Reduced the pay of some employees during the past year?					
13.	Is your senior management personally involved in ensuring the adequacy of your organization's system of internal accounting control?					
14.	Are your senior officers and key management personnel required to sign an annual representation letter indicating that they have followed and enforced the organization's system of internal control?					
15.	Have independent public accountants qualified their opinion of your organization's financial statement and system of internal accounting control?					
16.	Is it the policy of your organization to pay equal to, or better than, the prevailing wage in the community?					
17.	Does your organization publicize to all your employees the individuals to whom they should report unusual circumstances or questionable activities occurring in the organization?					
18.	Is your computer center accessible to individuals outside the organization through communication lines?					
19.	Has your data center acquired and installed security software to protect on-line access to your computer center?					
20.	Is it the policy of your organization to prosecute employees and other parties who commit fraud or crime against your organization?					
21.	Is it the policy of your organization to reprimand employees who fail to follow the policies and procedures of the organization?					
22.	Does your organization have well publicized policies regarding the personal use of its computer equipment?					

Fig. 4-1. Continued

No.	Criteria	Applicability				Comments
		High	Avg.	Low	None	
23.	Does your organization distribute guidelines about safe computing?					
24.	Does your organization have a publicized policy towards software copying and software piracy?					

No.	Criteria	Applicability				Comments
		High	Avg.	Low	None	
1.	Are the major financial applications of the organization computerized?					
2.	Is the financial data managed independently of the applications that use that data (the organization has a database administration function)?					
3.	Must the functions within a system meet important conflicting needs of several organization units?					
4.	Is the timing of application such that everything must work perfectly for the applications to accomplish their stated objectives?					
5.	Do the systems apply new, difficult, and unproven technology and techniques on a broad scale so that the systems are aggressively pioneering the use of new technology?					
6.	Does the data processing function have more than a two-year backlog of work to accomplish?					

Fig. 4-2. Application criteria.

No.	Criteria	Applicability				Comments
		High	Avg.	Low	None	
7.	Are the users generally dissatisfied with the data processing function?					
8.	Do the application users have reasonable expertise: a. In data processing? b. In the capabilities and limitations of their application systems?					
9.	Are unresolved transactions (i.e., those placed in a suspense account) resolved within a reasonable period of time?					
10.	Are system errors promptly corrected and re-entered into application systems?					
11.	Are financial applications reconciled to independently maintained control totals?					
12.	Are all warning messages and control reports regularly reviewed by supervisors and appropriate action taken based on the information presented?					

At a minimum, it is recommended that the checklists be completed by the following people:

- Environmental assessment checklist
  - ~ Internal auditors
  - ~ Corporate comptroller
  - ~ Data security officer
  - ~ Data processing manager
  - ~ One key user
- Application assessment checklist
  - ~ Two to five key data processing users
  - ~ Two to five EDP project leaders
  - ~ Database administrator
  - ~ Computer operations manager

These checklists contain criteria that have a correlation to computer crime. The individual completing the checklist must determine for each criterion whether the applicability is high, average, low, or none at all. Guidance in selection applicability follows

High applicability   The organization and environment meets or exceeds the criterion in every aspect.

Average applicability   The criterion generally fits the organization, although some aspects of the criterion may not apply.

Low applicability   The criterion is generally not typical of the organization, although some aspects of the criterion are representative of the environment in which the business functions.

No applicability   The criterion is not representative of the business or the environment in which the business operates.

The individual responsible for completing the checklist should add comments whenever there is some doubt about the category of applicability selected, or if the respondent wishes to clarify the reasons for the selection. When more than one individual completes the checklist, this type of information may be valuable in resolving differences.

If several individuals complete the checklist their responses should be averaged and then categorized into one of the four applicability categories. The vulnerability assessment checklist is not meant to be a high-precision document, but rather one that indicates degrees of vulnerability. Therefore, forcing the categorization into one of the four categories will not adversely affect the use of the information.

Analysis of computer crimes

History is a good teacher. The lessons learned in previous computer crimes can be applied to preventing and detecting future computer crimes. It is critical that the appropriate information be gathered so that the lessons that have been paid for in financial and other losses can be used to reduce the incidence of computer crime.

The collection of information relating to computer crime is a five-step process as follows.

1. Assign responsibility for data collection. One unit in the organization should be assigned the responsibility to collect information about computer crimes. The internal audit department, or the comptroller's function, are logical places to assign this responsibility. The fulfillment of this responsibility requires the establishment of computer crime data collection procedures (a formal process to collect the information) and the appropriate interaction and follow-up to ensure that the procedures are followed.

2. Design the data collection instrument. A standardized method needs to be developed to collect information about computer

crimes. Two general approaches are recommended. First, a narrative form can be prepared and disseminated to document suspected and actual computer crimes. Second, a checklist can be developed and periodically disseminated to gather computer crime statistics.

A narrative data collection form for computer crime should contain the following information:

~ Area in which the crime occurred (geographical and organizational)
~ Description of the crime
~ Perpetrators involved in the crime
~ Loss incurred
~ Disposition of the crime

A sample computer crime checklist is provided in Fig. 4-3 at the end of this chapter. This checklist is designed to be disseminated to parties who might be involved in computer crime prevention, as well as areas where it is known that computer crime has occurred. The checklist is designed to be easy to complete and, at the same time, to provide sufficient information to determine vulnerabilities that may result in computer crimes in the organization.

3. Collect computer crime data. The responsible organization must ensure that the appropriate data regarding computer crimes is collected. Parties most likely to be involved in computer crime should be contacted, notified of the data collection procedure, supplied with the appropriate forms, and requested to supply the needed information. The responsible organization should follow up to ensure that information regarding computer crimes is supplied.

4. Collect data on computer crimes outside your company. It is important to collect data on computer crimes outside your company. If companies like yours have been assaulted using a specific avenue of attack, it is critical that you are aware of and are prepared for this type of attack. There is no substitute for continued and conscientious research to prepare your organization to handle computer threats.

5. Analyze the collected data. The information collected on computer crime should be carefully analyzed. If a checklist is used, analysis becomes easy. If the narrative form is used, the information cannot be quantitatively accumulated, but should be accumulated into categories for analysis.

Remember that any time you add software to your system, you can change your vulnerability profile. For example, if you add a module to provide electronic mail via phone access, and you have not had modems previously, you now add the potential for dial-in access and attack. Each time you add software to your system you need to redo your checklists.

Evaluating the organization's vulnerability

It is not uncommon for organizations to find no computer crimes reported. This is attributable to two reasons:

1. The lack of a good definition of computer crime, and failure to contact the right people, results in no computer crimes being reported when they actually have occurred

2. There, in fact, has not been any computer crime

However, organizations with no computer crime should be suspicious. It is highly unlikely with the widespread use of computers and the widespread losses associated with fraud that an organization would be spared from this type of crime.

INSTRUCTIONS:

1. Read the instructions.
2. Make sure all entries are clear and legible.
3. Enter explanatory material where applicable.

Prepared By: _____ Date: _____

Location: _____

---

1. Department: _____
2. Case Number:_____
3. How was alleged computer crime discovered? (check one only)

    a. — Routine Audit, Inspection, Investigation, or Review

    b. — Specially Requested Audit, Inspection, or Review

    c. — Employee (knowledge gained through work)

    d. — Former Employee

    e. — Manager/Supervisor

    f. — Contractor Personnel

    g. — Former Contractor Personnel

    h. — Security Personnel

    i. — Private Individual (not former employee)

    j. — Anonymous Informant

Fig. 4-3. Sample computer crime checklist.

k. — Consumer Complaint

l. — Paid Informant

m. — Unsuccessful Bidder

n. — News Media

o. — Alleged Victim

p. — Confession by Perpetrator

q. — Law Enforcement Investigation — State/Local/Federal

r. — Not Applicable

s. — Other (specify)_____

t. — Unknown

4. If (a) or (b) were checked in question #3, indicate whether it was an

a. — Audit

b. — Inspection

c. — Investigation

d. — Internal compliance or eligibility review

5. If (a) or (b) were checked in question #3, indicate

Audit Number:_____

Date:_____

Job (or report) Title: _____

6. In how many locations did the alleged computer crime activity take place?

Number of Locations: _____

7. If alleged computer crime occurred at only one location, provide appropriate information under principal location. If alleged computer crime activity occurred at more than one location, provide the principal location and the second most important location.

Principal Location:

City_____

State or County_____

Second Most Important Location:

City_____

State or County_____

Fig. 4-3. Continued

8. What is the functional area in which the alleged computer crime occurred (check one only)?

    a. — Procurement Award   k. — Inventory Control

    b. — Property Dispositions   l. — Mail Service

    c. — Payroll   m. — Cash Control

    d. — Inventory   n. — Procurement Monitoring

    e. — Sales   o. — Travel

    f. — Computer Resource   p. — Administrative Services

    g. — Programs   q. — Training and Education

    h. — Loans   r. — Personal Property Management

    i. — Stock   s. — Not Applicable

    j. — Personnel   t. — Other (please specify)

    _____

                                        u. — Unknown

9. Frequency of alleged computer crime activity:

    a. — Once   e. — 16-20 Times

    b. — 2-5 Times   f. — 21-25 Times

    c. — 6-10 Times   g. — Over 25 Times

    d. — 11-15 Times   h. — Unknown

10. Indicate the period of time over which the alleged computer crime activity took place:

    a. — Less than 3 Months   d. — 1 to 2 Years

    b. — 3 to 6 Months   e. — More than 2 Years

    c. — 6 Months to 1 Year   f. — Unknown

11. Approximately how much time had elapsed between the time the alleged computer crime act was committed and the time it was reported or discovered?

    a. — Less than 3 Months   d. — 1 to 2 Years

    b. — 3 to 6 Months   e. — More than 2 Years

    c. — 6 Months to 1 Year   f. — Unknown

12. At the time the computer crime was committed, who was responsible for the administration of projects involved in the crime?

    a. — Department Head   f. — Contractor

    b. — Corporate Officials   g. — Financial Institutions

    c. — Data Processing Officials   h. — Other (Please specify)

d. — EDP Project Leader   _____

e. — EDP Operations   i. — Not Applicable

                                                   j. — Unknown

13. Was the computer necessary (material) in committing the fraudulent activity?

     Yes __   No __

14. Participants in the alleged computer crime (check one only):

a. — Employees Only

b. — Employees in Conjunction with Others

c. — Contractor(s) Personnel

d. — Other Individual Citizens

e. — Other Corporate or Business Entities (such as lending institutions)

f. — Unknown

g. — Other (please specify)

15. Indicate the type of computer crime:

    _____

    _____

    _____

Employees: Complete this section only if (a) or (b) were checked in question #14.

16. How many employees were involved in the activity?

a. — One   d. — Over 20

b. — 2 to 5   e. — Unknown

c. — 6 to 20

17. Which of the following categories best describes the occupation or position of the employee(s) involved in the computer crime activity? (check one only)

a. — Accountants   k. — Regulatory Official

b. — Attorneys   l. — Logistics and Inventory Control Officials

c. — Auditors   m. — Clerical Workers

d. — Computer Personnel   n. — Skilled Craftsmen

e. — Contracting and Procurement Officials   o. — Semi-Skilled

f. — Top Policy-Making Management   p. — Laborers

g. — Managers or Supervisors   q. — Not Applicable

Fig. 4-3. Continued

h. — Staff	r. — Other (Please Specify)
i. — Investigator	s. — Unknown
j. — Law Enforcement Officer	

Other Organizations: Complete this section only if items (b), (c), (d), (e), or (g) were checked in question #14.

18.   How many organizations were involved in the computer crime activity?

a. — One	d. — Over 10
b. — Two	e. — Unknown
c. — 3 to 10	

19.   How many employees of other organizations were involved in the computer crime activity?

a. — One	d. — Over 10
b. — Two	e. — Unknown
c. — 3 to 10	

20.   Which category below best describes the employees of the organization(s) that were involved in the computer crime activity? (check one only)

a. — Company or Corporate Officers (President, Vice President, Treasurer, or Secretary)

b. — Plant Manager/Superintendent

c. — Professionals (Attorneys, Accountants, Engineers, etc.)

d. — Computer Personnel

e. — Sales Workers

f. — Skilled Craftsmen, Foremen, Skilled Trades, Skilled and Kindred Workers

g. — Operators (Semi-Skilled)

h. — Laborers

i. — Clerical

j. — Not Applicable

k. — Other (specify) _____

l. — Unknown

Non-employees Involved: This section should be completed only if items (b), (c), (d), (e), or (g) were checked in question #14.

21. How many individuals were involved in the computer crime?

a. — One	d. — Over 10
b. — Two	e. — Not Applicable
c. — 3 to 10	f. — Unknown

22.   Describe the role of the individual(s) at the time they were engaged in the fraudulent activities.

_____

_____

_____

Loss (or Potential Loss) Due to Computer Crime

23.   If the specific dollar amount of the loss has been identified, insert it below.

$ _____

If multiple violations, indicate total amount of loss:

$ _____

If the specific dollar amount of the loss is not available, please **estimate** the dollar amount of the loss incurred by the organization for this case:

a. — Less than $100

b. — $101 to $1,000

c. — $1,001 to $10,000

d. — $10,001 to $100,000

e. — $100,001 to $500,000

f. — $500,001 to $1 Million

g. — Over $1 Million

h. — Monetary Loss but unable to Estimate Loss.

i. — Not Applicable because no Monetary Loss Involved

24.   If the computer crime activity did not result in a direct dollar loss, indicate the effect that occurred or may occur (check one only):

a. — Potential harmful effects to the health or safety of individuals

b. — Received benefits for which ineligible

c. — Received benefits greater than entitled to

d. — Intended recipients did not receive benefits

e. — Potential harmful effect to organizations

f. — Not applicable

g. — Other (describe) _____

h. — Unknown

i. — Recipient did not receive intended benefits

j. — Unauthorized disclosure of information

25.   Indicate whether a final decision or determination on the alleged computer crime case has been made (closed case) or whether the investigation or prosecution on the alleged computer case has not been completed (open case).

a. — Closed case   b. — Open case

Fig. 4-3. Continued

26. Indicate whether administrative action, legal action, or both types of action were taken.

  a. — Closed Cases — administrative action only - no action taken

  b. — Closed Cases — administrative action only - some substantive action taken

  c. — Closed Cases-only legal action taken

  d. — Closed Cases-both administrative (substantive) action and legal action taken

  e. — Closed Cases-no action taken since participant is unknown

  f. — Closed Cases-type of action taken is unknown

  g. — Open Cases-administrative action only-no action taken

  h. — Open Cases-administrative action only-some substantive action taken

  i. — Open Cases-legal action only taken

  j. — Open Cases-both administrative (substantive) action and legal action taken

  k. — Open Cases-no action taken since participant is unknown

  l. — Open Cases-case is pending

27. Is the alleged "open" computer crime case under investigation or has it been referred to another area of the organization for investigation or prosecution? If so, who?

28. Is prosecution declined for this case, what was the reason give (check one only)?

  a. — Insufficient evidence for prosecution

  b. — No loss to organization

  c. — Dollar loss insignificant

  d. — Case lacks jury appeal

  e. — Statute of limitations

  f. — Insufficient staff resources

  g. — Lacks prosecution merit

  h. — Other (please specify) _____

  i. — Unknown

  j. — Declined in lieu of administrative action

29. Indicate the type of administrative action taken against employees (check all that apply):

  a. — No action taken (skip to question #32)

  b. — Employee dismissed

  c. — Employee suspended

  d. — Employee issued warning letter

e. — Employee issued letter of counseling

f. — Employee issued oral warning

g. — Employee demoted

h. — Employee transferred

i. — Formal loss recovery plan agreed to (indicate amount of planned recoveries)_____

j. — Employee resigned pending dismissal

k. — Not applicable

l. — Other

m. — Unknown

30. Indicate the type of administrative action taken against other organizations (contractors, corporation, nonprofit organizations, etc.) or individuals involved in the computer crime case (check all that apply).

a. — Suspended from doing business

b. — Debarred from doing business

c. — Contract/grant cancelled

d. — Issued warning and they agreed to take corrective action

e. — Formal loss recovery plan agreed to (indicate amount of planned recoveries)_____

f. — No action taken

g. — Negotiating reimbursement

h. — Employee dismissed

i. — Not applicable

j. — Other (please describe) _____

k. — Unknown

31. Why was administrative action taken rather than legal action (check one only)?

a. — Isolated incident

b. — Immaterial amount

c. — Minor infraction

d. — Evidence and documentation insufficient for legal action

e. — Legal agency declined case

f. — Statute of limitations

g. — Hardship cases

h. — Funds recovered

i. — Other (please describe)_____

j. — Unknown

Fig. 4-3. Continued

32. Indicate the reason no administrative action was taken in the alleged computer crime case (check one only):

    a. — Case investigated and dismissed because no evidence of computer crime found

    b. — Employees resigned and it was felt the matter was not worth pursuing

    c. — Statute of limitations

    d. — Fraud (or crime) committed and case investigated but no suspect found

    e. — Lack of adequate evidence and documentation

    f. — Not applicable

    g. — Other (please specify)_____

    h. — Unknown

Legal Action

33. Was this case prosecuted as a civil or a criminal case?

    a. — Civil case

    b. — Criminal case

    c. — Civil and criminal prosecution

    d. — Pretrial diversion

    e. — Court-martial

34. Indicate the outcome of the criminal prosecution.

    a. — Acquittal

    b. — Conviction (quality plea, nolo contendere)

    c. — Other (please specify)

    d. — Unknown

35. Indicate the outcome of the civil proceeding.

    a. — Judgment for plaintiff

    b. — Judgment for defendant

    c. — Case dismissed

    d. — Unknown

36. If the defendants were convicted, indicate the amount of fines, recoveries, and restitutions:

Fines: _____

Recoveries: _____

Restitutions: _____

Sentencing Data

37. a. Actual sentence (in months)   _____

b. Sentence suspended (in months)   _____

c. Portion of sentence to be served on probation (in months)   _____

d. Portion of sentence to be served in prison (in months)   _____

If more than one person sentenced, provide the following information on additional persons.

38. Second Person

a.   Actual sentence (in months)   _____

b.   Sentence suspended (in months)   _____

c.   Portion of sentence to be served on probation (in months)   _____

d.   Portion of sentence to be served in prison (in months)   _____

39. Third Person

a.   Actual sentence (in months)   _____

b.   Sentence suspended (in months)   _____

c.   Portion of sentence to be served on probation (in months)   _____

d.   Portion of sentence to be served in prison (in months)   _____

40. Fourth Person

a.   Actual sentence (in months)   _____

b.   Sentence suspended (in months)   _____

c.   Portion of sentence to be served on probation (in months)   _____

d.   Portion of sentence to be served in prison (in months)   _____

41. Fifth Person

a.   Actual sentence (in months)   _____

b.   Sentence suspended (in months)   _____

c.   Portion of sentence to be served on probation (in months)   _____

d.   Portion of sentence to be served in prison (in months)   _____

Fig. 4-3. Continued

Computer Vulnerability Exploited

42.   List risk from Section 3 (or other) that permitted the crime to occur.

_____

_____

_____

_____

43.   List detection method from Part 3 of Manual (or other, if applicable).

_____

_____

_____

5

Vulnerability assessment on a macro level

FRAUD IS LIKELY TO OCCUR IN ANY ASPECT OF AN ORGANIZATION'S manual and computer-based processing. In addition, the defrauder may be an employee, someone who conducts business with the organization, or an individual with no ties to the organization other than that individual's attempt to acquire resources illegally. The spectrum of methods and perpetrators is so broad that the task of addressing fraud appears almost unaccomplishable. For this reason, auditors generally state that the detection of fraud is not an audit responsibility.

This chapter provides an approach for selecting the high-probability points for fraud, as well as the people who are likely to defraud. The concept of a macro level assessment is to narrow the scope of computer crime vulnerabilities to a manageable level. Once a determination has been made that an organization is vulnerable to computer crime, a systematic approach is necessary to continually narrow the scope of the computer crime activities so the prevention and detection countermeasures are cost effective. This chapter explains the process and describes in detail the macro level segment of that process.

The risk of computer crime

The risk of computer crime exists wherever there is a computer. At a minimum, the processing resources of the computer can be misused, and at the upper end of the computer crime spectrum is the loss of large sums of money and destruction of computer resources.

Historically, organizations have failed to deal directly with computer crime because of the extremely large spectrum of possibilities. The predominant practice with regard to computer crime is to develop a system of internal controls and hope that those controls are effective against computer crime.

The recommended process is to identify the major computer crime vulnerabilities, and ensure that controls against those vulnerabilities are adequate. It is possible that, with a small amount of additional investigation and effort, the probability of computer crime can be significantly reduced.

The following is the recommended four-part process:

1. Identify vulnerability to computer crime. This step was discussed in the previous chapter. In some situations, and for some readers, this step may suffice. However, with the proliferation of computer crime across all classes of computer, from the personal machine to the mainframe, it would be wise for all computer professionals to consider the other three steps.

2. Narrow the scope of possible computer crimes. The potential possibilities for computer crime are too numerous to consider unless we narrow the scope to include only those high-probability points of attack. The same is true when we try to discern those people we need to consider as potential threats. Without this process there is a great likelihood that efforts will be made to guard against nonexistent threats and that some vulnerabilities will be left unguarded due to lack of resources.

3. Pinpoint those controls necessary to reduce computer crime at the high-probability penetration points. Besides finding those areas where true vulnerability exists, it is important to identify the strength of the control necessary to defeat the threat. For example, it makes little sense to install an auto-callback modem on a system that has little or no phone access. The appropriate level of threat response is vital for the same reasons that the problem must be limited to a reasonable scope: to avoid spending unnecessary dollars to combat a nonexistent threat and avoid having some high-risk vulnerability exposed for lack of dollars to cover it.

4. Develop computer crime countermeasures. The final product from your work with this book and the experts you have available should be a set of procedures that will enable your organization to deal with the threats of computer crime. Please remember that not all threats need to be handled, only those

which are pertinent to your situation. The last two chapters in this book are targeted toward detecting and preventing the occurrence of computer crime at your facility. Bear in mind that this is not a one-shot process, but must be done at regular intervals, updating your strategy to handle new threats and protect new systems.

Purpose of the macro vulnerability assessment

Macro in this context means large. Thus, the macro vulnerability assessment is a broad look at the computer crime risks. A *macroassessment* is a broad analysis of the penetration possibilities within an organization. This macroview will begin to narrow the scope of activities involved in preventing and detecting computer crime.

At the end of the macro vulnerability assessment, the following will be accomplished:

- All high-risk areas in the organization will have been reviewed
- The points where the high-risk systems can be penetrated will have been identified
- The individuals or categories of people who can commit computer crime will have been identified
- The most probable penetration points will have been determined
- The most probable perpetrators will have been determined

The computer crime assessment process can be viewed as a funnel. At the top of the funnel, the computer crime methods and perpetrators are almost unlimited. At the bottom of the funnel, the computer crime strategy can focus on the areas where penetration is most probable. The macroassessment part of the process works at the wide end of the funnel. It is the beginning of the process that will narrow the computer crime risk to one which can be addressed in a cost-effective manner.

Penetration point matrix technique

The technique used in conducting the macro vulnerability assessment is called penetration point analysis. The tool used in this analysis is the penetration point matrix. The matrix attempts to identify which individuals are most likely to commit a computer crime, and at what point within a computer application area.

The penetration point analysis is a four-step process as follows:

1. Identify high-risk computer applications or areas. The areas or applications for which penetration points can be established

need to be identified. It is most economical to perform the analysis of areas that pose a high computer crime risk.

2. Identify the most probable points of penetration. Those places within the vulnerable application, geographical locations, or organization areas where computer crime is most likely to occur should be identified.

3. Identify perpetrators. Those individuals that are most likely to commit computer crime should be identified.

4. Rate the probability of computer crime for each individual at each point. Establish the priority for application computer crime countermeasures.

Identifying high-risk applications/areas

Penetration point analysis begins by identifying the areas or applications which present a high vulnerability for a computer crime incident. These are the applications or areas that need to be more closely analyzed and for which defensive strategies need to be developed. It is important to note that this first step enables us to focus on those areas that represent a true risk, and in so doing, saving time and resources which would have been wasted examining in detail areas that represent little threat.

Applications that should be considered as high-risk computer applications are those that:

- Make dispersement of large amounts of money
- Receive or process large amounts of money
- Process highly marketable merchandise
- Contain valuable information, such as customer lists manufacturing processes, etc.
- Enable users to access reasonable media
- Are accessible by computer terminals
- Are accessible over commercial communications lines
- Allow users to load software from outside the machine

The types of areas that should be considered high-risk computer crime areas include:

- The data center
- The data library, both on- and off-site
- Programming areas containing copies of programs and other types of documentation
- The master terminal and other facilities in which privileged instructions can be entered and executed

- The system software generation function
- Personal computers, especially if networked

The high-risk selection process should begin with an inventory of all computer applications and computer areas. People knowledgeable in the resources controlled by those systems, as well as the potential threats that can be directed against those applications or areas, should select the high-risk applications and areas for further analysis. Two approaches can be used for this:

1. High-risk criteria. The selection group determines the criteria that will put an application or area into (or out of) the high-risk computer crime category. For example, it might be determined that if the risk of loss is under $10,000 and will not provide access to other areas or applications, it will not be considered for further analysis. Those applications or areas that meet this selection criterion will be subject to further evaluation.

2. Judgment. The individual or group analyzing the application areas determine which ones have a high-risk computer crime potential, and thus, should be subject to further evaluation.

Identifying the most probable points of penetration

Once the application or area has been selected, the penetration points at which a crime can occur need to be identified. These points are defined as any one of the following:

- Type of fraud or abuse that might occur
- Method used to commit the crime
- An act that can be performed to cause a loss to occur

A determination of the fraud, method, or act is the basis for determining the point or location where the computer crime is most likely to occur. The description of the fraud, method, or act should be in sufficient detail to describe the point of entry into the system. For example, a fraud might be to enter a duplicate invoice for payment. This describes the fraud, but also describes the point in the system where the crime occurs.

In determining the penetration points (fraud, method, or act) for an application system, it is suggested that the individual determining the points go through the system in an orderly fashion. The portions of the system that should be evaluated one by one are:

- Data origination
- Data authorization
- Data entry
- Data communications
- Processing

- Storage
- Data output
- Data usage

Some individuals find it beneficial to go through the parts of the application systems for each business event. A business event is a business transaction that will cause resources to be acquired or consumed. For example, in a payroll system, a business event would be hiring a new employee, giving an employee a raise, recording an employee's hours worked, producing a paycheck, and so forth.

The process requires that for each economic event (at each point in an application system) these two questions should be asked:

1. How could a computer crime occur with this event at this point in the processing?

2. What could happen with this event at this point in the system that could lead to a computer crime?

The end-product of this step is a listing of the points in an application system where computer crime could occur. These points will be used later in assessing the high-probability points where computer crime could occur.

If an area is being evaluated rather than an application, the same types of questions need to be asked, but rather than application segments, it is necessary to define the resources within the area. For example, if the computer room is the area in question, then the resources might include:

- Computer hardware
- Operating systems and other software systems
- Application output reports
- Application input data
- Master console
- Computer programs
- Systems input data
- New software applications
- Inserts of removable media

Identifying perpetrators

This step involves the identification of potential perpetrators, including the people who may be threats to the application or area. No one should be excluded, regardless of position in the organization or personal traits.

Being categorized a potential perpetrator does not imply that an individual may, in fact, commit a computer crime. A potential perpetrator is an individual who has an opportunity to commit a computer crime. Individuals should look on this as a positive step because, if the proper analysis is performed, the necessary countermeasures will be installed so that they will not be a prime suspect in the event that an actual computer crime does occur.

Potential perpetrators can be listed by the name of the individual, the function or job title of the individual, a group of people performing the same function or within the same category, organizational units, or broad categories of people. Examples of who might be considered potential perpetrators are:

- Joe Smith
- Corporate comptroller
- Accounts receivable clerks
- Payroll department ex-employees
- System programmers
- Customers who purchase inventory
- Hardware system maintenance personnel
- People having access to a touch-tone telephone
- Any employee with a personal computer with removable media

This step should identify all of the individuals or categories of people that have an opportunity to commit computer crime. Those that only have a minimal opportunity should be deleted as potential suspects, but they should be included for analysis purposes.

The process of identifying perpetrators includes the following tasks:

1. Identify resources that can be lost. For either an application or an area, the resources that can be stolen, destroyed, or modified need to be identified.

2. Identify who might want those resources. This is a preliminary step that attempts to identify all of the individuals or categories of people who might have an interest in acquiring, modifying, or destroying the resources. Obviously, the list of people would be restricted to those who can reasonably be expected to have a knowledge of the existence of the resources.

3. Identify those having an opportunity to commit a computer crime. From the above list, those who would have an opportunity to commit a computer crime are selected. It is this list that becomes the list of potential perpetrators who will be subject to further analysis and investigation.

Rating the probability of computer crime

A penetration point matrix is a tool used to identify the most likely point of computer crime and the most probable perpetrator. Again, we are talking in probabilities and not making an inference that the individual is a criminal or the point is an actual point of crime. The objective of the analysis is to ensure that controls are adequate at the most vulnerable computer crime points.

An example of the penetration point matrix is illustrated in Fig. 5-1. The penetration points identified in Step 2 are listed down the left side of

Application/Area Evaluated _____

Potential Perpetrator	People who have an opportunity to commit a computer crime					
Fraud, Method, or Act	1	2	3	4	5	Total Points
	V					
	W	2-W				
	X					
	Y		Each intersection is a penetration point.			
	Z					
(Points where a computer crime can occur)						
Total Points						

Fig. 5-1. Penetration point matrix.

the matrix, and the probable perpetrators across the top of the matrix. One of these matrices is prepared for each high-risk computer application or area. Thus, if Step 1 (see pages 70 and 71) had identified 10 high-risk applications and areas, 10 penetration point matrices would be prepared in this step.

After the matrix has been developed, the probability of penetration is evaluated. The evaluation process commences after all of the probable frauds, methods, or acts (penetration points) have been documented on the left side of the matrix with the probable perpetrators across the top of the matrix. The evaluator then looks at each point to evaluate the probability of computer fraud at that point by the potential perpetrator.

If there are 10 penetration points and 10 perpetrators, there are 100 penetration points. Each of these points is evaluated for the probability of a computer crime occurring at that point. For example, if the system was accounts receivable, the penetration point the issuance of a credit, and the potential perpetrator the accounts receivable clerk, we would evaluate that intersection.

The opportunity to commit a fraud should be evaluated according to the following weight values (a weight value is the degree of opportunity to commit computer crime).

- 3 = good
- 2 = fair
- 1 = poor
- 0 = none

Each intersection within the penetration point matrix is evaluated independently. The computer crime team assigns one of the four weight values to the opportunity to commit a crime. For example, in our previous illustration, the accounts receivable clerk has a good opportunity to commit computer crime using credits in our hypothetical accounts receivable system. If in Fig. 5-1 that penetration point was the block "2-W" then a "3" would be inserted in that block to indicate the opportunity that the accounts receivable clerk had to commit a computer crime using the point in the system at which a credit was issued. Obviously, this is a judgement on the part of the computer crime team based on their knowledge of the system and the ease with which a computer crime could be committed.

The analysis is continued until all of the intersections in the matrix have been evaluated. The evaluator selects one of the four opportunities and inserts the numbers 3, 2, 1, or 0 in the appropriate intersection. When the final intersection has been evaluated, this step is completed for the application or area in question. The next application or area is then evaluated, until all applications and areas have been evaluated. Please keep in mind, these estimates are only as good as the knowledge of the evaluation team.

Identifying a high-probability penetration point

Experience has shown that computer crime most often occurs at those points where there is the greatest opportunity to commit crime and by people with the greatest chances. The objective of the matrix is to identify the individual with the greatest opportunity and the point where the system appears weakest. Again, experience has shown that the weakest link in the system is the link that is most likely exploited by criminals.

To determine the most vulnerable point, the horizontal lines are totaled and the vertical lines are totaled. All of the weighted opportunity values are numbers. These numbers are accumulated horizontally on each line and the total put in the total point column. The rows are then totaled numerically and the total of each row put in the total point column.

The rows with the highest number of points should be indicated by circling or otherwise designating the row and the column. The intersection of the rows and columns with the highest numerical scores should be circled. These intersections are the high-probability penetration points. They indicate not only the point where computer crime is most likely to occur, but the most likely perpetrator. At this point these data should be considered secret and discussed only among the crime team and appropriate management.

Discretion should be used when determining the number of high-probability intersections. Normally, one row and one column receive the highest number of points. If there are other rows and columns within 10% of that numerical value, they should be considered a tie and indicated as high-number rows and columns. Actual experience shows that the average number of points in a computer system or area is less than 10. This is a manageable number and can be addressed through either preventive or detective countermeasures.

Penetration point case study

VSRS is a state pension system. It is a consolidated pension system covering most public employees in the state. The system covers over 235,000 members in 700 different reporting agencies and has assets in excess of $1.3 billion.

Between November and February two years earlier, the pension system was defrauded for over $110,000. No interim audit of VSRS had been performed. When the regular audit began, there was no clear evidence that a fraud was in progress; however, there was ample evidence to support a widespread exposure of fraud. Much of the discussion that follows regarding the VSRS system was obtained from interviews with personnel at VSRS through generalized audit questionnaires.

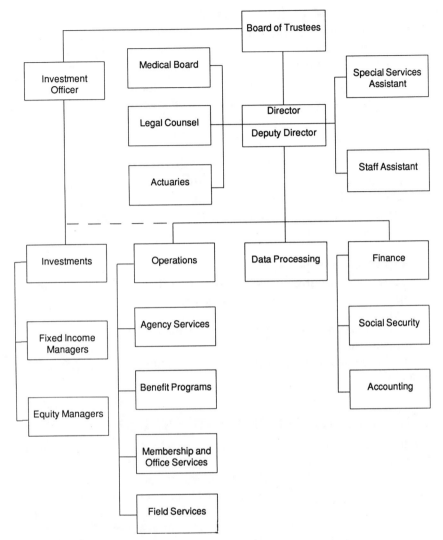

Fig. 5-2. Fraud case study supplemental retirement system.

The penetration point matrix was a tool used to identify the most probable point where a fraud might occur. The concept was used after the auditors recognized some potentially serious weaknesses in the pension system agency's financial and internal control activities.

Following the discussion of the case is a completed penetration point matrix (Fig. 5-5). However, you may find it helpful to attempt to develop a penetration point matrix from the case material. This will give you some experience in using the technique. Then you can compare your results to the one prepared in this case.

Background to the fraud

- Contribution system: This system processes retirement contributions for each member of the retirement system. Accounts are maintained at VSRS for each member of the system.

- Refund system: This system processes refund requests of retirement contributions made to VSRS. Refunds are made at the time of employment termination for those individuals not desiring to keep their retirement status.

Hardware and software environment

VSRS processes computer data via an RJE (batch) station located in the administration building of the retirement system. The computer installation located about 3 miles away is an IBM mainframe. Application programs are all written in COBOL.

Quantitative statistics

Member Contribution Account (MCA) file   An ISAM file containing about 315,000 accounts with total contribution balances of about $950 million.

Contributions processed   Three-million transactions for $100 million annually.

Refunds processed   Twenty-thousand transactions for $23 million annually.

Member contribution system

Contributions to retirement are made via payroll deductions with the state reporting on a semi-monthly basis; city and county school boards reporting on a monthly basis; and political subdivisions reporting on a quarterly basis. There are about 225 state agencies consisting of 80,000 employees; 148 city and county school boards consisting of 80,000 employees; and 385 political subdivisions consisting of 47,000 employees reporting to the system. This represents an annual volume of over 3 million transactions and over $100 million in contributions.

The accounting system used by VSRS to process this tremendous volume of accounting data is the member contribution system (MCS). The MCS is responsible for editing, processing, and updating retirement contribution balances in each member's respective member contribution account (MCA). Information contained in each of these computerized accounts includes employer reporting code, social security number, name, membership date, payroll date, birth date, service credit, account status, contribution balance, and interest balance. The MCS currently maintains over 310,000 member accounts on a computer file, which includes the records of active, inactive, retired, and deceased members.

When defined in relation to the total VSRS accounting function, the MCS should function as an operational subsystem providing accounting data for the central bookkeeping function. It is the primary purpose of the MCS subsystem to provide accurate and reliable information on a timely and efficient basis to central accounting. In an automated accounting system of this size and complexity, it is imperative that adequate application controls exist to ensure the integrity of data contained in the MCS computer file as well as the accuracy of the accounting information generated for central accounting. Adequate audit trails are also necessary for the auditor to be able to trace accounting transactions and to establish account balances.

New accounts are added to the MCA computer file as a result of the receipt of the VSRS-1 form (Member Information Report and Designation of Beneficiary) or the first contribution submitted by the employer. Accounts lose their active status when contributions are no longer being made to the account.

Contributions to retirement from school boards and political subdivisions include the submission to VSRS of a transmittal sheet, a check, and a contribution payroll report. The accounting section posts total contributions paid from the transmittal sheet to the cash receipts ledger, a depository certificate is prepared, and the monies deposited. The posting and depositing functions take place within a short period of time after the end of the payroll reporting period. However, the contribution payroll report which is used to update individual accounts on the MCA computer file may not arrive for several months after the payroll period.

Contribution payroll reports are processed by the payroll section of VSRS. These reports are edited for correction, reconciled to amounts posted in the cash receipts ledger, and updated in the respective MCA computer accounts. For balances that do not reconcile, adjustment forms are prepared and posted to the accounting ledger, and the reporting entity is notified. Form VSRS-1 is submitted with the payrolls for each new employee and is processed and filed. The reporting entity is notified of all VSRS-1 forms that have not been received, as well as any gross salary information that was reported incorrectly.

Control books containing a posting sheet for each reporting entity are maintained, with totals for retirement contributions posted manually. Also posted in these control books are reporting entity totals for refunds, transfers, retirements, and adjustment transactions processed in the MCA computer file. As a result, the control books maintain a current balance of total contributions and interest by reporting entity.

Contributions to retirement from state employees are made via semimonthly computer payroll tapes submitted by the state comptroller's office. The comptroller's office also submits a deduction register and a control report, which are used for balancing contribution payroll totals to contributions processed in the MCA computer file. Actual funds transferred to the retirement contribution and group life insurance accounts are reported to VSRS from the comptroller's office on a monthly basis. These reports show totals for each payroll in each state agency. They are used for posting to the cash receipts ledger by the central accounting section, and are reconciled with contributions posted in the accounts of the MCA computer file. Totals for retirement contributions posted to the MCA computer file for state employees are manually posted by the reporting agency to the control books.

Refunds and retirement transfers

Refunds of retirement contributions are made to members of the system who have terminated employment and filed a form VSRS-3 (Refund Request Application). For the situation in which an active member dies, refunds can be made to the estate or beneficiaries of that member. Adjustments to contribution account balances also may result in a refund to a terminated member or his estate or beneficiary.

VSRS processes an average volume of 18,000 to 22,000 refunds to individual members annually. The approximate dollar amounts of refunds processed annually are shown in Table 5-1.

Table 5-1. VSRS refunds processed annually.

Fiscal year	Amount ($ millions)
1	14.3
2	14.6
3	13.9
4	16.3
5	21.2
6	23.2

Peak loads for the processing of refund applications occur in the summer months when employment turnover is high, especially among teachers. In some instances, this can result in a single refund voucher containing several hundred individual refunds which is submitted for payment through the state comptroller's or state treasurer's office.

Teachers and employees of political subdivisions desiring a refund of contributions are required to file a VSRS-3 form, not more than 30 days prior to the termination of employment. Information to be filled out on the form by the individual includes social security number, name (both printed and signed), and names of any previous employers covered under VSRS. On this same form the employer is responsible for furnishing VSRS with the agency name, agency code, and contributions not yet reported to VSRS (from the last payroll submitted to termination). Upon receipt at VSRS, this form is reviewed for completeness by the refund section of the membership and office service department.

The VSRS-3s are then submitted to the data processing department to be keypunched, added to the computerized refund inventory file, listed on a "refund inventory" computer listing, and returned to the refund section with the VSRS-3s. The VSRS-1 forms (Member Information Report and Designation of Beneficiary) are removed from the VSRS-1 file, matched with the VSRS-3s, and filed in a pending file.

On a periodic basis, members requesting a refund have a display of their account printed from the computer file showing accounts to be refunded. If the account does not exist, a review is made of the payroll information shown on the VSRS-3 form and the payroll reporting status of the agency to determine whether the account should be added to the computer file. An account is added to the file when it is shown that the agency has not yet reported the first payroll contribution or submitted the VSRS-1 form for that individual's account. Amounts to be refunded are then based on contribution amounts shown on the VSRS-3 refund request application.

The bottom half of the VSRS-3 is used by the refund section to calculate the total refund amount. This is a total of the amounts shown in the computer account, and the amounts certified by the employing agency on the VSRS-3 as contributions subsequent to the last payroll contribution submitted to VSRS.

A voucher cover sheet with a voucher number is obtained from the accounting section. The VSRS-3s are batched and submitted to the data processing department where refund cards are keypunched from the VSRS-3s showing the amounts to be refunded. From these cards, a computerized voucher listing is produced and balanced to the batch total. The accounts from which the refunds are made are assigned a code to indicate that the amounts have been refunded from those accounts. The refund transactions are added to the computerized transaction file and removed from the refund inventory file. The refund cards are filed and are later used to deduct refunded amounts from the accounts at the time when all contributions have been reported for the respective accounts as indicated on the form VSRS-3.

The computer printed voucher and form VSRS-3 are returned to the refund section where the totals are verified, and the voucher cover sheet is attached to the voucher listing. The voucher is then submitted to the deputy director, director, or the administrative assistant for an authorized signature. The voucher is returned to the refund section where mailing envelopes are prepared and sent to the state treasurer's office. The original voucher is sent to the state comptroller's office. A carbon copy of the refund voucher is sent to the accounting section for posting to the cash disbursements ledger and returned for filing in the refund section. The comptroller prepares a warrant register from which the state treasurer's office produces the refund checks, stuffs the prepared mailing envelopes, and mails the refunds.

The processing of refunds for state employees is basically the same as those of political subdivision employees and teachers except for the following major differences.

- The VSRS-1 form is not removed from the file and matched to the refund request until after the refund has been issued.

- Because state agency contribution payroll reporting is very prompt, manually computing the amount of refunds from unreported contributions is not needed, and accounts do not have to be added to the computer file.

- Whereas refund cards are used to detect amounts from teacher and political subdivision accounts, a computer tape is used to perform the same function for the state employee accounts.

Refund adjustments that result in an adjustment to a member's contribution account or to a prior refund amount also result in the issuance of a refund check. Refunds of this type are initiated by an employee/employer request or from listings supplied monthly by the data processing department of inactive accounts with remaining contribution balances. The refund section reviews the account and, if necessary, reviews previous refunds issued from the account to establish the validity of the refund request and account balance. Written confirmations are also made with the employee/employer. Refund worksheets are prepared and batched with confirmation replies and displays of the computer accounts and sent to data processing for keypunching. The remaining process is the same as the regular refund process described previously, except that the outstanding refund is not recorded on the refund inventory file.

Refunds of member contributions to a beneficiary or estate resulting from the death of an active member are processed by the refund section of VSRS. Where the former member has not elected a survivor's option, a lump sum refund is made to the beneficiary or estate from the contribution account. Where a survivor's option has been elected, the contribution amounts are transferred to the retirement allowance account and an annuity is established. The refund process is similar to that of the regular refund process. However, refunds to members' beneficiaries, where members are covered under group life insurance, are not issued until Life of Virginia has made payment on the life insurance claim.

As indicated previously, refunded contributions are not deducted from accounts at the time of the refund. A reduction of individual balances does not take place until the last payroll for each respective account has been processed as indicated by the termination date on the VSRS-3 form. At the time the account balance is reduced by the refunded amount, the total of all refunds used to reduce these balances is posted in the control book. This is the same control book described previously which maintains total balances for retirement contributions and interest. Retirement transactions, where contributions and interest amounts are transferred to the retirement allowance account, are handled in a similar fashion.

Penetration point case solution

The penetration point matrix prepared for this case is illustrated at the end of this chapter. It was determined that the computer crime was committed by three members of a user department (i.e., refund clerks) through falsification of form VSRS-1. Through improper manipulation of the form, they were able to add fictitious accounts to the computer file to withdraw funds from those accounts and loot inactive computer accounts. The fraudulent transactions occurred over a 14-month period from November (year 4) through February (year 6).

Non-State Agency - Payroll Clerk:
Prepare Contribution Report for new employees, changes in salary, and contribution report for current employees and employees dropped from this system.

New Employee:
Fills out membership form "Member's Information and Beneficiary Designation." This form is then submitted to VSRS from the receiving agency, either with or without the first contribution report on which that employee is reported as a new employee.

Magnetic Tape Reporting:
Some agencies report contributions via magnetic tape together with a computer listing of all contributors.

Contribution Reporting Section:
Contribution Reports for agencies not reporting via magnetic tape are sent to keypunch section after a review of the file has been made to locate membership forms for new employees. For Tape Reporting Agencies, the keypunching, of course, is not done.

Data Entry Section:
Contribution Reports are entered via pseudo-batch processing.

Contribution Reporting Section:
Membership Forms for new employees are sent to keypunch. For new employees reported on the Contribution Report for which no Membership Form can be located, a letter is written to the agency requesting that a Membership Form be sent. A copy of the letter is filed.

Data Entry Section:
Membership Forms are entered.

RJE Operator:
Input files are submitted from Data Entry to RJE operator. The operator runs Program VSRMEMV4 to update the accounts on the Membership Contribution Account (MCA) file. The Membership Forms are sent to the Membership Form (VSRS-1) file room. A listing of updated accounts is discarded.

Note: The accounts are updated with three fields of data: Date of Birth, Sex, and Employment Date.

RJE Operator:
For those agencies on the Tape Reporting System, a payroll tape is run against the MCA file to produce a listing of adds, changes, and drops from the MCA, file as well as any errors in reporting. This run is made by executing Program VSRUPDTP.

For those agencies not on the Tape Reporting System, input files are loaded into program VSRMEMV4 and a listing of adds, changes, and drops, and any errors are produced.

Fig. 5-3. Auditor of public accounts-contribution system.

Fig. 5-3. Continued

Contribution Reporting Section:
Any errors in the listing of adds, changes, and drops are corrected and resubmitted.

Non State Agency – Accounting Clerk:
The Accounting Department of the Reporting Agency prepares a check Transmittal Form and check for the total amount of retirement contributions remitted to VSRS. According to law, these amounts must be sent to VSRS within 30 days after the payroll period has ended.

Note: There is a time lag between the submissions of the check to VSRS and the Contribution Report In some instances, a Contribution Report may not be submitted until two years after the payroll period has ended.

Accounting Department:
Upon receipt of the check, a deposit slip is prepared. From the deposit slip, the date of deposit and check amount are posted to the cash receipts ledger for that agency. A copy of the deposit slip is filed and a deposit with the bank is made. The Transmittal Form is also filed. The Contribution Reporting Section is notified.

RJE Operator:
The RJE Operator is notified by the Contribution Reporting Section to run Program VSRUPD01. This program prints the total contributions for the Reporting Agency for the payroll period.

Note: The contribution amount is recorded in a "transaction" field on the MCA file. The Totals Sheet is sent to the Contribution Reporting Section.

Contribution Reporting Section:
The Transmittal Form is obtained from the Accounting Department and the contribution totals are matched to the Totals Sheet and the Contribution Report.

If the amounts agree, the Transmittal Form and Contribution Report are filed.
If the contribution amount does not agree, a correction report is prepared. The original is mailed to the agency. A copy is sent to the Accounting Department.

Accounting Department
The correction amount from the Correction Report is posted to the Cash Receipts Ledger. The Correction Report is then sent back to the Contribution Reporting Section.

Contribution Reporting Section:
The Correction Report, Transmittal Form, and Contribution Report are filed.

Reconciliation Procedure:
At the end of each fiscal year, the Reporting Agency prepares a year-end adjustment and submits the documentation to VSRS. The Contribution Reporting Section prepares a year-end reconciliation.

RJE Operator:
After the Totals Sheet has been reconciled to the Transmittal Sheet and Contribution Report, an "Agency" record is created. With this record, the operator then runs Program VSRGVIN, which updates the member accounts on the file by the contribution amounts shown on the Contribution Report. Outputs from this program include the Duplicate Accounts Report, Missing Membership Data Report, and the Posting Sheet.

Contribution Reporting Section:
Clerks in the Contribution Reporting Section are responsible for correcting error listings and the reconciliation of the Posting Sheet to the Totals Sheet.

Duplicate Accounts Report:
This is a listing of all accounts within an agency which have identical names and social security numbers with at least 5 identical digits. This listing is reviewed and correspondence with the agency is made to determine if the multiple accounts are actually those of the same person.

Missing Membership Data Report:
This report lists those members with an account which has not had a VSRS Membership Form (VSRS-1) processed for it. This listing is reviewed and correspondence with the agency is made to determine the location of the form.

Posting Sheet:
The Posting Sheet shows the total VSRS contributions for the Reporting Agency. This sheet is checked to the Totals Sheet, and the amounts are verified for agreement.

If the amounts agree, then the total amount is posted to the Monthly Control Sheet in the Control Book and the Posting Sheet is filled.

Note: Before July year 5, the Posting Sheets were destroyed.

If the amounts do not agree (this is very rare), the updated amounts are reprocessed to show the state of account before the payroll update. The cause of error is then determined.

RJE Operator:
After the refunds are printed, the refund cards are sorted by agency code, and within agency code, by termination date. The cards are then sent to the Contribution Reporting Section where they are filed in the Refund Card File.

Contribution Reporting Section:
The Refund Card File is maintained by the Contribution Reporting Section. After each Contribution Report is processed for an employer's employees, the Refund Card File is searched, and any cards with a termination date equal to the date of the Contribution Report are pulled and submitted to the RJE operator.

Note: Contribution Reports may not arrive until as late as 2 years after the Contribution Reporting period. Therefore, Refund Cards could remain in the Refund Card File for as long as 2 years. The Refund Cards are used to deduct the Contribution amounts from the account.

RJE Operator:
The RJE operator runs Program VSRMEMV4 to deduct refunded contributions from the accounts. The amounts to be deducted are entered into a Refund Record. These records are held for the duration of the run.

Two reports are printed: the Refund Transaction Report and the Refund Totals Report. The Transaction Report is used for reference only and is filed in the Contribution Reporting Section.

Contribution Reporting Section:
The Refund Totals Report and the Statistics Reports are used for posting to the Control Sheet for the agency in the Control Book. The reports are then filed.

Note: The Control Book contains a Control Sheet for each Reporting Agency for each month. On each Control Sheet is recorded the beginning and ending month balances for Prior Contributions, Prior Interest, Current Contributions, and Total Amount. Any transactions affecting the balances (refunds, contributions, journal vouchers, etc.) are recorded. All entries represent agency totals.

NonState Agency – Payroll Clerk/Member:
Members of the system who are terminating employment and wish to withdraw their retirement contributions are required to file a VSRS-3 Refund Request Form not sooner than 30 days prior to the termination of employment. On this form, the employee's agency is required to identify any unreported contributions (contributions not yet reported to VSRS from the last Contribution Report submitted to termination).

Refund Section:
Upon receipt, the VSRS-3 is reviewed for completeness. If it is found to be incomplete or unsigned, it is returned to the agency.
Refund Requests (VSRS-3s) found to be satisfactory are batched for data entry.

Data Entry Section:
VSRS-3s are entered and submitted to the RJE operator.

Fig. 5-4. Auditor of public accounts-refund system.

Fig. 5-4. *Continued*

RJE Operator:
The RJE operator runs Program VSRRFINV. This program uses the Current Refund Files and Inventory Master File as input. The function of the program is to add all new requests for refund to the Inventory Master File. Reports produced include a Detailed Card Listing (used for reference only), inventory listings, and comparison listings.

Refund Section:
All reports produced by Program VSRRFINV are sent to the Refund Section for review.

Inventory Listing:
This listing is returned with the VSRS-3s. The listing shows for each applicant, the name, Social Security number, agency code number, termination date, and date the VSRS-3 was received. From the listing, all VSRS-1s are pulled from the file located in the agency services section of VSRS.

If the VSRS cannot be located, an "outsheet" is prepared by the refund clerk and placed in the VSRS-1 file indicating that the individual was refunded his contributions. The VSRS-3 is then processed as normal.

All Refund Requests (VSRS-3s) and VSRS-1s are placed in a pending file in Social Security number order and by termination date.

Comparison Reports:
Listing of members who have received a refund during the past two-year period are reviewed for possible duplicate refunds.
If the request is legitimate, the Refund Request will be processed as normal.
If the request is a duplicate, a letter of notification will be sent to the individual.

Refund Section:
On a periodic basis (usually weekly), the Refund Section requests the RJE operator run Program VSRREF02. This program lists all outstanding requests through a particular date (as entered on a control record).

RJE Operator:
The operator runs Program VSRREF02. A listing of all accounts to be refunded is produced. The listing shows, in Social Security number order for each applicant, the name, account status, agency code, prior contribution amount (as of the end of the previous fiscal year), prior interest (applied to contributions), current contribution amount (for current fiscal year), and current interest. Also shown is Total Refund Due, date of birth, and last date of Reported Contributions.

Refund Section:
The VSRS-3 Refund Requests located in the pending file are pulled and matched to the listing.
If the VSRS-1s had not been matched with the VSRS-3s, then two possible alternatives exist involving disposition of the Refund Request. If the Social Security number or agency code is wrong, the VSRS-3s is re-entered. If this is not the case, then it is assumed that the account does not exist on the MCA file.

For accounts not on the MCA file for which there is a Refund Request, a request is sent to the RJE operator to run Program VSRMEMV4 to add the new accounts. These VSRS-3s must have unreported contributions designated on the form. If not, the employing agency is called and the contributions are obtained.

Data Entry Section:
Records are created from the VSRS-3s.

RJE Operator:
Runs program VSRMEMV4 to add MCA accounts. Operator discards listing of accounts added.

Refund Section:
For Refund Requests where the VSRS-3s are matched to the VSRS-1s, amounts are verified to determine if they are up-to-date. If they are not up-to-date, the Reporting Agency is contacted for the information.

Refund Section:
From the "Accounts to be Refunded" listing, prior contributions, Prior Interest, Current Contributions, Current Interest, and the Refund Total are entered on the VSRS-3. Current Contributions include unreported contributions shown on the VSRS-3 form designated by the employing agency payroll clerk.

Accounting Department:
Accounting clerks are responsible for preparing Voucher Cover Sheets and stamping each voucher with a voucher number. Voucher numbers are assigned sequentially.

Refund Section:
Total refund amounts computed on the VSRS-3s are totaled on an adding machine tape, and the VSRS-3s are batched. The Voucher Cover Sheet is obtained from accounting. The voucher number is written on the adding machine tape and submitted with the VSRS-3s to the Data Entry Section. The Voucher Cover Sheet is kept in the Refund Section.

Data Entry Section:
The VSRS-3s are entered and "Refund Cards" are produced. Data entered includes name, Social Security number, agency code, termination date, prime contributions, prior interest, current contributions, current interest, and Total Refund Amount.

RJE Operator:
The RJE operator runs Program VSRRFBAL. This program produces a "Balance Refunds" report which lists all payees and the amount to be refunded. The total on this listing is compared to the total on the adding machine tape (plus unreported contributions) for agreement. If the totals do not agree, the operator locates the error, makes the correction, and reruns the program. If the Total Refunded Amounts agree, the computer operator then runs Program VSRRFNON to print the voucher listing. The operator then compares the "Balance Refunds" Report to the voucher listing for agreement. The "Balance Refunds" Report is then filed in the RJE room, and the refund voucher listing and VSRS-3 batch are sent to the Refund Section.

Program VSRRFNON also records all refunds on the current Refund Transaction File and accordingly removes all relevant outstanding refund requests from the inventory master file. Three statistics reports showing refund totals by agency code for prior contributions, prior interest, current contributions, and current interest are sent to the Contribution Reporting Section.

The RJE operator then runs Program VSRRFLST which prints a refund listing (cumulative to date for the current fiscal year), its Social Security number order, and its alphabetical order. Three listings are sent to the Refund Section.

Refund Section:
After the Refund Voucher Listing Interest Statement and the Refund Request Forms (VSRS-3s) are returned from the operator, the Voucher Total is verified to the Adding Machine Tape Total and the Voucher Cover Sheet is filled out with the Total Refund Amount. The voucher is then submitted for an authorized signature (both the original and a carbon copy).

VSRS Director or Deputy Director:
Voucher is reviewed and signed (both copies). They are then returned to the refund section.

Refund Section:
The bottom portion of the VSRS-3 containing the mailing address is separated from the form and stuffed into window envelopes. Interest statements are also inserted into each envelope.
The original Voucher Cover Sheet and Listing and the prepared mailing envelopes are sent to the State Comptroller's Office and State Treasurer's Office.
The carbon of the Voucher Cover Sheet and Listing are sent to the Accounting Department.

Accounting Department:
This Refund Voucher Total is posted to the Cash Disbursements Ledger. The voucher is then returned to the Refund Section.

Refund Section:
The Refund Voucher (Refund Voucher Listing and Cover Sheet) and the VSRS-3s are filed. The file is in voucher number order.

State Comptroller's Office:
Clerks in the Comptroller's Office enter each individual refund, assign a Warrant Number to each refund, and produce a Warrant Register which is submitted to the State Treasurer's Office.

State Treasurer's Office:
The checks are printed, signed, and stuffed into the prepared mailing envelopes. The envelopes are then mailed.

Potential Perpetrator Fraud, Method, or Act	Agency Payroll Clerk	Refund Clerk	Systems Programmer	Computer Analyst	RJE Operator	Contribution Reporting Clerk	Keypunch Operator	VSRS Management	EDP Auditor	Outsider or VSRS Former Employee	Total Points
Falsify or Forge Form VSRS-1	3	3	1	2	1	3	1	2	2	2	20
Fraudulent Contributions From Payroll Fraud	3	–	–	–	–	–	–	–	–	–	3
Inflate Contribution Report	—	–	–	3	–	–	–	–	1	–	4
Create Fraudulent MCA Account	—	–	2	3	–	–	–	–	3	–	8
Unauthorized Contribution Transfer	–	–	1	3	–	–	–	–	3	–	7
Create Fraudulent Multiple Accounts with Contributions	–	–	1	3	–	–	–	–	3	–	7
Computer Program Fraud To Create Fraudulent Account	–	–	1	3	–	–	–	–	2	–	6
Falsify VSRS-3 Refund Request	3	3	1	2	1	1	1	2	2	2	18
Falsify Unreported Contributions	2	3	–	2	–	–	–	–	2	–	9
Falsify VSRS-3 for Non-Existent Employee	3	3	–	3	2	1	1	3	3	2	21
Alter or Falsify Voucher	–	3	–	–	–	–	–	2	–	–	5
Destroy Fraudulent Source Documents	–	3	–	3	3	3	3	3	3	2	23
Destroy Output Containing Evidence of Fraud	–	3	–	3	3	3	3	3	3	2	23
Obliterate Computer Records	–	–	3	3	1	–	1	2	3	1	14
Total Points	14	21	10	33	11	11	10	17	30	11	168

Opportunity To Commit Fraud Weight Values
3 = Good   2 = Fair   1 = Poor   0 = None

Fig. 5-5. Fraud case penetration point matrix.

6

Prevention, detection, and investigation

VIRUS SOFTWARE IS PROBABLY THE MOST WIDELY DISCUSSED CLASS OF computer threat. No other form of software has made the cover of *TIME* magazine. In this chapter we will explore what makes up a virus. We will examine the threat posed by virus software. We will discuss the history of this form of software and examine how it has evolved over time. We will then look at how the virus threat affects your computer resources.

The last sections of this chapter will be devoted to exploring how to determine if your software has been infected and how to recover from an infection. We will examine some products on the market that will help with these tasks. Finally, a set of guidelines is provided to help avoid infection in the future.

What viruses are and why they are dangerous

Probably no class of computer software has ever received so much attention as have virus programs. Several theories have been advanced as to why this type of software is so popular. One very common theory describes virus software as AIDS for computers. It goes on to explain that like the AIDS epidemic, the epidemic of software infection is rampant in the U.S. This is another example of the way in which people tend to ascribe human traits to computers.

Let us dispel this myth. First, there are many forms of computer virus infecting different types of software on different machines. Second, in most cases, it is possible to recover from an infection. Third, many common software handling procedures can spread the virus. Fourth, not all virus programs are inherently evil or destructive. Cases exist of both benign virus programs and beneficial ones. Therefore, the choice of label for this class of software was unfortunate. Rather than a virus, a more correct description would probably be a parasite program.

Possibly because they are popular, the virus label is often incorrectly applied to other types of software attack. One example is the publicity surrounding the Burleson trial in 1988. Many papers reported that Burleson "infected his ex-employer's computer with a virus." This was not the case. Donald Gene Burleson built an extremely lethal time bomb that went off after he left the facility and wiped out 168,000 sales commission records. The software used in this attack was not a virus. However, because few people really understand what makes up a virus, many destructive assaults upon computers are labeled as viruses.

To qualify as a virus a program must meet one special criteria: the code in the program must be able to replicate or copy itself so as to spread through the infected machine or across to other machines. All destructive programs are not viruses, and all viruses are not destructive. Some are benign and are designed as harmless pranks or jokes. However, just because they are designed to be harmless is no guarantee that they will remain so.

As an example, look at the largest known infection by a single virus in a short time. The virus released across InterNet by Robert Morris was designed to be a slowly duplicating, harmless virus. However, he made a design mistake and rather than spreading slowly from computer to computer, doing no harm, his virus exploded across the network and tied up a history-making number of computers.

The history of the virus threat

The beginnings of the virus software are hidden in the history of the early days of computing at places like Stanford, MIT, Bell Labs, and Xerox. At first the challenge was to produce software that was more or less lifelike; software exhibiting some of the classic behaviors of living things. One of these characteristics is of course the ability to produce additional versions of the parent being. Real credit should belong to John von Neumann who thought up the idea of computer programs multiplying. He described these ideas in his paper "Theory and Organization of Complicated Automata." The next logical development of this idea was John Conway's program, "The Game of Life." Running this program the user would input a shape composed of asterisks, and the computer, using an elegant series of rules, would "grow" the shape. In this way, the computer program mimicked the expansion and growth of single-celled organisms, such as bacteria. Conway's program soon became available to programmers.

In the early 1960s, system programmers at several sites began building a new class of program. This program was designed to live in the memory (commonly referred to as core because the memory was composed of magnetic cores). These programs had the ability to replicate and destroy all other programs in the machine's memory. In a gamelike atmosphere, programmers would install two different versions of this type of program into different locations in the computer's memory and see which program destroyed the other. These contests were called core wars.

These were the first true virus programs. They were designed as games and were able to replicate and survive only in the memory of the machine into which they had been installed. Initially these core wars took place after hours, when the computer was not being used. After a session of core war, the programmers would turn off the computer, flushing memory. There was no way for these programs to spread to other machines or to disks because no link existed.

As these programs became more sophisticated, safety and control concerns had to be considered. When two of these creatures ran wild and took over a Xerox 530, the core war players stopped creating them. Because the number of core war players was small and well connected they decided to keep the detailed knowledge of self-replicating code to themselves. These professionals were aware of the potential damage that could result from undisciplined use of this knowledge. At this stage, the virus threat was merely a potential.

This potential was not reached for a few years, but the breeding ground for this threat was introduced in 1969, when Arpanet was created. It was designed to facilitate the transference of information between colleges, defense projects, and other researchers. It was this network that was strangled by the virus Robert Morris, Jr. released into it in 1988. When Arpanet was created the threat of a viral attack was fiction for most people. The only people who could even grasp the potential threat were those few programmers who had designed and built the core war programs.

Things changed drastically, in 1983, when Ken Thompson described the early core war programs at a meeting of the Association for Computer Machinery. In 1984, *Scientific American* published an article giving further information about this class of software and offered construction details on how to write them for a mere $2. Both students and faculty were quick to obtain this information, and for the most part it was used in a research context. However, nuisance infections soon occurred.

One of the first was a virus that spread throughout the universities called the Cookie Monster program, named after the Sesame Street character of the same name. When this particular virus attacked, the user's terminal went blank, then the words ''I want a Cookie'' appeared on the screen. The virus program went away when the user typed "Cookie," and whatever session was interrupted was soon restored. If "Cookie" was not typed in, the virus continued to demand "I want a Cookie." Although it was a bit of a nuisance, Cookie Monster was a relatively harmless virus program. It spread all across the country in just a few months. For the most part it was distributed by systems people. As long as the major computing power remained in the mainframe computers, the spread of the virus programs was rather limited and could usually only occur on machines with outside phone lines.

As the proliferation of personal computers (PCs) increased, however, a whole new domain became available to the virus programmers. Bulletin boards and other electronic communication networks were established, providing a variety of ways to spread virus programs. Simultaneously, the increased use of removable media (floppy diskettes) fostered a new medium with which to spread virus code. With mainframe computers, the only truly portable media were tape and cards. Most machines did not read or write removable diskettes, so there was less chance for infection through that methodology.

At first, only the IBM PC family was infected. This lead Apple owners to feel that they were somehow exempt. That changed late in 1988 when the Scores virus began infecting Macintosh computers at many government computer centers. A computer bulletin board spread the code of another Macintosh virus. From then on, both DOS (disk operating system) and Apple products had their fair share of virus attacks. The IBM PC DOS-type virus programs are most frequently spread by bulletin board infection. On the other hand, Apple-type virus programs seem to be spread most often by passing infected diskettes or through networks that have an infected Mac or diskette associated with it. All this leads up to the present when a misguided programmer like Robert Morris, Jr. can bring a whole network of machines to its knees with a simple, yet buggy, virus program.

Types of viruses

Virus code can be divided into three general categories based on the intent of the creator of the software. First, and probably least common, are the beneficial virus programs. Then there are the benign variety of programs. Please note that we are defining these categories of virus software based on the *intent* of the author of the program, not the outcome. Finally, we must consider the media darling, the beastly virus programs. Programs are often called snuffware or killware because of their operation. Now let us examine each of these categories in greater detail.

Beneficial virus programs

These programs follow the rules of a virus program in that they duplicate themselves many times within a system. However, they are probably constrained by design to live on only one system and not propagate across systems. Their function is beneficial and known to the user/owner of the system.

One such program infects each file on a target hard disk. Once a file has been infected, the virus compresses all the duplicate characters out of the file. When the file is later opened, the virus expands the file to its original size. This virus probably increases the storage capacity of a hard disk from 40 to 60%. If properly designed it is totally invisible to the user and yet works in a beneficial way to increase the user's resource utilization.

Benign virus programs

This classification includes many reporting and routing virus programs. There are many examples of this sort of virus program. For example, in 1987, the appropriately named Christmas Card virus came across the ocean from the European academic network and infected a 350,000 terminal IBM business network. All it did was display a Christmas card on the screen with the words "Happy Holidays" for each user as he/she logged into the system. Then the virus erased itself from the host computer. This program pointed out how vulnerable networks are, but did little or no harm.

Then there was the MacMag Peace virus. Again the name tells much about it. It was targeted at Macintosh computers and simply displayed the word "PEACE" on the screen on March 2, 1988. The virus then self-destructed with no known damage.

However, not all benign virus programs prove to be so when released. Robert Morris's program was supposed to sleep quietly in the infected computer until asked if it were there. It was then supposed to simply identify itself so he could track how far it had spread across the Arpanet. Unfortunately a last minute programming change caused the virus to replicate out of control once it had infected the host computer. In so doing, it actually shut down both the infected computer and finally a major portion of the network.

Beastly virus programs

This classification of virus programs is the one most often thought of when the topic of viruses is raised. These are the programs that cause and have caused untold damage. It is this group of programs which is being called the Black Plague of computing in the 1990s. The four classes of malevolent virus programs are discussed below.

Boot infections
(IBM DOS-type computers only)

These programs attach themselves to the first sector of the disk they have infected. This sector is used only by the operating system, so the user will not see it. One famous example of this type of virus is the Pakistani Brain virus. It was designed to be a nuisance for users of pirated software and induce them to buy a legitimate version of the software. However, it was quickly used as a platform by other, less ethically minded programmers. Usually this virus is loaded from an infected diskette (it has not been found on hard disks) and replaces some of the instructions initially used to load data from diskettes. If an uninfected diskette is loaded into the machine, the modified program will infect it. Some variants of this program also work in a time bomb mode. These will erase the contents of the diskette after a predefined number of disk insertions.

System infectors
(both PC and Macintosh computers)

This type of program infects system resources and actually becomes part of the operating system. On IBM computers the usual targets are IBM-BIO.COM, IBMDOS.COM, and COMMAND.COM. On the Macintosh any of the system resources files can be a target. An example of this class of program is the Lehigh virus. This is an interesting program in that it changes its mode of operation after an interval of quietly waiting in the COMMAND.COM file. After the virus replicates a specific number of times, the program becomes hostile and destroys all the files on the hard disk of the infected computer.

Application program infectors
(both PC and Macintosh computers)

This is the most commonly encountered type of virus. Most of the Macintosh virus programs fall into this category, as do most of the virus programs that are transferred across bulletin boards. These viruses infect any other application they can discover, and will most often either change the way the program works or destroy the infected program. One example is a virus that infects spreadsheet programs. Once infected, the virus causes the program to rearrange the digits in randomly selected cells. After a specific number of days, the program erases the contents of each spreadsheet opened by the infected application. Finally after another set period, the program erases all the spreadsheet files as well as the spreadsheet software itself. Many of this class of virus will infect applications and then attempt to destroy data on the hard disk. They do this by erasing the data, modifying the file allocation table, or doing either a high- or low-level format on the hard disk.

Data infectors

This is a very rare form of virus. It is usually found in spreadsheet data files. It causes the contents of the cells to be stored incorrectly or not to be stored at all. It usually looks like a strange formula in one cell of the spreadsheet. This form of virus is very difficult to write and has a limited application life. However, this class can do great damage to large computer organizations. These will become a more complex and challenging form of attack in the coming years.

Vulnerability

There is no computer that is immune to attack if that computer takes data or programs from the outside world. Unfortunately, it is no longer sufficient simply to use only commercial software and so be assured of having a virus-free environment. The infectors are penetrating the commercial sector as well. In 1988, the previously mentioned MacMag virus was widely disseminated in beta versions of the Aldus FreeHand program. Later that same year, a second set of beta copies of this same program were infected with a copy of the nVir virus. This infection was detected and the virus code was removed before the program was distributed. Therefore, we can see that even the most carefully guarded computer can still become infected. The size of the machine, really makes little difference.

Although there are more PCs available to malcontent programmers, and thus more virus programs for them, mainframe computers are not exempt. The Christmas Card virus was found to infect large IBM machines almost exclusively. While the control in a large machine and the environment which surrounds it are more stringent than that of a personal computer, the recent proliferation of networks brings this level of attack to the mainframe environment. If a PC on a network is infected with a virus (for example, a UNIX command module), and that module is used on the PC, on the mainframe, and on some Macintosh machines, then the whole network is potentially vulnerable.

Besides the network threat, there are more and more programs that can be used on both PCs and large machines. An example of this is a database package where a programmer works at home on his PC producing code written in DataFlex to run on both IBM and VAX mainframes. If this code is infected, the infection can spread to the large machines when the code is run. Here a program compatible with many classes of machine could be used to infect them all. Even so, in the near term, large machines will be the most virus free simply because they are more difficult to attack. On the other hand, if a virus is successful in an attack on a large computer, the result would probably be much more devastating than an attack on a PC.

Macintosh-type machines

Moving down the ladder of safety from virus attacks, we next come to the Apple products. We will discuss the Macintosh family of computers because they have received the widest coverage in the business community. Until late in 1988, Macintosh owners could look with amusement at the problems viruses and other such snuffware caused their IBM-using associates. Then a series of virus attacks came against the Mac. One of the most serious was called the Scores virus. This virus infected Macs at NASA, other government agencies, and finally in the U.S. Congress. It spread across the Mac-user community like a plague. Until Scores appeared, it was common practice to share software and utilities across the Mac community. Suddenly a Mac could be crippled by this insidious form of contagion from simply sharing a diskette.

At nearly the same time another virus called nVir began showing up in Macs across the country. A group of less-than-ethical programmers published the details of how to build the nVir virus. Suddenly a whole family of similar viruses began proliferating on Macs. One recent variety of Macintosh virus is the WDEF. It infects the desktop and causes frequent system crashes. Because of the increased use of Macintosh computers, virus developers are now designing more viruses for that platform. However, there are still fewer viruses available for this group of computers than for IBMs and their clones.

DOS-type machines

The most frequently targeted class of computer seems to be the DOS machines. Probably this has to do with the longer business life of these machines, and with the extensive bulletin boards developed for them. When speaking of DOS machines, you must realize that this is also the largest class of PCs. It ranges from true IBM personal computers through plug-in boards available for nearly all computers enabling them to run DOS programs.

This collection of computers, being the largest, plays host to many virus programs. For example, many of the previously mentioned viruses were designed to attack DOS machines. Many variants of the standard virus programs are also running rampant across the IBM community. This is caused by programmers dissecting a known virus and implanting a variant of the same code into another application.

One characteristic of the DOS-type virus is that, as a rule, it is more destructive than other viruses. While Macintosh viruses seem to try to crash the system or cause applications to stop working after a time, DOS virus attacks are usually against stored information. It is frequently the case that a DOS virus will attempt to erase all the data stored on the computer's disks, either by reformatting them or by altering the way the file allocation data is stored.

Probably there are some computers available that are relatively immune to virus attack. For example, it would be surprising if a virus surfaced that was designed to attack the Timex Sinclair or the Texas Instrument 99-A personal computers. These are older machines that have limited utilization. The newest machines and those that are used by business seem to be the most frequent targets for attack. They provide the greatest challenge as well as the greatest exposure.

Detection

There are several programs available which are designed to detect the presence of a virus in your system. Before discussing them, however, let us examine symptoms which could be caused by the computer having been infected. There are eight common clues pointing to infection by a virus. Please note there are other possible causes for these symptoms and the presence of one of them does not mean that the system is infected. These symptoms could be caused by some other agent. If a system is infected, one or more of these symptoms will be present.

1. Applications or other files suddenly grow in size. Because the virus adds instructions to the program, it becomes longer.

2. Application programs take longer to begin working or take longer to execute standard instructions than before. Another example of this is a program which suddenly "feels" different. If you are used to the time it takes your spreadsheet program to recalculate a column of numbers, and suddenly, for no reason it takes three times as long, that will "feel" different to you. Be careful about this symptom if it is the only one present. There are many possible reasons for this to occur, for example, expanding the database a program is trying to use.

3. There is unnecessary disk access or extra disk activity. Checking for this type of problem is one reason why there is a light which registers when disk access is taking place. If in the middle of an otherwise normal execution of a program you suddenly see the disk access light come on, you need to ensure that the program is indeed correctly writing data.

4. Files in some directories have unusual modification dates. Just like files that seem to grow for no reason, files having unaccounted for creation or modification dates should be suspect. For example, if you have a copy of a word processor on your system and all of the files are dated August 14, 1988, except one routine which has a date of June 23, 1990, this may be a sign that you ought to suspect that file may be infected. If you bought the package in January 1990, and you are sure that the file was not created normally by the program, you may be on the trail of an infected file.

5. If packages you regularly use suddenly fail to run due to lack of memory, some of your memory could be housing a terminate and stay resident (TSR) viral infection. TSRs are one popular method of attacking a system. The virus infects the system and is installed into memory along with other system software. Then when an opportunity to infect another file or diskette appears, the code is resident and ready to attack. TSR virus attacks are very hard to detect unless you have specialized software, but an

unexplained lack of available memory may point to this type of infection.

6. One of the most straightforward symptoms of a viral attack is that the system, or an application, crashes or stops working for no known reason. In the Macintosh environment this is one common symptom of an infection. In the DOS and mainframe worlds, there are other less obvious symptoms, but this remains one of the best and most straightforward. If an application has been corrupted by a virus, you cannot expect that program to run normally and still carry the infection. In most cases, once a program or application is infected it will begin to run erratically or stop running altogether.

7. If the hard disk suddenly is unavailable or stops working in the middle of a computing session, there is a possibility that the data on the disk has been destroyed by a virus. This is one of the most common attack points in DOS systems. Any damage to the COMMAND.COM file, such as from a low-level format of the hard disk will cause this. When a program looks to the system for some data, there is no system on the hard disk to use. There is no data left on the hard disk either. A virus infecting an application program can erase all the files on the hard disk while the application is running.

8. One of the common places to hide a virus is in the printer commands area. These commands are not always executed, and so a virus can remain hidden in this area with less chance of detection. If for no known reason, you have problems printing, it may be a sign that the print server associated software is infected by a virus.

Remember, if you experience one of these symptoms, you may not be infected by a virus. Most of these symptoms have other, less threatening possible causes. The list is provided to enable you to check your system to see if it is infected. Now, let us look at what actions are necessary should you discover that your system has been corrupted.

Recovery

If you feel your system has been infected by a virus, the most important step is to relax and refrain from a panic reaction. Often a suspected infection can be traced back to some new software or a new way of doing things. If you are relatively sure that you have been infected, there are six steps you need to take quickly.

1. Isolate your system. If you are using a modem to talk to another system, terminate the call at once. If you are part of a network,

disconnect from the network as soon as you can. Remember that you may be the source for contamination of other systems if you are tied to them. You must take care to keep your system isolated until you are sure you have eradicated the virus from all possible hiding places, or have ensured that your system is clean.

2. Carefully record all you can remember about the session. If you ran new software, write down the name and everything you can about it. Even commercial software may be infected, so if anything is new about the system you need to document it carefully. It is equally important to document everything you did during the session to help pinpoint where the infection could have come from. If any program behaved in an unusual manner, or any of the symptoms listed above were observed, carefully note that at this time.

3. Study the nature of the damage. You will be unable to recover from the attack and clean up your system unless you know the nature of the attack. If the virus simply destroyed files, then recovery is relatively simple. On the other hand, if the virus infected some of your application files, a more extensive recovery is necessary. Sometimes it is possible to recover files that have been erased by using file management software such as Norton Utilities. In other cases, only partial losses may have occurred and a full recovery is unnecessary. You will want to make notes about this information as well.

4. Notify other possible victims of the infection. If you were logged into a bulletin board, notify the system operator (SysOp) and other users. If you were active in a network at the time of the infection or any time shortly before the infection, notify all the other nodes, elements, or users on the network. This is an ethical responsibility. It also can help ensure that your system will not be reinfected after you have cleaned it up.

5. Get help from professional virus detectives. One source for help is the National Computer Security Association (NCSA) in Washington, D.C. They have a team of specialists that can help you track down and treat snuffware attacks. They also record the spread of the virus.

6. Clean up the problem and sanitize your system. This may be as simple as restoring damaged or destroyed files from a back-up set. If you feel an application has been infected, delete it and reinstall it from the original diskette. **NOTE:** It is very important that you remember to write-protect any media you are using to restore data or applications. If you fail to do this, your back-up or original diskette may become infected.

This is the first time that the idea of a back-up has been suggested. All computer users need to make regular and thorough back-ups of their data and application files. This is important not only in case of a viral attack, but in case of other losses as well. A single back-up is often insufficient. Many times a virus can be in a latent or waiting mode when the back-up is done. Then all you have accomplished is to reinfect your system with the same virus. A rotating set of at least three back-ups is recommended. However, one is better than none.

If files have been damaged but not destroyed, there are software packages available to search out the infecting code and recover the files that have been infected. Sometimes it is impossible to repair an attacked file and the file simply needs to be replaced. With other forms of attack it is possible to repair the damage. These software packages are frequently bundled with software that searches all the files looking for the tell-tale signs of infection. Most viruses can be identified by special, unique code within them. Virus detectors look for known signs and report to the user if they are discovered.

In other cases, if the files have simply been deleted or erased, packages like Norton Utilities can go into the disk and restore most, if not all, of the files. Simple erasure represents a very mild form of attack. It is always worth trying to recover all possible files.

Antivirus products

The business of providing protection against viral attack has mushroomed in the past couple of years. In the mid-1980s, there were no protections necessary. Today there are over 100 vendors supplying some form of viral detection or prevention product. As the rate of infection increases, the demand for this type of software will probably lead the curve.

In this section we will discuss only those programs that are designed to enable the user to run programs and yet trap, identify, and prohibit a virus from attacking and damaging the system. Some of these programs work only on specific viruses, such as the nVir family or the Scores virus. Others look for all known viruses. Most of these programs prevent the virus from infecting the system, while informing the user that the system is under attack.

The most powerful subclass of protection products do the things the others do, as well as monitor the system for activity indicating that a virus is present. One example of this type of product, used in the DOS environment, is the Dr. Panda package. It consists of three detection and three prevention programs, and an excellent book on virus programs. This product looks for suspicious activity in a running system. For example, one program watches for programs that issue disk format or file allocation table modifications. These are prevented and a message is sent to the user to notify him/her of the situation. Another part of the Dr. Panda set checks for the establishing TSR (terminate and stay resident) code. If the program is not part of the start-up file, Dr. Panda prevents it from installing into memory. The third monitoring job this software performs is watching for changes in the size of executable programs. If an existing application is going to be modified, this software informs the user and waits for permission to continue with the change. This class of protection is very valuable. Many programs are available to fill this need.

Similar programs exist on the Macintosh side. One is SAM, an acronym for Symantic Antivirus for Macintosh. This is similar in design to the Dr. Panda system. It has both detection and prevention software. The prevention software is very comprehensive and can prevent changes to both code and INIT resources. SAM is very easy to use and can provide an excellent level of protection for the Mac. One nice feature is that if allowed to, SAM will check each diskette as it is inserted in the Mac. This takes a little time to run, but the protection from virus programs seems well worth a few seconds wait.

As the level of sophistication of virus programmers grows, so grows the ability of the programmers to prevent viral attacks. Sufficient protection in 1989 becomes obsolete in 1991, because the virus builders have learned a trick or two. It is important for users to remain aware of the current level of viral attack for their type of computer and to keep software on that machine that will protect it against the state-of-the-art attack.

Safe computing

All the protection in the world is not as good as safe computing practices which are put in place and followed carefully. The most important aspect of safe computing is using common sense. Be aware of possible routes of infection and work to eliminate or reduce the chances. Below are a set of twelve guidelines to help establish a safe computing environment. Add to this list, but have a good reason for subtracting anything. In most cases, eliminating a step from the plan will produce a vulnerable area.

1. Back up applications and data on a regular, rotating basis so if infection occurs, reliable clean copies of the programs will exist to replace the infected ones.

2. Run virus checking software before doing back-ups. This will help ensure that the back-up copies are clean.

3. Never work with original master diskettes, keep them safe and clean for restoration. Always make a working copy of originals, and always write protect the original diskette before putting it into your computer.

4. Don't use pirated software. This is one source of infections. If you want to see an application, buy your own copy from the

originator. This gives you the best chance of an infection-free program.

5. Don't accept software from strangers. Software is usually expensive and is rarely given away with no ulterior motive. Be very careful of programs you download from bulletin boards or other public sources. On professional machines, a "no bulletin board" rule makes good sense.

6. If you must use it, run suspect or untested software only on floppy disk. Disconnect or disable the hard disk before you run the new program, and monitor what happens.

7. Avoid rushing to install new software (from any source other than a publisher) on your hard disk. Remember that a great many virus programs have a latency phase during which no harmful activity occurs. Give new software a chance to prove itself before sending it to the hard drive.

8. Don't ever make suspect or untested software public. This includes uploading it to a bulletin board or even using it on a machine connected to a local area network (LAN).

9. Become a knowledgeable user. Get familiar with the size of your programs, how they normally run, and other data about them (such as the correct creation date). Understand when your programs should be writing to the disk, and when they should not be.

10. If your system becomes infected, share that information as widely as possible. Let anyone who could possibly have been infected with your virus know that you have one. This includes bulletin boards and other users on the LAN, if you are tied to one.

11. Buy a quality virus detection and prevention program, and keep it active on your system whenever possible. This will not keep the virus from your door, but it may prevent it from setting up housekeeping in your system.

12. Keep a sense of perspective about viral attacks. Not every program on your local bulletin board contains a virus. Not all viral attacks are going to destroy all the data in your machine. And even if the worst happens, and a virus performs a low-level format on your hard disk, it is still only data that has been lost. People have not died, and the sun will shine tomorrow. You can learn much from this sort of situation, but only if you are in a frame of mind to do so.

7

Vulnerability assessment on a micro level

A VULNERABILITY IS A WEAKNESS IN THE SYSTEM OF INTERNAL CONTROL that enables a threat to become a loss. The assessment process as described in the previous chapters has been a risk/threat look at computer crime. The process has been designed to identify the magnitude of the computer crime risk, and then determine which points and perpetrators provide the highest probability of committing the crime. This chapter evaluates the countermeasures in place to stop the identified perpetrators at the high-risk points from committing computer crime.

The true threats, or vulnerabilities, are those for which the controls are inadequate or lacking. In the computer crime case study presented in the previous chapter, it was the control weaknesses that permitted the crime to occur. This chapter will look at the different segments of the computer system to determine whether controls are adequate at the identified high-risk points.

Cost-effectiveness of computer crime controls

This chapter explains how to determine whether a computer crime threat is controlled. The concept implies that if controls are adequate the assessment job is complete. However, the risk of overcontrol may cause as large a loss as could be encountered if computer crime were to occur.

In the past, adequacy of control has meant anything from adequate, to more than adequate, to much more than adequate, to exorbitant. While overcontrol may be more effective than adequate control, it can also be very costly. Unfortunately, adequacy is a judgmental decision, and the person making that decision may feel more comfortable in an overcontrolled situation than in a situation that is adequate. Let's look at the costs and benefits of controls (Fig. 7-1).

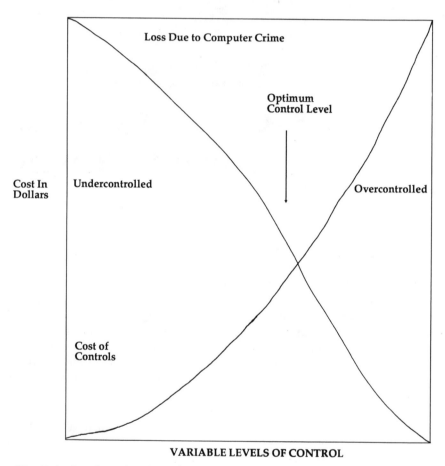

VARIABLE LEVELS OF CONTROL

Fig. 7-1. Cost benefit of controls.

The benefit of controls is reduction in potential loss due to computer crime. The costs of controls are the expenses incurred in developing, installing, and operating the controls that will reduce the risk of computer crime. The optimum level of control is that combination of controls which reduce the computer crime loss to the lowest level (the least amount of funds lost). This definition uses as the base of the loss, the totality of the loss due to computer crime, plus the cost of controls as expressed in the following formula:

LOSS DUE TO THE RISK OF COMPUTER CRIME = DOLLAR LOSS ATTRIBUTED TO THE OCCURRENCE OF COMPUTER CRIME + COST OF CONTROLS IN PLACE ATTRIBUTABLE TO REDUCING COMPUTER CRIME

Figure 7-1 illustrates that as the loss due to computer crime decreases, the cost of control increases. The point where the two lines intersect is the point where $1 spent for controls will reduce the loss attributable to computer crime by $1. Below that point, less than $1 will be expended on controls to reduce the loss attributable to computer crime by more than $1. As you back down the cost of control line, it is an undercontrolled situation because it is more economical to spend money for controls than it is to incur computer crime losses. To the right of the optimum control level, the organization would be spending more on controls than they are gaining in the reduction of computer crime. This means that the controls are uneconomical, although the organization may still want to spend that money because of the psychological aspect of a strong control system. There is nothing wrong with this decision as long as the organization realizes that the controls themselves are not strictly cost effective.

The cost/benefit concept of controls is easy to understand, but frequently difficult to implement. Implementing the concept requires that organizations be able to estimate:

- The loss attributable to computer crime in dollars
- The cost of controls
- The reduction in the loss due to computer crime by the addition of a control
- The reduction in the loss due to computer crime of a combination of controls

Even though the concept is difficult to implement, the principles need to be kept in mind during the control assessment process. If situations occur where controls appear weak or inadequate, the obvious solution is to strengthen controls. On the other hand, when controls appear more than adequate, the group performing the assessment must seriously consider whether it is in the best interest of the organization to delete some of the controls.

The control identification process

The control identification process requires the assessment team to examine the area of application under review. The choice of the word "micro" indicates that the assessment team must take a close look at the details of the system to understand whether controls are adequate. A detailed look is normally more time-consuming than a macro look, although the macro look may require a greater knowledge of the functioning of the system and the way in which the organization conducts business.

The micro control analysis is a four-step process as follows.

1. Identify and determine the magnitude of the penetration points. This process should have been completed by the conclusion of the macro vulnerability assessment. These are the points of risk at which the control assessment will be directed.

2. Identify controls. The controls identified are those effective in reducing the loss due to computer crime at each penetration point being assessed.

3. Estimate the strength of the controls. This step determines how effective each individual control will be in reducing a potential computer crime loss.

4. Determine which penetration points warrant further investigation. This last step determines the adequacy of control to reduce the risk of computer crime at each penetration point. Where the risks are not adequately reduced, a decision must be made as to whether additional preventive controls are needed. Another option is an investigation undertaken to detect whether or not a computer crime has occurred.

Determining the magnitude of the penetration points

The result of the macro vulnerability assessment should be a list of penetration points for further investigation. As was discussed earlier, the identification of the high-risk penetration points is the key to the computer crime vulnerability assessment. If too many points are selected, the process becomes too time-consuming and cumbersome to be effectively and economically completed. On the other hand, if important penetration points are eliminated from further investigation, the true high-risk penetration points may be overlooked. Note that the penetration point matrix is not a high-precision instrument, but rather a tool for differentiating the high-, from the medium-, from the low-risk penetration points.

The following advice may be helpful in selecting the penetration points. Attempt to group point scores into clusters so that they represent high-, medium-, and low-risk penetration points. Small differences in points should generally be disregarded. For example, if the points cluster in the 30 to 36 range, 18 to 23 range, and below 8 points, these would be the three obvious high-, medium-, and low-risk clusters. A few penetration points falling between these clusters should be forced into one or the other cluster. Concentrate the computer crime assessment process on the high-risk cluster first.

If a large number of penetration points remain, determine if several points in the same row, or several points in the same column, cannot be adequately assessed by a single investigation, rather than multiple investigations. For example, if the same fraud method could be perpetrated by both a current employee and an ex-employee, the question should be asked if a combined investigation, in which the perpetrator could be a current or past employee, would not suffice for investigating several points at once to determine the most probable method of computer crime.

Remember to use your common sense during the selection process. Those companies that produce protective software, and many of the popular media writers seem compelled to create an environment of paranoia. In this age when headlines seem to scream that our systems are soon to be penetrated, it is wise to keep a cool head. Some members of management may over commit to security measures. It is the task of the investigation group to accurately determine threat potentials. To highlight the potential for over reaction, one Fortune 500 company carefully installed an elaborate callback system on their computer at the insistence of the CEO. The only drawback to this wonderful protection scheme was that there were no modems on the computer to protect. Rather than making an accurate estimate of potential threats, the CEO had read of hackers breaking into computers using phones. To combat this threat the article suggested the use of callback devices, which the CEO ordered purchased. This response probably cost the company significantly more than one or two break-ins would have.

Identifying controls

The identification of controls is an investigation process. The computer crime team is looking for any method, procedure, policy, or act that will reduce the probability of computer crime occurring at the identified penetration point. All of the identified controls must be directed at the penetration point being investigated.

The process suggested for identifying penetration points is to go through the application system segment by segment, or go through an area resource by resource. The same process is recommended for identifying controls. For example, if the penetration points are in the data origination part of the computer system, then the controls identified should relate to data origination.

An extensive listing of the types of controls that might be found in the different application segments and areas are listed in Figures 7-2 through 7-10. The lists of controls can be used as checklists in the control identification investigation. If the investigator chooses not to use the

Controlled Data Origination Document Log

Controlled Input Document Containment

Data Entry Copy

Data Orgination Accountability

Data Origination Document Sequencing

Data Origination Procedure Manuals

Data Origination Prompting

Formal Data Origination Procedures

Retaining Documents at Orgination Point

Retaining Source Documents

Source Document Cross-Referencing

Source Document Retention Period

Tagging Transactions

Voiding Source Document

Fig. 7-2. Origination controls.

Fig. 7-3. Authorization controls.

Authorization Hierarchy	Object Program Change Authorization
Authorization Scanning	Passwords
Authorization Verification	Password Entry Suppress Print
Authorization Verification Matrix	Program Profile
Automatic Security Violation Shutdown	Resource Identification
Automatic Time-Oriented Sign-Off	Secure Output Storage Holding Areas
Data Element Profile	Security Classification
Evidence of Authorization	Security Profile Sign-Off
Magnetically Encoded Cards	Security Violation Review
Multiple Signature Authorization	Signature Authorization
Network Polling Profile	Source Program Change Authorization

Standards Override Authorization	User Identification
Supervisor Sign-On After Shutdown	User Profile
Terminal Profile	User Sign-Off
Terminal Sign-Off	Voided Control Document Retention
Terminal Sign-On	

Fig. 7-4. Data entry controls.

Batch Header Listing	Invalid Character Checks
Batch Identification	Key Device Feature Standards
Controlled Data Entry Document Log	Key Verification
Convention Compliance Audits	No Data To Enter Confirmation
Cut-Off Checks	On-Line Prompting
Data Entry Accountability	Physically Secure Terminals
Data Entry Copy	Positive Identification of Data
Data Entry Logging	Prenumbered Data Entry Forms
Data Entry Priority Structure	Range Checks
Data Entry Prompting	Reauditing Corrected Data
Data Entry Warning Messages	Redundant Data Entry Equipment
Data Checking	Redundant Entry of Data Elements
Delayed Processing	Retaining Data Entry Documents
Duplicate Entry Checks	Screen Standards
Error Suspense Re-Entry	Self-Checking Data Elements
Formal Data Entry Procedures	Simultaneous Data Entry
Immediate Display of Terminal	Size Checks
Input Transaction Identification	Special-Purpose Data Origination Forms
Installation Convention Checks	Terminal Feature Standards
Interactive Editing	Transaction Accounting
Interfield Consistency Checks	User Data Entry Scheduling
Internal Batch Identification Record	Utilization of Default Options

Automatic Callback

Communication Control Log

Communication Priority Structure

Echo Checking

Message Intercept

Message Transaction Verification

Preformatting Data Entry

Redundant Communication Equipment

Self-Checking Transmissions

Store and Forward Transmissions

Terminal Handshaking

Transmission Address Verification

Fig. 7-5. Communications controls.

Fig. 7-6. Process controls.

Abnormal Processing Log	Field-by-Field Editing
Accounting Period Cut-Off	Formal Recovery Procedures
Active Data Dictionary	Formal Restart Procedures
Arithmetic Proofs	Hang-Up Action Log
Automated Control File	Initial Program Load Logs
Computer Rerun Analysis Log	Limited Batch Size
Control Total Adjustments	Manual Footing and Crossfooting
Critical File Activity Report	Monitoring Accounting Controls
Cut-Off Date Identification	Object Code Modification Authorization
Default Processing	Operating Procedure Manual
Dual Processing	Operating Priorities
Emergency Processing Messages	Operator Intervention Procedures
Excessive Activity Report	Operator Message Log

Operator Message Procedures	Restart Point Standards
Overflow Indication	Restart/Recovery Logging
Parallel Simulation	Scanning Computer Console Log
Privileged Instruction Profile	Scanning Job Control Cards
Process Priority Structure	Scheduled Processing
Process Prompting	Sequence Checking
Process Warning Messages	System Change Standards
Processing Benchmarks	Systems-To-System Totals
Program Instruction Tracing	Too Little Activity Report
Reasonableness Check	Transaction Processing Logs
Redundant Process Equipment	Transaction Processing Override Log

Fig. 7-7. Storage controls.

Storage - Off-Line	Storage - On-Line
Application Data Disposition Procedures	Bait Records
Data Storage (Off-Line) Copy	Computer Media Erasure
Data Storage (Off-Line) File Labels	Computer Media Usage Indicator
File Control Totals	Data Conflict Matrix
File Disposition Segregation	Data Dictionary
File Disposition Report	Data Storage (On-Line) Copy
File Update Simple Accounting Proof	Data Storage (On-Line) File Labels
Physical Inventory of Accountable Documents	Deadlock Resolution
Redundant Data Storage (Off-Line)	Dormant File Control
Voided Control Document Retention	Employee Account Analysis
	File Completion Check
	File Conflict Matrix
	File Control Totals
	File Header Record
	Hash Totals

Fig. 7-7. Continued

Storage - Off-Line	Storage - On-Line
	Manual Footing and Crossfooting
	Master File Changing Log
	Master File Standards
	Physical Inventory of Computer Media
	Record Hash Total
	Redundant Storage (On-Line)
	Split Files
	Structured Hash Totals
	Suspense Record Control

Fig. 7-8. Output controls.

Dual Report Distribution	Redundant Output Equipment
End of Report Indication	Redundant Output Report Totaling
File Retention Status Report	Report Anticipation Check
Formal Control Reconciliation Procedures	Report Description
Limiting Report Copies	Report Distribution Confirmation
Listing of Reports Prepared	Report Distribution Log
Negotiable Document Containment	Report Frequency Code
Output Copy	Report Preparation Date
Output Handling Procedures	Report Receipt Confirmation
Output Prioritization	Retaining Output Documents
Output Priority Structure	Sequential Delivery Number
Output Report Delivery Standards	Sequential Page Numbering
Output Report Labeling	Shredding Computer Waste
Output Security Classification	System Output Logs
Output Warning Messages	Transmission Labeling
Print on Demand	Turn around Documents
Printer Accuracy Test	Voiding Printer Alignment Documents
Printer Form Replenishment Control	Warning Message Feedback
Printer Overrun Wastage	
Processing Period Covered	

Fig. 7-9. Use of data controls.

Aging Open Item	Override Log
Anticipation Control Totals	Post-Installation Audit
Anticipation Scanning	Redundant Independence Control Total
Application System Totals	Remote Terminal to Central Facility Reconciliation
Audit Trail Pointers	Report Sensitivity Code
Computer-Generated Transaction Accounting Totals	Report Transaction Inclusion List
Continuous Negative Configuration	Report Use Procedures
Error Suspense File Analysis Report	Scanning Computer-Generated Transactions
Exception Reporting	Sequence Number Control List
Formal Report Use Configuration	Simple Accounting Proof
Independent Control Total	Transanction Dump
Operator Scanning	User Opinion Sampling
Output Sample Analysis	User Transaction Sampling

Fig. 7-10. General purpose controls.

Accountable Document Reconciliation	Control Coordinator
Administrative Procedure Manual	Control Menus
Anticipation Audits	Control Personnel Training
Audit Trail	Control Point Identification
Audit Trail Checklist	Cut-Off Date Reviews
Audit Trail Procedures	Data Administrator
Authorization Lists	Database Administrator
Automated Error Suspense	Data Encryption
Automated Training Procedures	Data Processing Area Visitor Policy
Base Case Testing	Detailed Error Descriptions
Before and After Images	Distribute Schedules
Computer-Generated Record Identification	Documentation Reviews
Consolidation Identifiers	Dormant Account Control
Control Checklist	Dual Custody of Forms

Fig. 7-10. Continued

Employee Performance Benchmarks

Employee Screening-Current Employees

Employee Screening-New Employees

Error Alert Report

Error Correction Reason Code

Error Description Reports

Error-Handling Logs

Error History File

Error Notification Document

Error Sequencing

Error Suspense Listings

Error-Tracking Analyst

Expiration Dating

Financial Chart of Account Identifiers

Formal Error-Handling Procedures

Formal Security Policy

Formal Training

Group Security Classification

Housekeeping Procedures

Identification Badges

Independent Control Transmission

Independent Reconciliation

Individual Security Clearances

Input/Output Transaction Reconciliation

Issue Corrective Action Document

Job Accounting

Job Description

Job Rotation

Loss of Business Insurance

Management Problem Analysis

Mandatory Vacation

Monitoring Error Processing

Multilevel Charging

Object Program History

Observed Computer Operations

Observed Document Destruction

Observed Terminal Usage

Off-Site Storage

Operator Intervention Procedures

Operator Training

Organize Control Group

Override Code

Penalties for Violation of Procedures

Preventive Maintenance Standards

Privacy Classification

Problem Anticipation Notification

Procedure Page Dating

Process Flow Monitoring

Program Identification

Program Version Number

Prompting

Property Insurance

Quality Assurance Analyst

Read-Only Hardware Features

Reason Codes

Recommended Corrective Action

Redundant Processing Facility

Removal Identification

Restricted Access to Storage Areas	Supportive Error Message Information
Retention Date Index	Surprise Audits
Risk Identification	System Development Checklist
Risk Quantification	System Testing Checklist
Rotation of Job Duties	System Analyst/Programmer Training
Scanning Terminal Usage Logs	Test Equipment Use Procedures
Security Officer	Training Benchmarks
Security Policy	Transaction Conflict Matrix
Security Pouch	Transaction Dating
Sensitive Area Control Policies	Transaction Folio Number
Sensitive Document Destruction	Transaction Splitting Identifier
	Transmittal Document
Separation of Duties	Updating Action Lists
Signature Plate Security	User Acceptance Testing
Source Program Change Log	User Acceptance Testing of System Changes
Source Program History	
Step-By-Step Totals	User Chargeback
Suggestion System	User Training
Supervisor Sign-Offs	Visual Document Scanning

checklists, then inquiry can be used, or the investigator can study control or other documentation in an effort to identify the controls.

The identified controls should be listed on the penetration point assessment worksheet (Fig. 7-11). This worksheet should be completed for each penetration point being investigated. Up to this point, the worksheet should contain a description of the penetration point, the potential perpetrator, and the magnitude of the risk expressed in either qualitative terms such as high, medium, or low; or quantitative terms such as $100,000.

A detailed description of each of the controls explaining what the control does; the evidence it produces; the strength of the control; whether the control is preventive, detective, or corrective; the evidence it produces; and the advantages and disadvantages are contained in FTP's *Internal Controls Manual*.

Penetration Point: _____

Potential Perpetrator: _____

Magnitude of Risk: _____

Controls	Strengths

Assessment of Risk:

Recommended Controls (Preventive):

Recommended Investigation (Detective):

Completed By:_____ **Date:**_____

Fig. 7-11. Penetration point assessment worksheet.

Estimating the strength of the controls

A strong system of internal controls is the number one deterrent to computer crime. Control systems can be considered as one of the following two types:

Control chains   The system of internal control is viewed as a chain comprised of many links. It is the interconnection of these links that provides the needed protection. The perpetrator penetrates the point where the link is the weakest. Therefore, in the design of control it is important to have all controls of about equal strength. Monies expended to make one control very strong is wasted because the perpetrator will attack the weakest link.

Concentric circles   In this system, control is viewed not as a chain, but as a series of rings that must be broken through in order to commit a computer crime. Therefore, the more extensive the grouping of control circles, the more effective the system of controls. This concept puts a number of locks on the door, perhaps all of medium strength, as opposed to one very strong lock. The chain concept uses one very strong lock.

The importance of the strength of the control will vary depending on which theory is accepted. In practice, it is reasonable to assume both theories work, but it is necessary to be continually aware of the potential weak link because perpetrators will penetrate at the weakest point of control.

One of the better methods to assess the strength of controls was developed by Touche Ross & Co. This assessment method is illustrated in Fig. 7-12. This matrix divides controls into the following categories:

- Preventive: Controls that stop computer crime from occurring.
- Detective: Controls that identify the fact that a computer crime has occurred.
- Corrective: Controls that provide evidence about computer crime or take action to reduce losses once the crime has been detected.
- Discretionary: Controls which may or may not be performed. These are normally manually performed controls and one can never be sure that the procedures will actually be implemented when necessary.
- Nondiscretionary: Controls will be performed at the appropriate time or upon the appropriate stimuli.

Figure 7-12 shows the strength of the control based on which of the

METHOD OF IMPLEMENTATION	TYPE OF CONTROL		
	PREVENTIVE	DETECTIVE	
		With Corresponding CORRECTIVE	Without CORRECTIVE
DISCRETIONARY	-Blank or C- Least effective, generally manual controls applied at front end of processing. However, moderately efficient.	-B- Moderately effective manual controls probably least efficient controls.	-C- Least effective and possibly dangerous since users rely improperly on them. Very inefficient.
NON-DISCRETIONARY	-C or B- Moderately effective, generally EDP controls, applied at front end of processing. Probably most efficient controls.	-A- Most effective, generally controls which are computerized and applied before processing can take place. Moderately efficient.	-Blank- May have some remote effectiveness, but probably little. Highly inefficient.

Source: Touche Ross & Company

Fig. 7-12. Effectiveness and efficiency of controls matrix (courtesy of Touche Ross & Company).

six descriptions the control matches. The strength of the control is as follows:

- A = very strong
- B = strong
- C = weak
- Blank = not effective

In addition to the strength of the control, a brief description of the efficiency of the control is also supplied. Efficiency is a measure of the amount of resource that must be expended in order to accomplish the control objective (i.e., an objective is to prevent, detect, or correct the computer crime situation).

Each of the controls identified in Fig. 7-11 must be assessed to show their strength. The assessment would be "A," "B," "C", or "Blank" (use a hyphen to indicate ineffective). Let's look at a couple of controls to determine how this would be accomplished.

Training   The objective of training is to prepare people to prevent some wrongdoing from occurring, thus it is a preventive control. The use of what is learned in training is discretionary. Therefore, if you look up a preventive discretionary, the chart shows that it will either be weak or ineffective. This is a judgement based on the type of preventive discretionary control. If the training looks reasonable, it would be classified as weak. If the training itself is poor, then it would be considered ineffective.

Electronic sensor in the computer room   An electronic sensor is a detective control in that it will detect movement in the comptuer room during off hours. Since it is operating continuously, it is a nondiscretionary control. When we look this up in Fig. 7-12, we find that if there is a corrective countermeasure, the control is very strong; while if there is no corrective countermeasure, the control is ineffective. This means that if the electronic sensor is connected to a security force or the local police, the corrective measure is alerting and calling security personnel to the computer room. On the other hand, if the sensor is connected to an audible alarm, but there is nobody present to answer it, that control should be considered ineffective.

At the end of this step, the identified controls in Fig. 7-11 are assigned a strength. The strength is used as part of the process of determining the adequacy or inadequacy of the controls to reduce the computer crime risk at the penetration point being evaluated.

Determining which penetration points warrant further investigation

The last step of the micro vulnerability assessment is determining the true vulnerability at the most probable point of penetration. Based on this assessment a judgement is made as to whether additional controls should be added, a computer crime investigation commenced, or a combination of the two.

The assessment process is one of judgement. Figure 7-11 has been designed to support that judgement. The penetration point is identified, the potential perpetrators are identified, and the magnitude of the computer crime risk is stated. The controls in place to reduce the computer crime risk at the identified point have been described and the strength of those controls determined.

The assessment process is the equivalent of placing the computer crime risk on one side of a scale and the controls on the other. If the controls balance the risk, the optimum level of control has been achieved. If the risk is greater than the controls, an undercontrolled situation exists. The remedy is more controls or investigation. If the controls far outweigh the risk, an over-controlled situation exists, and deletion of some controls might be considered.

The following questions may be helpful in assessing the adequacy of control:

- Can a few key controls reduce the risk to an acceptable level? Look for the key controls, those that are normally considered to be strong or very strong.

- Are the controls directed at the identified perpetrator? Some average to weak controls may be effective if they are directed at the identified perpetrator.
- Do the controls reinforce one another? Do they present a ring structure so that if the first control fails, the second will be effective; and if the second fails, the third will be effective; and so on?
- Do the controls balance the risk? If it is a high risk, are there strong controls?

At the end of this step, the last three blocks in Fig. 7-11 should be completed as follows:

Assessment of risk   The determination of whether the risk is adequately controlled, overcontrolled, or undercontrolled.

Recommended controls (prevention)   If the computer crime risk is undercontrolled, additional controls may be recommended to prevent a loss from occurring. On the other hand, if the risk is overcontrolled, the removal of some of the controls may be recommended.

Recommended investigation (detection)   If the controls appear weak in relation to the magnitude of the risk, an investigation may be warranted to determine whether an actual computer crime has occurred. The type and extent of investigation recommended should be included.

In most cases, and on most systems, it is a good idea to check at regular intervals for signs of tampering. Even if your security system seems adequate, the sophistication of computer criminals is growing daily. What keeps out the intruders today may not be sufficient tomorrow. Along this same line, it is essential that your security force keep in close contact with security groups of sites like yours. In this way, you will quickly be apprised of current threats.

Computer crime case study continued

The computer crime case involving the VSRS system described in the previous chapter concluded with the penetration points being identified. The next step after this is the assessment of the adequacy of controls to reduce those risks. In this case, the investigation was conducted by state auditors.

The state auditors concluded that there were the following control weaknesses:

- Organizations: No middle management existed. They did not support a system of good internal control. The data processing department had too much control.

- Management policy: Did not support an adequate system of internal control.

- Records management: Was not well defined. No importance was placed on retention of documents or computer files.

- Physical security: Extremely weak. Was not adequate to prevent unauthorized access to the building.

- System development controls: No standards existed for project management and review.

- Accounting controls: Reconciliation could not be performed. Manual accounting ledgers and computer accounts could not be reconciled.

- Documentation: For computer systems, operations, and user procedures, documentation did not exist.

The auditors also evaluated each of the penetration points and found controls to be weak at all of the points, although weaker at some than others. The result of the auditors' findings and the recommended controls are shown in Fig. 7-13.

As a result of this assessment, the auditors decided to conduct a fraud investigation. Their investigation concentrated on the high-risk penetration points and resulted in the detection of an actual fraud and the prosecution of the perpetrators. As previously stated, the fraud was conducted by three members of the user department.

Penetration Point	Fraudulent Method Or Act	Position and Expertise Of Most Likely Perpetrators	Impact of Controls In Place	Recommended Controls To Reduce Fraud Threat
P1	**Falsify or Forge SRS Membership form SRS-1.** The SRS membership form should be submitted from the new employee through the employing agency. Supplies of blank SRS-1 forms are kept at each agency. The SRS-1 form can be completely falsified by either the payroll clerk of the reporting agency or an individual with access to blank SRS-1 forms. The SRS-1 form is a means of establishing a computer account (MCA) at SRS.	**Agency Payroll Clerk** – has access to forms and knowledge of how they are properly filled out. **Informed Individual** – this person would include a former employee or SRS employee.	No control over blank SRS-1 forms. No control over SRS-1 forms submitted without a contribution report and no exisiting account with SRS.	Security control of blank SRS-1 forms. Accounts should not be added to the file based on SRS-1 without a contribution. All SRS-1's must accompany the contribution report.
P2	**Payroll Fraud In the Reporting Agency** – If a payroll fraud is occurring in the reporting agencies payroll system, then fraudulent contributions would be paid into the MCA account. This could possibly be looted at a later date by the perpetrator.	**Agency Payroll Clerk** – has access to contribution payrolls (reports) submitted to SRS.	No controls within SRS could prevent or detect a payroll fraud in a reporting agency.	None

Penetration Point	Fraudulent Method Or Act	Position and Expertise Of Most Likely Perpetrators	Impact of Controls In Place	Recommended Controls To Reduce Fraud Threat
P3 &4	**Fraudulent Computer Program Code** - Programs SRS UP001 and SRGVIN could have fraudulent code which would be used to inflate amounts reported on the contribution report to agree with the amount on the transmittal sheet when this is an error in reporting contributions by the agency. The inflated amount would be deposited in a fraudulent account.	**Computer Programmer or Analyst** - must have access to the transmittal sheet and contribution report before the program is run.	There are no controls in place to prevent access to these documents. There is no control over access to program libraries. There are no log controls.	Control access to program libraries. Implement log controls for access to hard copy source listings.
P5	**Create Fraudulent MCA Account** - This involves creating a computer account completely without any supporting documentations and without any trace of how the account was added.	**Computer Programmer or Analyst** - must have access to program libraries and data files.	No access controls exist to prevent access to data files or program libraries.	Control access to program libraries. Implement computer files control procedures.

Fig. 7-13. Case study penetration points.

Penetration Point	Fraudulent Method Or Act	Position and Expertise Of Most Likely Perpetrators	Impact of Controls In Place	Recommended Controls To Reduce Fraud Threat
P6	**Transfer Contributions From Other Accounts on the File to a Fraudulent Account** - This would be performed by an unauthorized computer program. Inactive accounts would be chosen as best for looting, however, older active accounts with large balances could be skimmed off. Accounts looted must be within the same agency.	**Computer Programmer or Analyst** must have access to program libraries and data files.	Control Sheet - Controls amounts by agency total; therefore, looting must be within accounts of the same agency. Owner of looted account could tip off this fraud scheme.	Control access to program libraries and data files. Control access to computer listings of accounts and their status.
P7	**Create Fraudulent Multiple Accounts with Equal Negative and Positive Contribution Balances** - This would be performed through an unauthorized computer program offsetting balances in fraudulent accounts. Accounts must be those of the same agency.	**Computer Programmer or Analyst** must have access to program libraries and data files.	No data control or access control exists except the control sheet which controls amounts by agency total.	Control access to program libraries and data files. Do not allow account with a negative balance to appear on the file or accounts with negatives should be subject to immediate review.

Penetration Point	Fraudulent Method Or Act	Position and Expertise Of Most Likely Perpetrators	Impact of Controls In Place	Recommended Controls To Reduce Fraud Threat
P8	**Creation of Fraudulent Computer Account Within a Computer Program (As Opposed to Creation of the Account on the File)** - Fraudulent code in two programs, SRREFO2 and SRRFBAL, would have to exist to make the user think that the account was on the file.	**Computer Programmer or Analyst** must have access to program libraries.	No access controls to program libraries exist. Control sheet file controls (by agency per mos.) would not detect this fraud if computer listings used to post totals to control sheet suppressed fraudulent transactions.	Control access to computer program libraries.
P9	**Falsify SRS-3 Refund Request Form** - The SRS-3 refund request form should be submitted by terminating employees through their agency. Supplies of blank SRS-1 forms are kept at each agency and at SRS. These forms could be easily falsified for the purposes of fraudulently withdrawing money from the contribution accounts.	**Agency Payroll Clerk** has access to blank forms and knowledge of inactive accounts. **Refund Clerk** also has access to blank forms and knowledge of inactive accounts.	No control over blank SRS-3 forms. Computer listings of account status and balances are easily accessible within SRS. Microfilm copies are made once a month and are used as references for information in each department within the agency.	Control physical access to blank SRS forms. Control access to computer accounts. Control access to computer listings of accounts and their status.

Fig. 7-13. Continued

Penetration Point	Fraudulent Method Or Act	Position and Expertise Of Most Likely Perpetrators	Impact of Controls In Place	Recommended Controls To Reduce Fraud Threat
P10	**Falsify Unreported Contributions on SRS-3 Form** - This method is similar to that of the one outlined above except, in this method the perpetrator is greedy and wants to withdraw more money than what is in the account which is being looted. An inactive account would be the target of this fraud.	**Refund Clerk** has access to blank SRS-3 forms. This would be the only person able to perpetrate this fraud because unreported contributions cannot be made into an inactive account. Any perpetrator, other than the refund clerk, could not commit this fraud because the refund clerk would detect it when editing the refund request.	No control over blank SRS-3 forms. Inactive account data is easily accessible.	Unreported contributions should not be allowed to be designated on the SRS-3. Control access to computer listings of accounts and their status.

Penetration Point	Fraudulent Method Or Act	Position and Expertise Of Most Likely Perpetrators	Impact of Controls In Place	Recommended Controls To Reduce Fraud Threat
P11	**Falsify SRS-3 Refund Request Form For NonExistent Employee** - This method involves filling out the SRS-3 form with unreported contributions which fall completely within the date of employee termination and the date of the last contribution report which was submitted by the agency. The SRS then would have no record of this employee and would add the fictitious account to the computer file based on the SRS-3 form.	**Agency Payroll Clerk** has access to blank forms and knowledge of when the last contribution report was submitted to SRS. **Refund Clerk** - same as stated above for the agency payroll clerk.	No control over blank SRS-3 forms.	Unreported contributions should not be allowed to be designated on the SRS-3 form. Accounts must not be added to the computer file solely on the basis of the SRS-3 refund request.
P12	**Alter or Falsify Refund Voucher** - This method involves altering transactions on the refund computer listing of already fraudulent refund transactions. Since the voucher is signed and returned to the Refund Section, this provides an excellent opportunity to alter the voucher.	**Refund Clerk** must have access to the authorized voucher and sufficient time to make alterations before submitting it to the State Comptroller's Office.	Alterations should be detected by processing clerks in the State Comptroller's Office.	Authorized voucher should be sent directly to the State Comptroller's Office. Strict editing of vouchers must exist in the State Comptroller's Office.

Fig. 7-13. Continued

8

Developing a
vulnerability profile

THE VULNERABILITY ASSESSMENT PROCESS CONCLUDES WITH AN assessment report. This section describes how to organize and present the material developed during the computer crime vulnerability assessment. The objective is to provide a computer crime profile so that countermeasures can be developed for the high-risk areas.

The challenge of preventing and detecting computer crime has been the cost-effective allocation of countermeasure resources. The answer to this dilemma is to identify the areas where computer crime is most probable, and then allocate resources to prevent and detect computer crime at those points. The computer crime profile that will be developed using the guidelines presented in this chapter is the basis on which preventive and detective computer crime countermeasures should be developed.

Computer crime profile analysis

At the conclusion of the vulnerability analysis, a report or profile needs to be prepared showing the organization's vulnerability to computer crime. The profile is a report to management outlining a detailed plan of action. Earlier in this book was a general plan of action. The vulnerability assessment will customize that plan for your specific organization.

The computer crime profile report should consist of the following five parts.

1. Organizational computer crime risk. Shows the susceptibility of the organization to computer crime. This vulnerability characteristic is based on the assessment of the criteria that correlate to high computer crime vulnerability. The rational judgement of security professionals can be very valuable here.

2. Individual application vulnerability. This segment of the profile shows the detailed computer crime vulnerability for each application system. The profile illustrates the most probable perpetrator and the most probable points of penetration.

3. Computer crime perpetrator candidates. This part of the profile consolidates all the opportunities provided to perpetrators to commit computer crime at the target site. The basis is that the individual with the greatest opportunity is the one most likely to commit computer crime. Because this assessment looks at perpetrators' accessibility to all application systems, the assessment will vary from that of the perpetrators for individual applications.

4. Computer crime penetration point candidates. This part of the profile attempts to rank the penetration points to indicate which has the greatest vulnerability organization-wide. Again, knowing this, the resources for computer crime countermeasures can be applied to the applications or areas with highest risk.

5. Customized computer crime plan of action. The general plan of action outlined earlier needs to be customized, outlining specific steps to take based on the computer crime vulnerability assessment.

Organizational computer crime risk

The organizational computer crime risk is an organization's vulnerability to crime based on its organizational characteristics. The presence of these environmental criteria have been shown to have a high positive correlation to the incidence of computer crime. The organization's environmental criteria correlate with the computer crime vulnerability checklist in chapter 4 (Fig. 4-1). Chapter 4 described who should complete these assessment questionnaires. This chapter describes how to develop the risk profile.

The computer crime vulnerability assessment checklist for environmental criteria (Fig. 4-1) contained 21 questions. The applicability of each criterion was rated by one or more individuals. A numerical score for each individual should be calculated by assigning three points to each criterion checked for high applicability, two points for each criterion checked for average applicability, one point for each criterion checked for low applicability, and zero points for each criterion checked for "no" (none) applicability. The environmental criteria vulnerability score worksheet (Fig. 8-1) can be used to calculate the risk score for each rater.

The worksheet is completed by transferring the number of check marks in each of the four applicability columns from Fig. 4-1 to Fig. 8-1. For example, if three of the 21 criteria are checked "highly applicable," this is then multiplied by the weight (three) to give a total score of nine. When the four applicability categories have been calculated, the four scores should be totaled to develop a total environmental criteria risk score. The score will be in the range of 0 to 57.

The risk score is interpreted as follows:

- 40 to 57 = high risk
- 22 to 39 = medium risk
- 1 to 21 = low risk
- 0 = no risk

Once the risk score for each rater has been determined, it can be converted into a graphical representation. This graphical representation will show variations between low, medium, and high risk without using the precision of mathematics. An example of a computer crime risk profile is illustrated in Fig. 8-2. This figure shows four raters (A, B, C, and D) and the average of all four. The risk score for each rater is approximated on the scale, and then the four risk scores are averaged to show the average score for all four raters.

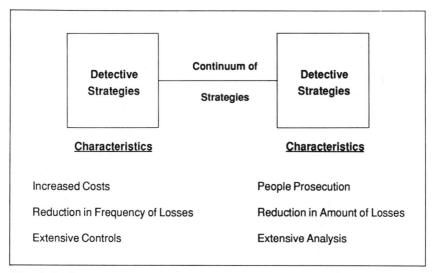

Fig. 8-1. Computer crime countermeasure continuum of strategies.

No.	Phase	Description
1	Planning	Setting Objectives, Defining Scheme, Participants, Methods, and Roles
2	Execution	Physical Movement of Goods, Information, or Ownership of Resources
3	Concealment	Misrepresentation or Manipulation of Data or Accounts to Prevent the Crime and/or Criminal from being detected
4	Conversion	Changing the Assets Stolen from what it was to what is wanted

Fig. 8-2. Four phases of computer crime.

Individual application vulnerability

Profiles can be developed for each computerized application subject to computer crime. Chapter 4 briefly described how applications can be evaluated to determine whether or not they are subject to computer crime. The key criterion is the value of the assets, both tangible and intangible, controlled by the application system.

The first look at application computer crime vulnerability is determined by evaluating the results of Fig. 4-2. The assessment is similar to that just completed for the overall organizational computer crime vulnerability using environmental criteria.

The application computer crime vulnerability risk score is calculated in the same manner as the organizational computer crime vulnerability.

Figure 8-3 can be used to calculate the individual application risk score for each rater. The interpretation of the total risk score is as follows:

- 40 to 57 = high risk
- 22 to 39 = medium risk
- 1 to 21 = low risk
- 0 = no risk

The same profile as prepared for the organizational risk can also be prepared for the application's computer crime vulnerability risk. Figure 8-3 will show the scoring of each rater and the average risk for the application.

An application system profile should also be prepared. This profile will show the application risk plus the high-risk perpetrators and the high-risk penetration points. The application risk is the average risk determined using Fig. 4-2. The most probable perpetrator and penetration points are determined from the analysis suggested in chapters 5 and 6. The results of all of these assessments can be recorded in Fig. 8-4.

The potential perpetrators and penetration points are identified on the penetration point matrix developed for each application system. A description of how to develop this penetration point matrix was included in chapter 5.

The degree of risk comes from the total penetration point scores, horizontally and vertically. However, the score must be normalized before it can be converted to high, medium, or low risk. This is because both the number of penetration points and the number of opportunities will vary from application to application, thus the total number of penetration points will vary.

To calculate a normalized score:

1. Identify the maximum number of points for both the perpetrators and penetration points.
2. Develop a scale for the maximum number of points for both the perpetrators and penetration points so that the one-third and two-third points on the scale are known. For example, if 20 points is the maximum score, the one-third point would be approximately 6 and the two-third point, 13.
3. Label the one-third point the low-risk score, and the two-third point the average-risk score.
4. Convert the perpetrator score and the penetration point score into the appropriate level of risk.

Those perpetrators who have the highest risk should be placed on the risk profile (Fig. 8-4). Normally, this would be five or less perpetrators. The high-risk penetration points are then placed on the application profile. Again, this would normally be five or less penetration points.

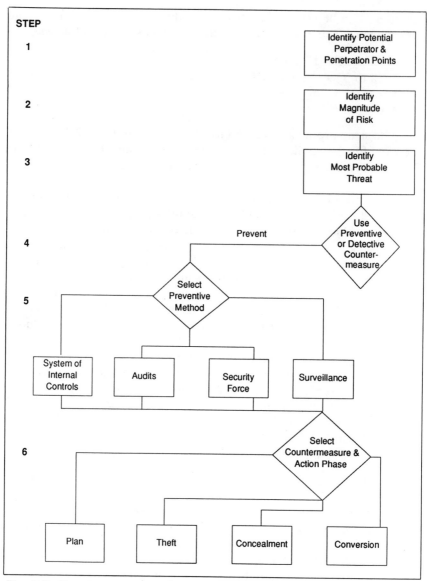

Fig. 8-3. Countermeasure selection process.

The degree of risk based on the normalization score is shown on the profile by the height of the bar for each penetration point and perpetrator. These can be listed randomly or in descending degree of risk. The name of the perpetrator/penetration point can be written into the bar, as in Fig. 8-4, or at the bottom, whichever appears more appropriate.

Upon completion of this analysis, a risk profile is prepared for each application with a computer crime vulnerability. The objective of the pro-

COMPUTER CRIME THREATS MATRIX
(THEIR PROBABLE IMPACT AND COUNTERMEASURES)

No.	Threat	Loss of Assets	Destruction/Plant	Destruction/Media	Disclosure	Disruption	System of Internal Controls	Audits	Security Force	Surveillance
		Probable Impact					Preventive Countermeasures			
	Data Input Threats									
1.	Undetected, unreasonable, or inconsistent source data	x					x			
2.	Key entry changes not detected	x								x
3.	Misinterpretation of record formats	x								x
4.	Fraudulently adding, deleting or modifying data	x								x
5.	Inserting or deleting transactions	x								x
6.	Modification of personal data	x						x		
7.	Emergency entry of transactions	x					x			
8.	Improper use of error correction procedures	x					x			
	Misuse By Authorized End-Users									
9.	Sale of privileged information				x				x	
10.	Acquisition and sale of complete list of information				x				x	
11.	Theft of services	x					x			
12.	Destruction or modification not for personal gain		x	x		x				x
13.	Sell information to an unauthorized individual				x				x	
	Uncontrolled System Access									
14.	Theft of data or programs	x			x				x	
15.	Destruction of EDP facilities		x						x	
16.	Unauthorized access to EDP facility	x	x	x	x	x			x	
17.	Unauthorized access through remote terminals	x			x		x			
18.	Unauthorized access through dial-in lines	x			x		x			
19.	Inadvertent revealing of passwords	x			x					x

Fig. 8-4. Computer crime threats matrix.

Fig. 8-4. Continued

20.	Piggybacking a terminal	x				x					x
21.	Password not voided when employee terminated	x				x		x			
22.	Unauthorized access	x				x					x
23.	Undetected repeated attempts	x				x		x			
	Ineffective Security Practices										
24.	Poorly defined authorization access	x				x		x			
25.	Incomplete enforcement of security	x	x	x	x	x				x	
26.	No follow-up on unusual conditions	x				x	x	x			
27.	Repeated processing of the same event	x						x			
28.	Careless handling of sensitive data					x					x
29.	Lack of follow-up on potential security violations	x	x	x	x	x			x		
30.	Lack of management follow-up	x	x	x	x	x			x		
	Procedural Errors Within The EDP Facility										
31.	Ignoring operational procedures	x							x		
32.	Operations manager or supervisor circumventing operational controls	x							x		
33.	Lapses of security during reorganization and recovery	x			x		x			x	
34.	Failure to protect files during maintenance				x	x			x		
35.	Inadequate supervision during non-working hour shifts	x			x	x	x				x
36.	Control overrides	x						x			
37.	Inadvertently or intentionally mis-labeling storage media				x	x				x	
38.	Failure to erase sensitive information					x		x			
39.	Output routed to wrong individual					x					x
	Program Errors										
40.	Key data stored in programs	x						x			
41.	Trojan Horse routines	x							x		
42.	Programs readily accessible	x								x	
43.	Program theft	x								x	
44.	Program time bombs			x			x		x		

No.	Vulnerability								
45.	Ghost program versions	x		x		x			
	Operating System Flow								
46.	Operating system control weakness	x		x		x			
47.	Disable operating system control	x					x		
48.	Failure to SYSGEN controls	x	x	x		x			
49.	Lack of copy protection			x		x			
50.	Unauthorized modification to the operating system	x						x	
51.	Unbroken audit trail	x				x			
52.	On-line system crash protection	x						x	
53.	Unauthorized processing in a supervisory mode	x	x	x	x	x			
	Communication System Failure								
54.	Lack of positive identification	x		x		x			
55.	Unauthorized monitoring			x				x	
56.	Unauthorized acts at remote terminals	x							x
57.	Unauthorized modification of communication software			x		x			
58.	Wire tapping			x				x	
59.	Unauthorized takeover	x		x					x
60.	Stealing encryption keys	x		x				x	
61.	Spoofing	x					x		
62.	Replaying messages	x					x		

file is to enhance computer crime prevention and detection. Knowing the degree of risk within the application and the most probable perpetrators points out the amount of computer crime attention each application should receive.

Perpetrator candidates

The opportunity for perpetrators to commit computer crime is partially related to the number of systems to which they have access. The more systems a perpetrator has to defraud, the more opportunity there is to commit and conceal a crime. Thus, while there is not an exact multiplier effect in being able to penetrate multiple systems, having those multiple opportunities does increase an individual's opportunity to commit computer crime.

To calculate an individual's total opportunity, each risk score should be normalized to a risk score of zero to three. This can be done from the individual profiles by allocating a three to high risk, a two to medium risk, a one to low risk, and zero to no (none) risk. The risk score for each perpetrator is then normalized to zero to three. For this exercise, the risk score of every perpetrator should be normalized, not just those illustrated in the Fig. 8-4 risk profile.

The normalized risk score for each perpetrator is then summed. This is done by adding together the risk score for that perpetrator for each computerized application being evaluated. The total scores are then put in descending sequence from high to low.

The perpetrator with the highest total risk score is ranked #1 and listed first on Fig. 8-5. The perpetrator with the second highest score is ranked #2, and the process continues until all the perpetrators are listed on Fig. 8-5. Comments need to be added where appropriate. At the conclusion of the analysis, all the potential perpetrators are ranked.

Penetration point candidates

This part of the profile ranks penetration points in the same manner as perpetrators are ranked. The penetration point scores for all of the penetration points must first be normalized to a score of zero to three. The penetration points can then be scored to show the opportunity at a single point to manipulate multiple systems.

For this part of the profile to be meaningful, one of the following two strategies must be used in identifying penetration points.

1. Common names. An overall naming convention for penetration points must be adopted so that when the same penetration point appears in multiple systems it is readily identified. Note that the variances in systems make this difficult to do, and conscientious effort is required.

2. Generalized penetration points. After all of the applications have been rated, the penetration point should be put into categories. For example, some of the categories might be preparation of input documents, approval of input documents, error

POTENTIAL PERPETRATOR RANKING WORKSHEET

Rank	Perpetrator	Comments

Fig. 8-5. Potential perpetrator ranking worksheet.

correction, updates of master records, and so forth. Once this has been done, the common categories of penetration points can be scored and ranked.

The ranking for penetration points is performed in the same manner as ranking for perpetrators (see Fig. 8-6). The total risk scores are ordered

HIGH-RISK PENETRATION POINTS RANKING WORKSHEET

Rank	Penetration Points	Comments

Fig. 8-6. High-risk penetration points ranking worksheet.

with the highest score receiving the highest ranking and the lowest score the lowest ranking.

An alternative to ranking the high-risk penetration points is to rank the applications or areas. This is done by listing the applications in order of their application risk score using the values calculated from Fig. 4-2.

Customized computer crime plan of action

A generalized computer crime plan of action was presented as management strategies in Fig. 2-2. A seven-step process was suggested in chapter 2 for selecting a strategy to manage computer crime. This general strategy can now be customized based on the areas of high computer crime risk in the organization.

The computer crime profile will show:

- The organization's computer crime vulnerability
- The vulnerability of individual applications
- The ranking of the potential perpetrators according to degree of computer crime risk
- The ranking of penetration points according to the opportunity they provide
- The ranking of applications by degree of computer crime risk (optional)

The management computer crime strategy attempts to assess the threat category of both people and systems. The detailed profile offers the following additional information to enable the initial strategy to be accepted, rejected, or modified:

- Confirm that the strategy is consistent with the high-risk perpetrators
- Determine that the strategy is consistent with the high-risk applications and penetration points

Customizing the strategy can be done as follows:

1. Allocate resources to computer crime. The degree of computer crime risk can be used as the basis for allocating countermeasure resources.
2. Customize people strategies. The plan of action directed at preventing or detecting people who commit computer crime can now be customized toward specific individuals or groups of individuals.
3. Customize system strategies. The plan of action directed at preventing or detecting systems used in committing computer crime can now be customized toward specific systems or groups of systems.

Although much of this chapter pertains to large organizations with many employees and many computers, there are significant portions which should be considered by personal computer (PC) users as well. For example, a penetration point analysis of the usual personal system would reveal possible attack vectors from three sources. First, and most common, is penetration by downloading of software. This can entail either a trap door program or an infection by a viruslike program. Next is infection by contaminated media. If an infected diskette is loaded into your machine, the security of your computer has been compromised. Finally, your machine is susceptible to security violations by co-workers. Leaving your machine unattended while you are at lunch could be just the invitation a less-than-ethical co-worker needs to, at the least, begin perusing your files. At the other extreme, an unauthorized user could corrupt your operating system or erase some of your files.

Having a PC rather than a large mainframe does not eliminate the threat of computer crime. On the contrary, with the spread of local area networks (LANs), an additional source of contamination and attack is becoming prevalent.

Computer security is the responsibility of anyone who has access to a computer. It should not be left solely to the large-computer users. Each PC can become a source of infection and a vector for contamination. Safe computing is a necessity in any computer.

9

Detecting computer crime

THE MAJOR OBJECTIVE OF ANY COMPUTER CRIMINAL DETECTION PROGRAM is to reduce the amount of financial loss for a company. There are two ways this loss can be limited: by reducing the number of computer crimes committed and by reducing the exposure in any one crime. This chapter brings together several different, yet related, concepts concerning the detection of computer crime. First, we will examine the general detection process, as well as the way informants are used. Then, we will consider how to investigate a complaint. Next, we will look at ways to investigate actual crime. Finally, we will look at the process of analyzing computer crime.

Detection strategy

The reason for a detection strategy is to determine if a computer crime has been committed. This may sound odd, but many times it has been almost impossible to determine exactly what crime was committed, even though all the parties involved knew that a crime had taken place. Computer crimes are often as nearly invisible as a crime can become.

The strategy for detecting computer crime should incorporate the following objectives.

- Limit the loss. The goal should be to detect the loss as early as possible so as to limit the amount of damage and maximize the opportunity to catch the criminal and recoup the loss.

- Detect those crimes that cannot be prevented. In any situation, there are possible crimes that defy prevention. A good detection policy aids in spotting these crimes.

- Limit the cost of detection. It is usually easier to detect a computer crime than it is to prevent it. Therefore, early detection is very important.

- Utilize the existing capability in the software. Many systems have some sort of software to check and validate users. Some have audit trail capability. Explore the existing system and use the tools available. Remember that the system must be usable when you are finished. Don't build such a complex security system so that normal users can't access the system.

- Make prosecutions of computer criminals public. Often a company does not wish to make it known that they have been attacked. It is important to send a message to computer criminals that nefarious activity will not be tolerated.

Cost of computer crime detection

There are four primary ways to become aware of a crime. These are listed below, along with the associated costs for each. It is a fact of life that computer crime will happen. Therefore, the job is to find the crime and isolate it with the least possible cost.

- Information: In most cases, there is no cost because people will come forward and volunteer information on potential crimes.

- Complaints: People seem willing to complain about the flaws in the software. If an application suddenly becomes difficult to use, it may be due to a virus infection. These individuals have no direct cost and can become powerful allies if treated with respect.

- Investigations: The system should be investigated by the staff that is most familiar with the software. Frequent random audits will show whether the system is safe or has been compromised.

- Analysis: A large portion of detection time is spent looking at data gathered during recent computer program runs. Always be on the lookout for unusual or extraordinary occurrences. It may be necessary to obtain help from a computer crime consultant to unravel a sophisticated criminal event.

Figure 9-1 is a matrix of 62 potential threats. It lists possible avenues of attack, their probable impact, and countermeasures to offset the threat. The first set of columns lists the possible cause of the crime. The next set lists the potential countermeasures. This table should become part of the security staff's regular procedure.

COMPUTER CRIME THREATS MATRIX
(THEIR PROBABLE IMPACT AND COUNTERMEASURES)

No.	Threat	Probable Impact					Detective Countermeasures			
		Loss of Assets	Destruction/Plant	Destruction/Media	Disclosure	Disruption	Informants	Complaints	Investigation	Analysis
	Data Input Threats									
1.	Undetected, unreasonable, or inconsistent source data	x								x
2.	Key entry changes not detected	x						x		
3.	Misinterpretation of record formats	x						x		
4.	Fraudulently adding, deleting, modifying data	x								x
5.	Inserting or deleting transactions	x								x
6.	Modification of personal data	x							x	
7.	Emergency entry of transactions	x						x		
8.	Improper use of error correction procedures	x						x		
	Misuse By Authorized End-Users									
9.	Sale of privileged information				x			x		
10.	Acquisition and sale of complete list of information				x			x		
11.	Theft of services	x							x	
12.	Destruction or modification not for personal gain		x	x		x		x		
13.	Sell information to an unauthorized individual				x			x		
	Uncontrolled System Access									
14.	Theft of data or programs	x			x			x		
15.	Destruction of EDP facilities		x						x	
16.	Unauthorized access to EDP facility	x	x	x	x	x			x	
17.	Unauthorized access through remote terminals	x			x					x
18.	Unauthorized access through dial-in lines	x			x					x
19.	Inadvertent revealing of passwords	x			x			x		

Fig. 9-1. Computer crime threats matrix.

Fig. 9-1. Continued

20.	Piggybacking a terminal	x			x		x			
21.	Password not voided when employee terminated	x			x					x
22.	Unauthorized access	x			x			x		
23.	Undetected repeated attempts	x			x					x
	Ineffective Security Practices									
24.	Poorly defined authorization access	x			x				x	
25.	Incomplete enforcement of security	x	x	x	x	x			x	
26.	No follow-up on unusual conditions	x			x	x				x
27.	Repeated processing of the same event	x								x
	Ineffective Security Practices (continued)									
28.	Careless handling of sensitive data				x		x			
29.	Lack of follow-up on potential security violations	x	x	x	x	x				x
30.	Lack of management follow-up	x	x	x	x	x				x
	Procedural Errors Within The EDP Facility									
31.	Ignoring operational procedures	x							x	
32.	Operations manager or supervisor circumventing operational controls	x							x	
33.	Lapses of security during reorganization and recovery	x		x		x			x	
34.	Failure to protect files during maintenance			x	x				x	
35.	Inadequate supervision during non-working hour shifts	x		x	x	x			x	
36.	Control overrides	x								x
37.	Inadvertently or intentionally mis-labeling storage media			x	x				x	
38.	Failure to erase sensitive information				x				x	
39.	Output routed to wrong individual				x			x		
	Program Errors									
40.	Key data stored in programs	x								x
41.	Trojan Horse routines	x							x	
42.	Programs readily accessible	x								x
43.	Program theft	x					x			
44.	Program time bombs			x		x		x		

45.	Ghost program versions	x		x			x	
	Operating System Flow							
46.	Operating system control weakness	x		x			x	
47.	Disable operating system control	x				x		
48.	Failure to SYSGEN controls	x	x	x			x	
49.	Lack of copy protection			x			x	
50.	Unauthorized modification to the operating system	x						x
51.	Unbroken audit trail	x						x
52.	On-line system crash protection	x				x		
53.	Unauthorized processing in a supervisory mode	x	x	x	x			x
	Communication System Failure							
54.	Lack of positive identification	x		x	x			
55.	Unauthorized monitoring			x		x		
56.	Unauthorized acts at remote terminals	x						x
57.	Unauthorized modification of communication software			x			x	
58.	Wire tapping			x		x		
59.	Unauthorized take-over	x		x		x		
60.	Stealing encryption keys	x		x		x		
61.	Spoofing	x					x	
62.	Replaying messages	x						x

Building a network of informants

Most law enforcement professionals will admit that they rarely solve a crime. Rather they are able to find individuals who know what happened. Finding these witnesses is the largest part of their crime solving job. Likewise it is important for the computer security specialist to cultivate a group of individuals who can act as ancillary eyes and ears to detect computer crime. We will call this group a network of informants.

To build this network the security specialist needs to contact a wide variety of people in different jobs. It is not enough to simply rely on the programming staff, but rather it is important to cultivate relationships throughout the company.

Investigatory staff

One important factor is the makeup and conduct of the investigatory personnel. You should use professional staff whenever possible, drawing from auditors, the security force, and the legal staff. If an investigation is improperly handled, especially the questioning of suspects, the company may be put at risk for legal action. In addition, the case against the perpetrator may be rendered void if his/her rights have been violated. In later sections of this chapter, we will examine these areas in greater detail.

Informant network

While some individuals will come forward and report a computer crime, most informants will need to be cultivated over a period of time. This is the long-range aspect of the network building process. It will not happen all at once. The security professional must be patient and careful, treating each individual as a special asset to the security department. Some of the groups from which the security specialist may wish to draw individuals include:

- Honest co-workers who witness a crime or the results of a crime and report it to the company.

- Management at all levels. Because management is charged with protecting the company, they are ready and willing to help. Remember that managers are a good source of information (as watchers), but are generally untrained for the more serious aspects of investigation.

- Designated informants should be selected informally. They may include members of the three groups who make up the investigatory group or may be individuals who seem to be in the right place at the right time. It is important that the identity of these informants be kept secure. If knowledge of their function is leaked, their effectiveness drops.

- Local law enforcement agencies may provide information as to the current makeup of the area's crime. Especially important is data on attacks against similar computer sites. Using the data available from local and federal law enforcement agencies can serve to keep the security professional up to date on current threats and countermeasures.

- Knowledgeable third parties are sometimes very valuable and important in the collection of data. They will have insights into the behavior of the staff. Be careful not to enlist the aid of anyone who is recently separated from one of the employees. In that situation, the possibility of a revenge report is too great to risk that exposure.

Key factors in building and maintaining a productive network are regular recognition and a sense of protection. Each informant must be aware that his/her name will never be used and so will never surface to serve as a target for the less-than-ethical members of the work force.

The cost of a network of informants is usually quite nominal. The money and time invested in this procedure are well worth the effort.

Maintaining an informant network

There are a number of different steps that need to be taken to maintain a network of informants. They are summarized in Fig. 9-2. Carefully study this figure because it provides an idea of the scope of the task, as well as some suggestions for increasing a network's effectiveness.

Figure 9-3 is the first set of countermeasures, and is based on the use of informants. In other sections of this chapter we will examine other countermeasures.

Complaint investigation

Many computer crimes have been identified by the user community. Taken as a group, knowledgeable users are one of the most important factors in recognizing computer crimes. This section looks at the complaints of users, which form the basis for this aspect of investigation.

Never before in the history of man has it been possible to make so much from so little. As a case in point, a large bank in Michigan was the site of a rather common early computer crime. A programmer for the credit card division altered the interest calculating portion of the program so that when it had to round off a portion of a penny in interest, that portion of the penny was added to the programmer's account. Detection would have come at the end of the month when his statement was printed; 11 boxes of transactions. Each month he carefully suppressed the printing of his statement. Detection came when the bank decided to run the statements a day early, a day the programmer was on vacation. When the 11 boxes were delivered to his office, his secretary took the matter to his boss, believing an error had occurred. This triggered an investigation and the programmer was brought to justice. However, it is not known how much money he stole. There have been guesses of a figure in the millions, but no one knows for sure. If the secretary had remained silent, this crime may have gone undetected for years. Here we see the value of listening and acting on customer and employee complaints.

THREAT: Emergency Entry of Transactions

PROBABLE IMPACT: Loss of Assets

RECOMMENDED PREVENTIVE CONTROL METHOD: System of Internal Controls

No.	Potential Vulnerability	Countermeasure Needed			Suggested Countermeasure	Crime Action Phase
		Yes	No	N/A		
1.	Have procedures been established on what types of transactions will be entered on an emergency basis?				Develop a listing of the conditions that would warrant entering transactions on other than the normal basis.	Planning
2.	Has a list of individuals who are authorized to enter transactions in the computer system on an emergency basis been defined?				Determine from management who has the authority to enter emergency transactions.	Planning
3.	Are procedures established so that only authorized individuals can enter authorized emergency transactions?				Develop a matrix showing the emergency type transactions and the individuals who can enter them, and then develop procedures to verify that the entry is in conformance with those procedures.	Theft Act
4.	Is a listing of all emergency transactions that are entered into the system prepared?				Modify computer sytems so that all transactions entered, other than through the normal means, are listed for later review.	Concealment
5.	Does supervision regularly review the reasonableness of emergency transactions?				Establish procedures so that management reviews all emergency transactions.	Concealment

Fig. 9-2. Potential countermeasures based upon informants.

THREAD: <u>Emergency Entry of Transactions</u>

PROBABLE IMPACT: <u>Loss of Assets</u>

RECOMMENDED DETECTIVE CONTROL METHOD: <u>Informants</u>

No.	Potential Vulnerability	Countermeasure Needed			Suggested Countermeasure	Crime Action Phase
		Yes	No	N/A		
1.	Do personnel within the area defraud the system by entering fraudulent transactions through the emergency procedures?				Inquire of data entry personnel who is responsible what type of transactions are being entered on an emergency basis.	Concealment
2.	Are fraudulent transactions subject to normal controls when they are entered on an emergency basis?				List the transactions being entered on an emergency basis and verify their correctness.	Concealment
3.	Will inadequate controls over emergency transactions enable the process to be abused?				Interview supervisors to determine the type of control over emergency procedures and the adequacy of control.	Planning
4.	Do employees know that the emergency procedures are being violated but do not bring the matter to the attention of supervisors?				Randomly talk to a large number of employees in order to probe potential emergency transaction procedure violations.	Concealment

Fig. 9-3. First set of countermeasures based upon informants.

Fig. 9-3. Continued

THREAT: Improper Use of Error Correction Procedures

PROBABLE IMPACT: Loss of Assets

RECOMMENDED DETECTIVE CONTROL METHOD: Informants

No.	Potential Vulnerability	Countermeasure Needed			Suggested Countermeasure	Crime Action Phase
		Yes	No	N/A		
1.	Are fraudulent transactions entered through the error correction procedures?				List a sample of high-risk corrected errors and verify that the correction is proper.	Concealment
2.	Do employees know that error correction procedures are being violated but do not bring that matter to the attention of supervisors?				Talk to a random number of employees to probe of potential error correction violations.	Concealment
3.	Do users recognize that there is an error correction problem but do not associate it with computer crime?				Review the program change requests submitted by users for potential error correction violations.	Concealment
4.	Do the originators of transactions recognize that a problem has occurred but do not associate it with computer crime?				Review sources of user complaints over error corrections for potential computer crime symptoms.	Concealment
5.	Are errors caused in the error correction procedure exploited for fraudulent purposes?				Review the handling of errors caused by the correction of errors to ensure that they are not used for improper purposes.	Concealment

THREAT: Sale of Privileged Information

PROBABLE IMPACT: Disclosure

RECOMMENDED DETECTIVE CONTROL METHOD: Informants

No.	Potential Vulnerability	Countermeasure Needed			Suggested Countermeasure	Crime Action Phase
		Yes	No	N/A		
1.	Do law enforcement agencies know privileged information has been sold but do not report it to the organization?				Maintain an interface with the local police force so that they will alert the organization to potential sales of organizational privileged information.	Conversion
2.	Does the marketing force know that privileged information is in the market place but do not report it to the appropriate group?				Inquire among marketing personnel of their awareness of organizational privileged information in the market place.	Conversion
3.	Are perpetrators permitted to acquire privileged information because the risk is not recognized?				Identify potential perpetrators and monitor their activities.	Execution
4.	Are users aware that privileged information has been compromised but do not report it?				Inquire of users the probability of privileged information within their function being compromised.	Concealment
5.	Are individuals aware that privileged information has been compromised but do not report it?				Post a reward for information leading to the conviction of perpetrators of privileged information.	Concealment

Fig. 9-3. Continued

THREAT: Acquisition and Sale of Complete List of Information

PROBABLE IMPACT: Disclosure

RECOMMENDED DETECTIVE CONTROL METHOD: Informants

No.	Potential Vulnerability	Countermeasure Needed			Suggested Countermeasure	Crime Action Phase
		Yes	No	N/A		
1.	Is information compromised and the organization not aware of it?				Include bait records on key computer files. A bait record is an individual or organization on the file which is fictitious but established so that if it is ever contacted the fact that the file has been compromised will be known.	Concealment
2.	Is the file offered for sale on the market place but the individuals offered the information do not come forward and disclose the offer?				If the compromise of a computer file is suspected, contact friendly third parties regarding their knowledge of the availability of that information.	Concealment
3.	Are individuals aware that the file has been compromised and is for sale but do not come forward with that information?				Offer a reward for information leading to the arrest and conviction of individuals who have compromised computer files and offer them for sale.	Concealment
4.	Are marketing personnel aware that the information is available in the market place but do not notify the investigators of that fact?				Probe marketing personnel to determine their knowledge of availability of organizational information.	Concealment

THREAT: Destruction or Modification Not For Personal Gain

PROBABLE IMPACT: Destruction of Plant, Destruction of Media, Disruption

RECOMMENDED DETECTIVE CONTROL METHOD: Informants

No.	Potential Vulnerability	Countermeasure Needed			Suggested Countermeasure	Crime Action Phase
		Yes	No	N/A		
1.	Do employees destroy organizational property without recognizing the countermeasures that will be taken against them?				Post a sign indicating the organizational policy against individuals who destroy company property.	Concealment
2.	Do employees witness destruction but not report it?				Publicize a hot-line telephone number for the purpose of employees reporting problems anonymously or in a manner that assures their identity will be protected.	Concealment
3.	Does sabotage occur but is diagnosed as an error or omission?				Interview parties associated with the destruction of property in order to determine the true cause.	Concealment
4.	Are disgruntled employees stopped before they cause damages?				Continually inquire among employees regarding who is strongly disgruntled with the organization so that appropriate countermeasures can be taken against that individual.	Concealment

Fig. 9-3. Continued

THREAT: Sell Information to an Unauthorized Individual

PROBABLE IMPACT: Disclosure

RECOMMENDED DETECTIVE CONTROL METHOD: Informants

No.	Potential Vulnerability	Countermeasure Needed			Suggested Countermeasure	Crime Action Phase
		Yes	No	N/A		
1.	Is the loss of information detected by data processing personnel but no action is taken?				Regularly interview the data librarian about potential losses of information.	Concealment
2.	Are potential perpetrators of selling information controlled?				Through inquiry and informants, identify potential perpetrators of selling information so that the action of those individuals can be observed.	Concealment
3.	Are individuals aware that information has been taken or sold but do not inform the appropriate individuals?				Develop and publicize a hot-line for the purpose of reporting potential loss or sale of information.	Concealment
4.	Do operators suspect that improprieties are occurring but do not report it?				Include in the computer operators' job description the responsibility to be alert to potential losses of information.	Planning

THREAT: Theft of Data or Programs

PROBABLE IMPACT: Loss of Assets and Disclosure

RECOMMENDED DETECTIVE CONTROL METHOD: Informants

No.	Potential Vulnerability	Countermeasure Needed			Suggested Countermeasure	Crime Action Phase
		Yes	No	N/A		
1.	Are programs stolen from the organization sold through software houses?				If the theft of software is suspected, friendly software houses should be contacted regarding the sale of that software and the market place.	Conversion
2.	Do individuals buy programs and data and not know they were stolen?				Imbed a copyright or other notification in the program or data indicating the source and ownership of the data.	Conversion
3.	Are data and programs taken from the organization and theft is not known?				Incorporate bait records in the data and programs so that the notification of those individuals will alert the bait individuals to the fact that resources have been stolen.	Concealment
4.	Are programs and data removed from their computer center without detection?				Imbed magnetic sensors in computer media so that, if it crosses a protected threshold, alarms will go off indicating the theft of that media.	Concealment

Fig. 9-3. Continued

THREAT: Inadvertent Revealing of Passwords

PROBABLE IMPACT: Loss of Assets and Disclosure

RECOMMENDED DETECTIVE CONTROL METHOD: Informants

No.	Potential Vulnerability	Countermeasure Needed			Suggested Countermeasure	Crime Action Phase
		Yes	No	N/A		
1.	Do users properly control passwords?				Interview users regarding the type of security procedures they have over passwords and investigate potential vulnerabilities.	Concealment
2.	Are individuals aware of the importance of protecting passwords?				Install signs and other means to create an awareness on the part of users to protect passwords.	Concealment
3.	Are individuals aware that passwords have been compromised but do not make that fact known?				Install telephone hot-lines so that individuals aware of the fact that passwords are compromised will know who to call to report that violation.	Concealment
4.	Do individuals lose or compromise their passwords but do not notify the proper individuals of same?				Create an awareness on the part of individuals that if their password is compromised they should inform security personnel so that their current password can be deleted and they can be issued a new password.	Concealment

THREAT: Piggybacking a Terminal

PROBABLE IMPACT: Loss of Assets and Disclosure

RECOMMENDED DETECTIVE CONTROL METHOD: Informants

No.	Potential Vulnerability	Countermeasure Needed			Suggested Countermeasure	Crime Action Phase
		Yes	No	N/A		
1.	Do users forget to shut down a terminal and fail to notify supervisors of that fact?				Individuals should be instructed that if they inadvertently forget to shut down a terminal that they should make supervisors aware of that fact so that potential violations can be determined.	Planning
2.	Are criminals able to use a terminal because it has not been properly shut down?				After "X" seconds or minutes of no activity at a terminal, it should be automatically shut down. Note that the volume of complaints should be monitored and the shut-down time varied accordingly.	Planning
3.	Do criminals piggyback a terminal and perform operations under the authority of the previous terminal user?				Periodically prepare a list of all the actions performed by users of terminals and confirm with them that all those users are authorized.	Concealment
4.	Are employees in the vicinity of a terminal aware that it is being piggybacked but do not inform the appropriate individuals?				Periodically, the employees in the vicinity of the terminal should be queried regarding the potential improper use of that terminal.	Concealment

Fig. 9-3. Continued

THREAT: Careless Handling of Sensitive Data

PROBABLE IMPACT: Disclosure

RECOMMENDED DETECTIVE CONTROL METHOD: Informants

No.	Potential Vulnerability	Countermeasure Needed			Suggested Countermeasure	Crime Action Phase
		Yes	No	N/A		
1.	Will individuals witness the careless handling of sensitive data but not inform management of that event?				Post signs indicating the importance of handling sensitive data correctly and the action to be taken should the misuse of sensitive data be noticed.	Concealment
2.	Will individuals observe the careless handling of sensitive data but do not want to personally report the incident to a member of supervision?				Install a hot-line and create an awareness of the number so that individuals can call anonymously and report the careless handling of sensitive data.	Concealment
3.	Will data processing personnel be aware of the mishandling of sensitive data but choose not to report it?				Periodically interview the people in the data processing area who might observe misuse of sensitive data to ask about those conditions.	Concealment
4.	Will sensitive data be readily available in the market place and yet the organization not be aware that data has been compromised?				Request Marketing, and other third parties that might be aware of the loss of sensitive data, to report that data to the organization. In addition, these individuals may be periodically surveyed to determine whether they are aware of the compromise of any sensitive data.	Concealment

THREAT: Program Theft

PROBABLE IMPACT: Loss of Assets

RECOMMENDED DETECTIVE CONTROL METHOD: Informants

No.	Potential Vulnerability	Countermeasure Needed			Suggested Countermeasure	Crime Action Phase
		Yes	No	N/A		
1.	Are programs sold on the outside market?				Inquire through computer stores and other groups that sell programs as to whether programs of the organization in question are being brokered.	Conversion
2.	Are organization programs sold to competitors?				Inquire of friendly competitors whether they have been offered the organization's programs for sale.	Conversion
3.	Are programmers aware that they cannot take programs with them when they leave employment?				Require programmers and other people having access to programs to sign a statement indicating that the programs are the property of the organization.	Planning
4.	Do individuals know that programs are being stolen but fail to bring that matter to the attention of supervisors?				Use signs or hot-lines to indicate management's desire to be informed of program thefts.	Concealment
5.	Do third parties buy programs from the organization, not recognizing that they are stolen?				Include within every program source code a copyright statement or other information indicating the source of the program and that it is not for sale or use by other parties.	Conversion

Fig. 9-3. Continued

THREAT: Disable Operating System Control

PROBABLE IMPACT: Loss of Assets

RECOMMENDED DETECTIVE CONTROL METHOD: Informants

No.	Potential Vulnerability	Countermeasure Needed			Suggested Countermeasure	Crime Action Phase
		Yes	No	N/A		
1.	Are operators aware that operating system controls have been disabled but do not notify management of that fact?				Periodically interview operators to determine if they are aware of potential situations where controls were disabled and to alert them to report situations involving the disabling of control should it occur.	Concealment
2.	Do programmers ask that operating system controls be disabled to facilitate the system processing?				Ensure that system programmers are aware that programmers cannot authorize disabling operating system controls. Attempt to determine if they are aware of these conditions, and if so to report them to management.	Concealment
3.	Are users aware that unusual processing is occurring which appears attributable to lack of operating system controls?				Implement user complaint reports for unusual conditions and direct those reports to an independent party for follow-up action.	Concealment
4.	Are computer operations personnel aware that operating system controls are disabled but do not want to report that fact personally to their supervisor?				Install a hot-line for operations personnel to call to report unusual conditions which will let them report those conditions anonymously.	Concealment

THREAT: Lack of Positive Identification

PROBABLE IMPACT: Loss of Assets and Disclosure

RECOMMENDED DETECTIVE CONTROL METHOD: Informants

No.	Potential Vulnerability	Countermeasure Needed			Suggested Countermeasure	Crime Action Phase
		Yes	No	N/A		
1.	Do authorized terminal users know that unauthorized users are using the communication facilities but do not inform supervisors of that fact?				Periodically inquire among users whether or not the communication facilities are being abused.	Concealment
2.	Do computer operators recognize that there is unauthorized use of communication facilities but do not notify management of that fact?				Periodically inquire among the operators to determine their knowledge of unauthorized use of communication lines.	Concealment
3.	Do users of communication facilities recognize that they are not being adequately challenged for positive identification but do not notify management of that fact?				Notify users that security protection is their partial responsibility and that they should notify management if the procedures are violated or appear inadequate.	Planning
4.	Do the communication carriers recognize that the system is being abused but do not notify the organization of that fact?				Periodically meet with the communication carriers in order to identify potential security violations of communication facilities and to look for new countermeasures.	Concealment

Fig. 9-3. Continued

THREAT: <u>Wire Tapping</u>

PROBABLE IMPACT: <u>Disclosure</u>

RECOMMENDED DETECTIVE CONTROL METHOD: <u>Informants</u>

No.	Potential Vulnerability	Countermeasure Needed			Suggested Countermeasure	Crime Action Phase
		Yes	No	N/A		
1.	Do unauthorized individuals tap into communication lines?				Investigate all complaints about communication personnel activity that may indicate wire tapping is occurring.	Concealment
2.	Do individuals tap into wires and no one notifies supervision that it has happened?				Place signs and notify people that any tampering with the communication lines is unauthorized and should be reported to management.	Concealment
3.	Are complaints about communication reception that might indicate wire tapping has occurred investigated?				Develop procedures that will monitor for wire tapping if communication complaints indicate that wire tapping may be occurring.	Planning
4.	Are communication companies called for problems but cannot identify the cause?				Problems that cannot be detected by the communication company should be investigated for potential wire tapping.	Concealment

THREAT: Unauthorized Takeover

PROBABLE IMPACT: Loss of Assets and Disclosure

RECOMMENDED DETECTIVE CONTROL METHOD: Informants

No.	Potential Vulnerability	Countermeasure Needed			Suggested Countermeasure	Crime Action Phase
		Yes	No	N/A		
1.	Does an unauthorized individual take over the terminal after an authorized user leaves it but before it has been shut down?				Automatically shut down the terminal after a predetermined amount of inactivity.	Planning
2.	Do unauthorized individuals physically take over a terminal from an authorized user?				Place terminals in locations where they can be observed by other individuals.	Planning
3.	Does an individual taking over a terminal commit unauthorized acts?				Develop a user profile and if the acts performed are outside that profile shut down processing or reverify the authenticity of the user.	Concealment

Fig. 9-3. Continued

THREAT: Stealing Encryption Keys

PROBABLE IMPACT: Loss of Assets and Disclosure

RECOMMENDED DETECTIVE CONTROL METHOD: Informants

No.	Potential Vulnerability	Countermeasure Needed			Suggested Countermeasure	Crime Action Phase
		Yes	No	N/A		
1.	Are encryption keys stolen and no action is taken?				Initiate a procedure so that, if an encryption key is stolen, a new key will be used immediately.	Planning
2.	Are encryption keys stolen and no one is aware of the fact that they are stolen?				Keep encryption keys under the control of a custodian so that the loss would be immediately detected.	Concealment
3.	Are employees aware of the need to protect the encryption keys?				Place signs or use other means of communicating with employees on the importance of keeping encryption keys secure.	Concealment
4.	Are individuals aware that encryption keys are in the possession of a specific individual but do not inform management?				Place signs or use other means of communication to indicate the importance of immediately notifying supervision if they detect an encryption key in the possession of the wrong individual.	Concealment

Problems with customer complaint investigation

The use of customer complaints poses two significant problems. The first is simply tracking all the complaints. They may be delivered to one of several groups in the organization, so tracking and accountability can be difficult. The second is identifying those complaints that may stem from a potential security event, not just from normal business practices.

Recommendations of reasonable use

Three suggestions make it reasonable to use complaints as a basis for investigation. These are:

1. Funnel all the complaints through a central clearing house. Don't allow any individual group to handle their own complaints. Ensure that all complaints are sent through one group.
2. Require that all complaints be formally documented and, when possible, sequentially numbered. This allows for greater accuracy in the information that is collected and passed on.
3. Categorize the complaints to identify those that could be the result of computer crime.

Significant cases of complaints

The types of complaints that should trigger the interest of the computer crime investigative group include:

- Questions about accuracy and timeliness in internal transactions
- Problems with the accuracy of the data being sent to customers
- Missing or late financial data
- Any computer-generated data that has been altered manually
- Any complaints about accounts which, though correct, show unexplained transactions

Countermeasures using complaints

Customer complaints will usually be fielded in several different departments. The complaints may involve everything from wrong sizes to a mix-up on deliver dates. Even though seemingly small, all should be considered and a judgement made. The key countermeasures that apply to computer crime include:

1. The first countermeasure has been discussed before: centralize the complaint function. This will reduce the possibility of the perpetrator intercepting the complaint and destroying it or fixing the cause for the complaint.
2. Get on the carbon copy list for all management hate mail. Hate mail could contain leads to criminal activity.

3. Work with the customer relations staff. They can be a boon in pointing out problems.

4. That part of the staff which is computer literate should be given the opportunity to review all system/program change requests within their sphere of expertise. This review should be random and announced to the staff.

5. Interface with the marketing group and collect customer complaints from them.

6. The audit department can collect problems from customers while confirming the client's financial data.

Figure 9-4 is designed to show the many ways investigation of customer complaints can be used in the data processing environment.

Computer crime investigation

Investigation of computer crime can be viewed in two different ways depending on when the investigation is undertaken. Investigation of a postfacto crime should include the local police and, possibly, federal officers as well. This form of investigation should be handled by professional law enforcement officers because of the complex nature of our legal system and the ease with which a small mistake can allow the perpetrator to go free. This section will discuss the type of internal investigation that should take place before a crime has occurred or to determine if there has been a crime. When a crime is detected, the proper authorities must be contacted immediately, and proper precautions taken to make sure the evidence is not disturbed. This is crucial to the apprehension and prosecution of computer criminals.

The case for rigorous investigation and prosecution

All too frequently the statistics on computer crime are often accompanied by the statement that many businesses are reluctant to report a computer crime. If a crime is not reported, the criminal is not prosecuted. Computer crime is growing each year; if we fail to prosecute and publicize, we are simply encouraging more criminals. Lurid stories of the huge profits to be made can tempt knowledgeable users. This temptation coupled with little reported repercussion from the victim paves the way for increased crime.

Steps in the investigative process

Investigation differs from auditing. There are five major steps in investigation, which are discussed below. They may necessitate the use of outside

THREAT: Key Entry Changes Not Detected

PROBABLE IMPACT: Loss of Assets

RECOMMENDED DETECTIVE CONTROL METHOD: Complaints

No.	Potential Vulnerability	Countermeasure Needed			Suggested Countermeasure	Crime Action Phase
		Yes	No	N/A		
1.	Are authorized amounts changed by key entry personnel?				Conduct a random sample of key data entered into the computer system and manually verify that it is equal to the amount that should have been entered according to the source transactions.	Concealment
2.	Are problems reported about input transactions but no action taken, permitting improper data to be processed?				Review call-in lists and other documents recording user complaints to ensure that appropriate action has been taken on all complaints.	Concealment
3.	Are potential computer crimes reported, but the individual responsible for the crime intercepts the complaint and makes the adjustment?				Review the types and frequency of adjustments made based on customer complaints to ensure that they are due to errors and omissions and not computer crime.	Concealment
4.	Do marketing personnel receive complaints from customers and other parties with which they come in contact, but not report that information to the appropriate investigative groups?				Develop a procedure for documenting user complaints by the marketing force so that they can be forwarded to the appropriate investigative group.	Concealment

Fig. 9-4. Vulnerability countermeasure Tables No. 79–85.

Fig. 9-4. Continued

THREAT: Misinterpretation of Record Formats

PROBABLE IMPACT: Loss of Assets

RECOMMENDED DETECTIVE CONTROL METHOD: Complaints

No.	Potential Vulnerability	Countermeasure Needed			Suggested Countermeasure	Crime Action Phase
		Yes	No	N/A		
1.	Do users of application systems abuse vulnerabilities and record formats to circumvent system controls?				Review the adequacy of data validation edits, as they relate to ensuring that defined record formats are complied with.	Concealment
2.	Do users recognize vulnerabilities due to violation of record format rules but not consider it a computer crime threat?				Review the program change requests submitted by users to determine if the weakness being addressed by the change might be a symptom of a computer crime.	Concealment
3.	Do problems caused by using record format vulnerabilities to commit computer crime result in errors, but they are not properly investigated?				Review data errors that may be symptomatic of record format vulnerabilities as a source of clues to potential computer crimes.	Concealment
4.	Are problems encountered in the environment investigated relating to data definitions that may be symptomatic of computer crime?				Review changes to the data dictionary for key financial fields to identify if they might be symptomatic of potential computer crimes.	Concealment
5.	Do users recognize problems occurring in their system due to data violations but do not connect those problems to potential computer crimes?				Evaluate documented user data complaints as a source of potential computer crime symptoms.	Concealment

THREAT: **Theft of Services**

PROBABLE IMPACT: **Loss of Assets**

RECOMMENDED DETECTIVE CONTROL METHOD: **Complaints**

No.	Potential Vulnerability	Countermeasure Needed			Suggested Countermeasure	Crime Action Phase
		Yes	No	N/A		
1.	Do operators suspect that computer services are being used for unauthorized purposes but do not volunteer that information?				Periodically interview operators to determine if they suspect potential threats of computer services.	Concealment
2.	Do employees recognize that what they are doing is in violation of organizational policy?				Post signs at points where computer services are accessible stating the authorized and unauthorized use of those services.	Concealment
3.	Do employees recognize that computer services are being misused, but do not know to whom those violations should be reported?				Develop a special telephone hot line to make it convenient for employees to report potential theft of computer services.	Concealment
4.	Are users charged for the theft of services, but do not report the unaccounted for use of the computer?				Periodically confirm with users that all the time charged to them is valid.	Concealment
5.	Do the normal accounting systems account for services that have been stolen?				Reconcile the authorized and legitimate uses of the computer as accumulated by the accounting systems, and compare that to the total use of computer services as recorded by the vendor of the hardware. Investigate differences.	Concealment

Fig. 9-4. Continued

THREAT:　Unauthorized Access

PROBABLE IMPACT:　Loss of Assets, Disclosure

RECOMMENDED DETECTIVE CONTROL METHOD:　Complaints

No.	Potential Vulnerability	Countermeasure Needed			Suggested Countermeasure	Crime Action Phase
		Yes	No	N/A		
1.	Do individuals recognize the importance of unauthorized access to the organization?				Put a sign in key places which states the company policy regarding unauthorized access, and advise those individuals who are aware of the fact that it is an unauthorized access but fail to report it, that they should report it.	Concealment
2.	Do users fail to recognize that access to their system has been penetrated?				Periodically confirm to users who have access to their resources, so that they can confirm authorized access.	Concealment
3.	Are DP personnel aware of potential violations of access but do not take any action?				DP personnel should be periodically interviewed to determine whether or not they suspect potential access violations.	Concealment
4.	Do users fail to report suspected access violations?				Users should be periodically surveyed in order to identify their suspected access violations.	Concealment

THREAT: Output Routed to Wrong Individual

PROBABLE IMPACT: Disclosure

RECOMMENDED DETECTIVE CONTROL METHOD: Complaints

No.	Potential Vulnerability	Countermeasure Needed			Suggested Countermeasure	Crime Action Phase
		Yes	No	N/A		
1.	Is output data inadvertently routed to the wrong individual?				Periodically confirm that recipients of data do not receive the wrong data.	Concealment
2.	Is the distribution function aware that data is being routed to the wrong individual, but they do not take appropriate action?				Review the complaints received regarding improper distribution to determine whether appropriate action has been taken.	Concealment
3.	Is the delivery function uncertain regarding whom they should deliver computer-produced data to?				Indicate predominantly on all delivered reports the individual to whom the report is directed.	Planning
4.	Are outputs intentionally routed to wrong individuals so that they have access to privileged information?				Output data should be placed under security control and only released to the recipient when that recipient can provide appropriate identification, such as passwords.	Planning

Fig. 9-4. Continued

THREAT: Program Time Bombs

PROBABLE IMPACT: Destruction of Media and Disruption

RECOMMENDED DETECTIVE CONTROL METHOD: Complaints

No.	Potential Vulnerability	Countermeasure Needed			Suggested Countermeasure	Crime Action Phase
		Yes	No	N/A		
1.	Do programmers that terminate include routines designed to disrupt or destroy media?				Instruct the programmers taking over programs to review the code and bring to the attention of supervision unusual coding.	Concealment
2.	Are disruption and destruction of media viewed as errors and omissions as opposed to deliberate destruction?				Investigate all complaints that may potentially be sabotage by employees.	Concealment
3.	Do operators bring to the attention of supervision unusual matters, but no investigation is taken?				Conduct investigations where appropriate based upon operator complaints of unusual conditions.	Concealment

THREAT: Unauthorized Monitoring

PROBABLE IMPACT: Disclosure

RECOMMENDED DETECTIVE CONTROL METHOD: Complaints

No.	Potential Vulnerability	Countermeasure Needed			Suggested Countermeasure	Crime Action Phase
		Yes	No	N/A		
1.	Are the communication facilities monitored but monitoring is unknown?				Determine if the communication carrier can test the lines to determine whether they are being monitored.	Concealment
2.	Are problems that may be attributable to monitoring investigated?				Evaluate communication complaints to determine whether they might be caused by unauthorized monitoring.	Concealment
3.	Do complaints arrive about improper activity around communication facilities, but they are not investigated?				Carefully scrutinize complaints about unauthorized acitivity around communication facilities to ensure that the activity is not associated with monitoring.	Concealment
4.	Are complaints voiced about the reason why communication personnel are on the premises, but the complaints are not investigated?				Investigate all communication personnel on the premises to determine that their presence is not associated with monitoring.	Concealment

agencies to ensure that proper and usable procedures are followed. The five steps in the investigation process are

1. Set the investigation objectives
2. Plan the investigation
3. Conduct the field work
4. Analyze the results and draw conclusions
5. Take action appropriate to the results

Set the investigation objectives

An investigation can be conducted as a preventive measure, to determine if the computer has been the victim of a crime, or when a crime has occurred. Before beginning, certain objectives and goals must be defined. The most important question is what to do if a crime is discovered and the perpetrator identified. There are five objectives, each of which requires a different approach.

1. Prosecute the perpetrator(s). This entails involvement of outside agencies and requires careful and detailed procedures under the guidance of those agencies. Evidence needs to be carefully and completely defined. If this is the goal, it would be wise to bring in law enforcement personnel as soon as a crime is detected.

2. Dismiss the perpetrator(s). If this is the only goal, sufficient evidence needs to be gathered to confront the individual(s) responsible and either dismiss them or force their resignation. It is essential that the legal staff be involved to ensure sufficient evidence is compiled to satisfy the legal requirements of the state.

3. Reprimand the perpetrator(s). In this case, only enough evidence to identify the perpetrator with a high level of confidence is required. The main concern is that the responsible individual be correctly identified to avoid a countersuit charging defamation of character.

4. Take civil action against the perpetrator(s). In this type of investigation, there has to be an attempt to compile sufficient evidence against the perpetrator to enable your company to recoup losses caused by the crime. This type of investigation may be included within the scope of one of the other investigations. If this is your sole objective, the investigation need only proceed until the perpetrator agrees to repay the loss.

5. Ignore the perpetrator(s), secure the system. This seems to be one of the popular objectives. In this type of investigation it is important to identify the perpetrator, but only to enlist his/her cooperation in closing the chink in the computer's armor that allowed the crime to take place. It is important to understand

that this objective does nothing to prevent further crimes of a slightly different nature. Nor does it provide incentive for the criminal to change his/her behavior. It may provide a small measure of security for the system.

Plan the investigation

The actual considerations of the investigation are determined by the goal(s) established. Some factors that need to be evaluated are:

- To what degree will law enforcement agencies be involved?
- What security measures are needed during the investigation?
- Who will be assigned/involved in the investigation?
- How large is the investigation budget?
- What work program will be used during the investigation?
- What form of investigation will be used for each lead?
- Which automated tools will be used during the investigation?
- Which witnesses, if any, will be contacted?
- Who are the preliminary suspects?
- What types of evidence need to be collected?

Because some of the evidence of a computer crime is very volatile, it is a good idea to determine the answers to these questions well in advance of an actual crime investigation. For example, one of the important tools for investigation is the operator log. This log is often purged and the listing destroyed soon after it is produced. If this log has been identified as important, one of the first steps in the investigation must be to secure this log. This is one reason why the plan for the investigation must be completed long before the investigation takes place.

Conduct the field work

There are four general types of field work that must be performed to conduct a computer crime investigation. The degree to which each of these methods is used is determined by the investigation plan and the objectives of the investigation. When it becomes obvious that a crime has been committed, and if the objective is prosecution, law enforcement personnel should be contacted at once. The four types of field work are:

- Analyze documents. In this phase, the investigating centers on gathering and analyzing documentation.
- Interview witnesses. If individuals who have knowledge of the crime or the conditions surrounding the crime are available, they should be interviewed in an attempt to gather additional information.
- Conduct observations. This is an important part of the field work. It is critical to observe the activities of both the suspects and others who perform similar duties. However, observations

are not limited to simply watching people. This phase also includes examination of logs and other software related to the case.

- Interview suspects. Again, if the objective is prosecution, this step should only be attempted with the aid of professional law enforcement personnel.

Analyze the results

Once the field work has been completed, the information collected must be analyzed to determine exactly what happened. Some of the possible conclusions that could be drawn include:

- Whether a crime has been committed. It is possible that the situations leading to the investigation were the result of some unintentional activity on the part of an innocent user. The most frequent cause for what appears to be computer crime is simply carelessness on the part of legitimate users.
- If there was indeed a crime, who committed it?
- The magnitude of the crime.
- Recommendations of the actions to be taken.

Take action appropriate to the results

If management has not taken an active role before this phase, they must be consulted to determine what action to take. Action should not only be taken against the perpetrator, but also to institute whatever steps are necessary to prevent a recurrence of the same type of crime.

Investigative countermeasures

Several types of documentation are important in the tracing of a computer crime. These include

Job accounting logs   These record information on computer usage and access. The extent of the information contained in them varies from vendor to vendor and from installation to installation. Where possible, without impacting the working environment adversely, they should be made as complete as possible.

Database management system logs   If established, database management system logs can show before and after images of the database to indicate the changes that have taken place. Some also show the user who made the change.

System security logs   If the system is so equipped, and these logs are enabled, system security logs can show a wide variety of information.

In the most basic usage, only log-ins and log-outs are recorded. However some systems, like the Digital Equipment Corporation VAX/VM, have elaborate security logging tools. These will enable the recording of such details as file accesses.

Operator logs Operator logs are usually of great importance because they show which jobs were run and in what order. In addition, they show the errors that occurred during the running of any job. Normally they are not retained for long periods, so it is important to procure them quickly.

Depending on the system and the parameters used when the system was started, it is possible to have an excellent audit capability. It is important that the most complete audit system possible be instituted as soon as possible. The information services group should be consulted to determine the level of audit possible without producing significant negative impacts on productivity.

Figure 9-5 lists a set of threats which can best be detected and substantiated through the use of investigation.

Comptuer crime analysis

Analysis is one of the least often used tools for the detection of computer crime. Often, the reason for not undertaking it is the extensive background required to perform an analysis properly. When properly applied, analysis can prove to be a very powerful tool in the fight against computer crime.

Conducting an analysis

A special individual or team must be assembled to perform the analysis. Members of the information services unit directly involved should not be in charge of the analysis. A team should be brought in from outside that particular information services unit to conduct the analysis. If it is decided to use any one individual, he/she will need to be well versed in several areas. Criteria to be considered when using the computer as an analysis tool include:

- The skills of the investigators
- The investigators' knowledge of the area being analyzed
- The classes of data available for use by the investigators
- The analytical tools available
- The understanding of the investigative process

THREAT: Modification of Personal Data

PROBABLE IMPACT: Loss of Assets

RECOMMENDED DETECTIVE CONTROL METHOD: Investigation

No.	Potential Vulnerability	Countermeasure Needed			Suggested Countermeasure	Crime Action Phase
		Yes	No	N/A		
1.	Do employees process fraudulent amounts through their own personal accounts?				Based on the area of suspected fraud, investigate the accounts of employees in that area.	Conversion
2.	Do employees start fraudulent activities, and they are not detected?				Monitor employee accounts over two different periods and investigate the variances between the two periods.	Conversion
3.	Do employees use internal debits and credits to transfer funds into their own personal account?				List all transactions in employees accounts that are questionable and investigate the propriety of those transactions.	Conversion
4.	Do employees divert normal transactions into their personal accounts?				List transactions going into the employee accounts and send them to the originating area to validate the authenticity of the transactions.	Conversion

Fig. 9-5. Vulnerability countermeasure Tables No. 86–105.

THREAT: Destruction of EDP Facilities

PROBABLE IMPACT: Destruction of Plant

RECOMMENDED DETECTIVE CONTROL METHOD: Investigation

No.	Potential Vulnerability	Countermeasure Needed Yes	No	N/A	Suggested Countermeasure	Crime Action Phase
1.	Will the EDP facility be destroyed and clues lost?				Employees should be instructed that after any destruction, evidence should not be moved or destroyed until an appropriate investigation can be undertaken.	Planning
2.	Will potential perpetrators of destruction be identified under an anonymous call, but that information not recorded?				Instruct computer operators that anonymous telephone leads should be recorded and that the operator should probe for additional information.	Planning
3.	Will the services of law enforcement agencies and fire detection agencies be utilized in the investigation of the destruction of EDP facilities?				Develop a procedure that involves local law enforcement and fire agencies in the investigation of the destruction of EDP facilities.	Planning
4.	Will the destruction of EDP facilities be viewed as a computer crime?				All investigations of the destruction of EDP facilities should include, as one of the hypotheses, computer crime.	Planning

Fig. 9-5. Continued

THREAT: Unauthorized Access to EDP Facilities

PROBABLE IMPACT: Loss of Assets, Destruction of Plant, Destruction of Media, Disclosure, Disruption

RECOMMENDED DETECTIVE CONTROL METHOD: Investigation

No.	Potential Vulnerability	Countermeasure Needed			Suggested Countermeasure	Crime Action Phase
		Yes	No	N/A		
1.	Are unauthorized individuals in the computer room but not detected?				Computer operations personnel and supervision should be instructed to challenge individuals who are not authorized members of the operation contingency.	Execution
2.	Are security personnel aware that unauthorized individuals have access to computer facilities?				TV monitors should be installed to enable security personnel to continually monitor the facility.	Execution
3.	Do unauthorized visitors gain access to the computer room during nonworking hours?				Electronic sensors should be installed to detect unauthorized visitors during nonworking hours.	Execution
4.	Do individuals gain easy access to the computer room because there is no protection prohibiting that entry?				Install a security guard or key-card entry system so that only authorized individuals can access EDP facilities.	Execution
5.	Are individuals detected, but their identities not known?				Install cameras to monitor unauthorized visitors.	Execution

THREAT: Poorly Defined Authorization Access

PROBABLE IMPACT: Loss of Assets, Disclosure

RECOMMENDED DETECTIVE CONTROL METHOD: Investigation

No.	Potential Vulnerability	Countermeasure Needed			Suggested Countermeasure	Crime Action Phase
		Yes	No	N/A		
1.	Are the authorization access rules enforced when they are not properly defined?				Investigate the adequacy of the authorization access definition to ensure that it is complete enough to be enforceable.	Concealment
2.	Is the actual enforcement of authorization rules in accordance with the owner's intent?				Investigate with the user to ensure that the actual enforcement of authorization access is consistent with the user's or owner's intent.	Concealment
3.	Is the extent of unauthorized access recognized because of the poorly defined authorization access rules?				Investigate, through a study of evidence produced by the operating environment, the degree of access to data processing resources which does not comply with the user's intent.	Concealment

Fig. 9-5. Continued

THREAT: Incomplete Enforcement of Security

PROBABLE IMPACT: Loss of Assets, Destruction of Plant, Destruction of Media, Disclosure, Disruption

RECOMMENDED DETECTIVE CONTROL METHOD: Investigation

No.	Potential Vulnerability	Countermeasure Needed			Suggested Countermeasure	Crime Action Phase
		Yes	No	N/A		
1.	Do security personnel enforce the security rules?				Periodically initiate a surveillance function to oversee the day-to-day enforcement of security procedures.	Execution
2.	Are the security measures inadequate to enforce the security rules?				Conduct an investigation of the security procedures to determine the adequacy of those procedures to achieve the stated security objectives.	Concealment
3.	Are the security measures ineffective against potential perpetrators?				Attempt to break security in order to determine if the security measures are adequate to detect that violation of security procedures.	Execution

THREAT: Ignoring Operational Procedures

PROBABLE IMPACT: Loss of Assets

RECOMMENDED DETECTIVE CONTROL METHOD: Investigation

No.	Potential Vulnerability	Countermeasure Needed			Suggested Countermeasure	Crime Action Phase
		Yes	No	N/A		
1.	Are data processing employees aware of high-risk operational procedures?				Identify the high-risk operational procedures and make employees aware of the importance of performing those procedures.	Planning
2.	Are employees permitted to ignore operational procedures without reprimand or punishment?				Identify the violators of operating procedures and determine that appropriate reprimand or punishment has occurred.	Concealment
3.	Do flagrant violations occur and are they ignored by the operation areas?				Periodically spend time in the operation areas observing which procedures are and which are not being followed. When procedures are ignored, inform the appropriate level of management about those violations.	Concealment
4.	Are employees aware of procedure violations but do not bring it to the attention of supervision?				Interview employees in the operation areas at random to probe for their knowledge of potential operations procedure violations.	Concealment

Fig. 9-5. Continued

THREAT: Operations Manager or Supervisor Circumventing Operational Controls

PROBABLE IMPACT: Loss of Assets

RECOMMENDED DETECTIVE CONTROL METHOD: Investigation

No.	Potential Vulnerability	Countermeasure Needed			Suggested Countermeasure	Crime Action Phase
		Yes	No	N/A		
1.	Are supervisors, through their privileged position, able to circumvent operating controls?				Periodically initiate surveillance of the supervisors in order to detect whether or not they are using their privileged position to circumvent operating controls.	Concealment
2.	Do supervisors perform improper acts by using facilities that are not normal for their position in the organization but, because of that position, are able to use?				Identify the types of facilities that should be used and then scan activity logs to determine if supervisors are using other types of facilities. If so, conduct appropriate investigations to determine the propriety of those users.	Concealment
3.	Are controls over supervisory activities inadequate?				Identify the risks unique to key supervisory positions and then determine whether or not, through investigation, the controls over those risks are adequate.	Concealment
4.	Do supervisors take advantage of opportunities available to them to commit computer crimes?				For key supervisory positions, identify the opportunities unique to that position and investigate to determine whether or not supervisors have taken advantage of those opportunities.	Concealment

THREAT: Lapses of Security During Reorganization and Recovery

PROBABLE IMPACT: Loss of Assets, Destruction of Media, and Disclosure

RECOMMENDED DETECTIVE CONTROL METHOD: Investigation

No.	Potential Vulnerability	Countermeasure Needed			Suggested Countermeasure	Crime Action Phase
		Yes	No	N/A		
1.	Are the security procedures inadequate during the reorganization and recovery process?				Observe the execution of the reorganization and recovery procedures to determine the adequacy of security during those procedures.	Concealment
2.	Are the prescribed reorganization and recovery security procedures inadequate to reduce the risks to an acceptable level?				Identify the types of security risks that are associated with reorganization and recovery and then determine, based on the risks, whether those security measures are adequate to reduce the risks to an acceptable level.	Concealment
3.	Will recovery and reorganization personnel deliberately fail to follow security procedures?				Review the logs of activity during the reorganization and recovery activities to determine whether or not appropriate security procedures have been followed.	Concealment
4.	Will data be added, deleted, or modified during the reorganization and recovery process without protection?				Execute the database verifier before and after the recovery or reorganization procedures to ensure that data has not been added, deleted, or modified during that process.	Concealment

Fig. 9-5. Continued

THREAT: Failure to Protect Files During Maintenance

PROBABLE IMPACT: Destruction of Media, and Disclosure

RECOMMENDED DETECTIVE CONTROL METHOD: Investigation

No.	Potential Vulnerability	Countermeasure Needed			Suggested Countermeasure	Crime Action Phase
		Yes	No	N/A		
1.	Are files adequately protected during maintenance by vendor personnel?				Observe vendors performing maintenance to ensure that they do not perform an unauthorized access to files.	Concealment
2.	Are vendor maintenance procedures inadequate to prevent them from accessing computer files?				Review the exposures the organization has for vendor personnel accessing computer files, and then determine if the procedures to prevent those exposures are adequate.	Concealment
3.	Do vendor personnel access computer files without detection?				Review the job accounting logs for periods during vendor maintenance to identify files that have been accessed during that period.	Concealment
4.	Do vendor personnel use operator commands to access computer files without detection?				Review operator logs during the periods in which vendor maintenance is occurring to detect inappropriate acts.	Concealment
5.	Are computers connected, via communication lines, to vendor diagnostic equipment which can access computer files without detection?				Ensure that vendor diagnostic computers cannot access the organization's computer without appropriate supervisory approval.	Planning

THREAT: Inadequate Supervision During Nonworking Hour Shifts

PROBABLE IMPACT: Loss of Assets, Destruction of Media, Disclosure, and Disruption

RECOMMENDED DETECTIVE CONTROL METHOD: Investigation

No.	Potential Vulnerability	Countermeasure Needed			Suggested Countermeasure	Crime Action Phase
		Yes	No	N/A		
1.	Do employees commit computer crimes during nonworking hours without appropriate detection?				Observe the actions taken by un-supervised employees during non-working hours to ensure they are not performing improper acts.	Concealment
2.	Are employees allowed to enter the computer area during supervised periods?				Attempt to access the computer area during supervised periods to determine whether controls prevent that access.	Concealment
3.	Are employees allowed in the com-puter area during unsupervised peri-ods?				Review the policies and procedures regarding unsupervised activities in the computer area. If the policy exposes the organization, make ap-propriate recommendations.	Concealment
4.	Will the computer be operated during unsupervised periods?				Review the operating logs to deter-mine whether or not the computer was operated during nonsupervised hours.	Concealment
5.	Will the computer be operated during nonsupervised hours, and at the same time, will the logs recording usage be disabled?				Reconcile the total computer usage, as recorded by the vendor, to the computer usage recorded by the job accounting logs. Investigate differ-ences.	Concealment

Fig. 9-5. Continued

THREAT: Inadvertently or Intentionally Mislabeling Storage Media

PROBABLE IMPACT: Destruction of Media and Disclosure

RECOMMENDED DETECTIVE CONTROL METHOD: Investigation

No.	Potential Vulnerability	Countermeasure Needed			Suggested Countermeasure	Crime Action Phase
		Yes	No	N/A		
1.	Is storage media mislabeled through inadvertent or intentional means?				Periodically spot check the storage media labeling to determine the validity of the labels.	Concealment
2.	Is storage media intentionally or inadvertently mislabeled due to inadequate labeling procedures?				Identify the mislabeling exposures and then determine whether or not the labeling procedures are adequate to prevent those exposures.	Concealment
3.	Do individuals deliberately mislabel tapes so that they can modify or obtain the information on the storage media?				Determine the most likely mislabeling suspects and then periodically conduct surveillance over those individuals to determine whether or not they are mislabeling tapes.	Concealment

THREAT: Failure to Erase Sensitive Information

PROBABLE IMPACT: Disclosure

RECOMMENDED DETECTIVE CONTROL METHOD: Investigation

No.	Potential Vulnerability	Countermeasure Needed			Suggested Countermeasure	Crime Action Phase
		Yes	No	N/A		
1.	Are sensitive files not erased because data processing personnel have not identified which files are sensitive?				Through interview with owners of the files, determine which files contain sensitive data.	Concealment
2.	Is sensitive data not destroyed during the erasure process?				Select a representative sample of erased sensitive files and list them to ensure that the sensitive data has been erased.	Concealment
3.	Do individuals return sensitive files to use and not erase them?				Observe the removal of sensitive files for erasure and ensure they are erased.	Concealment
4.	Is data on sensitive files disclosed after the file retention period because the data is not erased?				Determine the distribution of sensitive data storage media to ensure that it is not directed to inappropriate individuals.	Concealment

Fig. 9-5. Continued

THREAT: Trojan Horse Routines

PROBABLE IMPACT: Loss of Assets

RECOMMENDED DETECTIVE CONTROL METHOD: Investigation

No.	Potential Vulnerability	Countermeasure Needed			Suggested Countermeasure	Crime Action Phase
		Yes	No	N/A		
1.	Do programmers embed Trojan Horse Routines into their programs for execution at later times?				Perform an analysis on programs with software packages such as language optimizers to identify groups of nonentrant code for investigation.	Concealment
2.	Will programmers put Trojan Horse Routines into programs during routine maintenance?				Require supervisors to review the changed source code to verify that it is for authorized purposes.	Concealment
3.	Do disgruntled employees put Trojan Horse routines into programs to disrupt operations or damage data media?				Identify disgruntled employees and review their program code to ensure that it does not contain any potentially damaging routines.	Concealment
4.	Do terminated employees embed Trojan Horse Routines into their programs before they leave in order to activate them at a later point in time?				Review the programs of all terminated employees, line by line, to ensure that there are no Trojan Horse Routines embedded into their programs.	Concealment

THREAT: Ghost Program Versions

PROBABLE IMPACT: Loss of Assets and Disclosure

RECOMMENDED DETECTIVE CONTROL METHOD: Investigation

No.	Potential Vulnerability	Countermeasure Needed			Suggested Countermeasure	Crime Action Phase
		Yes	No	N/A		
1.	Are ghost copies of the authorized programs contained on the library?				Compare those programs contained on the production libraries for key systems, to the programs that should be on the production libraries for those key systems.	Concealment
2.	Are duplicate copies of the same program contained on the production library?				Do a comparison of program numbers on the production library, or programs on the production library, to identify duplicates.	Concealment
3.	Are high-risk programs, such as SUPER ZAP, included on the production library, but recorded under a different name and number?				Identify the high-risk utilities and do an object code byte-by-byte comparison to determine if those programs are on the library under different names.	Concealment
4.	Are extra programs included on the production library for key systems?				Do a comparison between the system that issues job/program numbers and the programs actually on the production library. Any unaccounted-for programs should be investigated.	Concealment

Fig. 9-5. Continued

THREAT: Operating System Control Weaknesses

PROBABLE IMPACT: Loss of Assets and Disclosure

RECOMMENDED DETECTIVE CONTROL METHOD: Investigation

No.	Potential Vulnerability	Countermeasure Needed			Suggested Countermeasure	Crime Action Phase
		Yes	No	N/A		
1.	Do control procedures ensure that the user exits provided in the operating system will not be used for unauthorized purposes?				Identify the uses made of the user exits and determine that they are authorized uses.	Concealment
2.	Will operating system weaknesses permit databases to be accessed for unauthorized purposes?				Analyze the job accounting log, the operator log, and the DBMS log for identifying potential improper accesses to the database file.	Concealment
3.	Will vendor-provided controls be generated into the operating system?				Develop management controls that provide for management reviews of the controls included and deleted in the generated operating system.	Planning
4.	Will computer operators circumvent operating system controls?				Analyze the operator log to identify operator actions that are designed to circumvent operating system controls. Investigate the cause and authorization for those actions.	Concealment

THREAT: Failure to SYSGEN Controls

PROBABLE IMPACT: Loss of Assets, Destruction of Media, and Disclosure

RECOMMENDED DETECTIVE CONTROL METHOD: Investigation

No.	Potential Vulnerability	Countermeasure Needed			Suggested Countermeasure	Crime Action Phase
		Yes	No	N/A		
1.	Does the system of operating controls take into account the risks associated with executing the operating system?				Implement a process that first identifies the operating system risks, and then select from among the available controls those which are directed at the identified risks.	Planning
2.	Are selected operating controls installed into the production version of the operating system?				Review the system generation documentation to ensure that the appropriate controls have been system generated into the production version of the operating system.	Concealment
3.	Does the lack of inclusion of operating system controls lead to losses?				Investigate the problems associated with the operating system and determine if they are attributable to the fact that the appropriate controls were not generated into the operating system.	Concealment
4.	Are controls not selected that could have been selected?				Evaluate the adequacy of what was and was not selected as controls for the operating system. Include those that appear to provide worthwhile benefits, but were not initially selected.	Planning

Fig. 9-5. Continued

THREAT: Lack of Copy Protection

PROBABLE IMPACT: Disclosure

RECOMMENDED DETECTIVE CONTROL METHOD: Investigation

No.	Potential Vulnerability	Countermeasure Needed			Suggested Countermeasure	Crime Action Phase
		Yes	No	N/A		
1.	Will copied files receive the appropriate protection, and if not, will management be aware of the lack of protection?				Develop a procedure that identifies all of the files that are copied so that they can be subject to the same protection as the original file.	Planning
2.	Are the procedures for protecting copies as strong as the procedures for protecting originals?				Develop a procedure which will provide the same degree of protection for copies as the originals.	Planning
3.	Can copied files be readily used for unauthorized purposes?				Periodically spot check the controls over copies of files to ensure that the copy is receiving adequate protection.	Concealment
4.	Will sensitive copied files be subject to the same erasure and destruction procedures as original files?				Review the disposition of the copied version of the file to ensure it receives the same disposition process as the original file.	Concealment
5.	Is there adequate protection to stop individuals from making a copy of a sensitive file?				Attempt to have a file copied to determine whether any authorization checks are required. If not, recommend that procedures be established to restrict the copy of files to authorized individuals.	Planning

THREAT: On-Line System Crash Protection

PROBABLE IMPACT: Loss of Assets

RECOMMENDED DETECTIVE CONTROL METHOD: Investigation

No.	Potential Vulnerability	Countermeasure Needed			Suggested Countermeasure	Crime Action Phase
		Yes	No	N/A		
1.	Does the operating system crash frequently, exposing the organization to problems during those periods?				Determine the expected number of crashes and verify whether or not the actual crashes have exceeded that number.	Concealment
2.	Do computer operation personnel provide appropriate protection during system crashes?				Observe the types of security procedures that occur during a system crash to determine whether or not they are adequate.	Concealment
3.	Are the recommended security procedures during a system crash adequate?				Review the procedures recommended to operations personnel to provide protection during a crash and determine whether or not they are adequate.	Planning
4.	Do the operations personnel understand and follow the protection procedures during a system crash?				Deliberately initiate an operating system crash to determine whether or not the operations personnel can provide the appropriate protection during the down-time period.	Planning

Fig. 9-5. Continued

THREAT: Unauthorized Modification of Communication Software

PROBABLE IMPACT: Disclosure

RECOMMENDED DETECTIVE CONTROL METHOD: Investigation

No.	Potential Vulnerability	Countermeasure Needed			Suggested Countermeasure	Crime Action Phase
		Yes	No	N/A		
1.	Do individuals make unauthorized modifications to communication software and management does not detect that modification?				Review the modifications that have been made to communication software to determine that they are all authorized.	Concealment
2.	Are changes, other than those developed by the vendor, made to communication software?				Sort the modifications to the communication system by source of modification, and identify those modifications submitted by other than the communication vendor.	Concealment
3.	Are the control procedures over communication software adequate?				Identify the communication system risks and determine whether or not the controls to reduce the risk of unauthorized modification to communication software is adequately controlled.	Planning
4.	Are unauthorized changes made to the communication software in conjunction with authorized changes?				Identify the changes made to communication software and determine from the vendor whether or not they are vendor-made changes. Investigate non-vendor changes.	Concealment

THREAT: Spoofing

PROBABLE IMPACT: Loss of Assets

RECOMMENDED DETECTIVE CONTROL METHOD: Investigation

No.	Potential Vulnerability	Countermeasure Needed			Suggested Countermeasure	Crime Action Phase
		Yes	No	N/A		
1.	Is the threat of spoofing recognized as a threat to be controlled?				Identify the spoofing threats and the magnitude of those threats to determine the need for countermeasures.	Planning
2.	Are users of communication facilities aware they are being spoofed?				Users should be instructed never to turn an open terminal over to an unknown individual without approval by management.	Planning
3.	Do criminals spoof users with a simulated version of a security system?				Users should advise supervision if they enter their password into the security system and the system then goes down and asks them to re-enter the password. An investigation should occur immediately about the possibility of spoofing.	Concealment
4.	Are users alert to spoofing and do not let it happen without realizing?				Signs should be placed around terminals warning users to shut them down immediately at conclusion of processing and not to turn them over to other individuals.	Concealment

The skills of the investigators

In order to be successful in the role of analyst, the computer crime investigator (or team) should possess the following set of background knowledge and skill, which have proven to be necessary for successful analysis:

- An understanding of the terminology of information services
- Being well versed in the principles and concepts of information services
- An ability to interpret data record layouts and the various file designs
- A more-than-passing knowledge of the principles and practices of computer systems design
- An understanding of system operations in a production environment
- An ability to design and write analysis programs, at least in a simple spreadsheet or database analysis package

Knowledge of the area under investigation

Besides general systems knowledge the investigator (or team) should have an extensive knowledge of the specific area that is being investigated. Some of the critical knowledge required includes:

- A detailed knowledge of the computer file and record layouts and contents
- A knowledge of the functions of the system under investigation
- An awareness of any external files that duplicate all or part of the systems data under examination
- A precise knowledge of the flow of data through the application
- A complete understanding of the way the audit trail is built and maintained for the application under investigation

Classes of data available

Many different classes of data are available: files, listings, input logs and output files from the program, and so on. An important aspect to be concerned about is that much of it is volatile because of short retention periods. If the analyst, or team, requires time to get up to speed, provisions should immediately be made to preserve any data that could possibly be of use in the analysis. Each investigation, and sometimes each system under investigation, will require a different set of data. It is important for the analyst to determine as soon as possible which files are needed in the investigation.

The analytical tools

Various types of tools are available to aid in the analysis. Their appropriateness for use in a specific investigation depends on the system under analysis and the experience level of the investigator. These tools include:

- Auditing software designed for this type of analysis
- Speciality utility programs written for the system under investigation
- Query language (if a database is used)
- Specialized report writers available from the system under investigation
- Programs designed for this analysis
- Analysis routines designed and prepared by the auditors

Additional information that may be available includes:

- Error listings from development and production runs
- Production histories and statistics from computer operations
- System reports and listings
- Auditor working papers and analyses
- Special analysis data from user departments

The investigation process

The steps in the analysis process are very similar to those used to design an application program. They include:

1. Determine the requirements of the analysis. Until requirements have been defined, it is impossible to analyze the system.
2. Design the analysis. A design should show how the required analysis reports will be produced, how the input will be analyzed, and how the process will be defined.
3. Design the analysis program. Build the program that will perform the analysis. This may include writing in one of the fourth-generation applications languages or in a standard programming language.
4. Test the analysis. Once built, the investigator must prove that the program follows the design and produces the desired outputs. If the results of this program are to be used to prosecute the perpetrator, the program must be proven to be factually correct. To do this the investigator may need to produce predefined data that will give a predefined output.

Computer crime analysis countermeasures

Using the tools available, the investigator can perform several powerful forms of analysis. These different types of analysis may be the only form of investigation possible, or necessary, for many types of computer crime. Common methods used to detect computer crime include

1. Comparison to a standard. An analysis program can compare application data to some predefined standard. Any deviation from the expected standard could point to problems with the program.

2. Trend analysis. Looking at the performance of the program along the lines of one factor can point to problems. For example, if the trend is to decrease run time as enhancements are made, and suddenly the run time increases, this may point to problems.

3. Gross profit test. This is usually done to point out problems in a particular area. For example, if the profit on a specific line has decreased, that may point to some loss attributable to computer crime.

4. Nonposted items. Analysis has shown that this is an area with high vulnerability. It is through this tool that funds are moved from one area in the company to another. It is easy to have funds start out for a specific area but not end up there. Diverted funds may only be detectable using computer-based tools.

5. Internal debits and credits. As with nonposted items, this facility allows funds to be moved within accounts in the organization. Individuals who have access to the creation of debit accounts have unique opportunities to manipulate large dollar data.

As with the other means to analyze computer crimes, this method presents some unique opportunities to recognize particular crimes. Figure 9-6 explores these methodologies.

THREAT: Undetected, Unreasonable, or Inconsistent Source Data

PROBABLE IMPACT: Loss of Assets

RECOMMENDED DETECTIVE CONTROL METHOD: Analysis

No.	Potential Vulnerability	Countermeasure Needed			Suggested Countermeasure	Crime Action Phase
		Yes	No	N/A		
1.	Are problems in the source data interspersed between such a large number of input source transactions that potential problems will not be easily detected?				Stratify the input transactions by categories that tend to identify improprieties; for example, amounts immediately under approval levels and variances from norm.	Concealment
2.	Could the same individual attempt to abuse the system through the entry of unusual, unreasonable, and unauthorized source data? Because these may be entered at random intervals, they may not be detected.				Sort questionable transactions by individual who entered those transactions. This assumes there is an accountability for transactions, and the sort will be by accountability. This will show the frequency of transaction entered by that individual.	Concealment
3.	Do the normal data validation routines detect unreasonable or inconsistent source data?				Develop specialized data validation routines and review source data that has been accepted by the system to ensure that it meets the investigator's requirements.	Concealment
4.	Could a group of improper transactions be entered within a short time span and not detected?				Compare the type, frequency, and magnitude of high-risk transactions entered in two different timeframes in order to detect variations between the two timeframes for further investigation.	Concealment

Fig. 9-6. Vulnerability countermeasure Tables No. 106–124.

Fig. 9-6. Continued

THREAT: Fraudulently Adding, Deleting, or Modifying Data

PROBABLE IMPACT: Loss of Assets

RECOMMENDED DETECTIVE CONTROL METHOD: Analysis

No.	Potential Vulnerability	Countermeasure Needed			Suggested Countermeasure	Crime Action Phase
		Yes	No	N/A		
1.	Is data added, deleted, or modified within transactions and not detected?				Sample key financial fields and compare the entered transaction to the source data in an attempt to identify fraudulent changes.	Concealment
2.	Is the entered source data the transactions originated by the user?				For selected vulnerable areas, list the data actually entered into the computer and send it to the originator to confirm that it is correct.	Concealment
3.	Is data entered correctly into the system unmodified during processing?				Compare the data in two different parts of the application system to determine whether or not it has been fraudulently changed during the processing.	Concealment
4.	Is transaction data fraudulently changed and not recognized by the user?				Compare entered transactions against an expected norm and list variances for follow-up purposes.	Concealment

THREAT: Inserting or Deleting Transactions

PROBABLE IMPACT: Loss of Assets

RECOMMENDED DETECTIVE CONTROL METHOD: Analysis

No.	Potential Vulnerability	Countermeasure Needed			Suggested Countermeasure	Crime Action Phase
		Yes	No	N/A		
1.	Are extra transactions entered into the system by re-entering a transaction twice?				Sort key transactions and compare to determine whether or not transactions have been duplicated.	Concealment
2.	Are variances in batch totals properly investigated?				Review all variances and batch totals to ensure they are not due to fraudulent purposes.	Concealment
3.	Are transactions added or deleted using internal debits and credits?				Review all internal debits and credits to ensure that internal system processing capabilities were not used to fraudulently add or delete transactions.	Concealment
4.	Do users recognize that transactions have been added or deleted?				Compare the list of processed transactions to the original source transactions to detect variances between what was entered and what was processed.	Concealment

Fig. 9-6. Continued

THREAT: Unauthorized Access Through Remote Terminals

PROBABLE IMPACT: Loss of Assets, Disclosure

RECOMMENDED DETECTIVE CONTROL METHOD: Analysis

No.	Potential Vulnerability	Countermeasure Needed			Suggested Countermeasure	Crime Action Phase
		Yes	No	N/A		
1.	Does the system record an unautho-rized access to a remote terminal but no action is taken on that violation?				Analyze the security logs for poten-tial security violations and investi-gate if appropriate.	Concealment
2.	Will users have their data accessed but not recognize that the accesser was an unauthorized individual?				Periodically prepare a list of who is accessing what information and send it to the individuals or groups who own the computer data to confirm that all accesses are authorized.	Concealment
3.	Do individuals access data and take their unauthorized action but their identity cannot be detected?				Insert a monitor software into the operating environment to look for unauthorized accesses, and initiate investigation up to the point where the access occurs.	Concealment
4.	Will individuals abuse the same termi-nal for unauthorized access?				Periodically analyze the type of ac-cesses by terminal so that the activi-ties occurring at a terminal can be analyzed.	Concealment

THREAT: Unauthorized Access Through Dial-In Lines

PROBABLE IMPACT: Loss of Assets, Disclosure

RECOMMENDED DETECTIVE CONTROL METHOD: Analysis

No.	Potential Vulnerability	Countermeasure Needed			Suggested Countermeasure	Crime Action Phase
		Yes	No	N/A		
1.	Do perpetrators call from unauthorized locations to obtain computer services and resources?				Implement a policy that disconnects call-ins from unknown locations and calls back to unauthorized locations prior to processing.	Execution
2.	Are resources consumed as a result of dial-in facilities and the individual using those resources not identified?				If thefts are suspected, use the communication carriers to trace the origin of the call-in facilities prior to authorizing access over those lines.	Execution
3.	Are some resources subjected to more computer crime, but the organization does not recognize the risk or need for allocation of more protection resources?				Quantify, by types, unauthorized access to dial-in lines, and then apply greater resources protecting the areas of high risk.	Concealment
4.	Do unauthorized accesses occur but those accesses are not known?				Analyze the type of accesses occurring and periodically confirm those accesses with the user to verify whether or not they are authorized.	Concealment

Fig. 9-6. Continued

THREAT: Password Not Voided When Employee Terminated

PROBABLE IMPACT: Loss of Assets, Disclosure

RECOMMENDED DETECTIVE CONTROL METHOD: Analysis

No.	Potential Vulnerability	Countermeasure Needed			Suggested Countermeasure	Crime Action Phase
		Yes	No	N/A		
1.	Are employees' passwords terminated after the employees leave?				Periodically compare terminations with password cancellations to ensure the two are synchronized.	Concealment
2.	Are passwords left open for long periods of time, after employees have terminated?				Age password by origination date, and investigate passwords which have been open for long periods of time.	Concealment
3.	Do passwords remain active long after there is no longer a need for those passwords?				Periodically age passwords by date of last usage, and investigate passwords for which there has been no usage for an extended period of time.	Concealment
4.	Is there a large number of violations of not terminating passwords when employees terminate?				Identify the number of employees whose passwords are not terminated at the time of termination. If a large number of violations occur, stringent action should be taken.	Concealment

THREAT: Undetected Repeated Attempts

PROBABLE IMPACT: Loss of Assets, Disclosure

RECOMMENDED PREVENTIVE CONTROL METHOD: Analysis

No.	Potential Vulnerability	Countermeasure Needed			Suggested Countermeasure	Crime Action Phase
		Yes	No	N/A		
1.	Are perpetrators allowed unlimited attempts to access resources without detection?				Periodically review logs with security information so that the number of invalid access attempts can be identified.	Concealment
2.	Does the data processing facility recognize which terminals are most susceptible to unauthorized access?				Stratify invalid accesses by terminal so that the terminals with high frequency of invalid access can be identified and subjected to more stringent controls.	Concealment
3.	Do perpetrators find success at certain terminals and continue to break access through those terminals?				Develop analyses that show the trend over a period of time for invalid accesses by terminals. Those terminals where invalid access is increasing over time should be subject to more stringent controls.	Concealment

Fig. 9-6. Continued

THREAT: No Follow-Up on Unusual Conditions

PROBABLE IMPACT: Loss of Assets, Disclosure, Disruption

RECOMMENDED DETECTIVE CONTROL METHOD: Analysis

No.	Potential Vulnerability	Countermeasure Needed			Suggested Countermeasure	Crime Action Phase
		Yes	No	N/A		
1.	If an unusual item occurs, will it be recognized as an unusual item?				Review the application characteristics and data definitions in order to identify the types of conditions that would be considered abnormal for the application. Write an audit software program that will review the transactions and/or master files to list those unusual conditions. Determine whether follow-up should have occurred and whether or not it did.	Concealment
2.	Will transactions remain in the application system and not be completed, or action occur for an extended period of time?				Stratify transactions within the applications system by the length of time they have been included in the system without completing the processing. If an extensive number of transactions are old, list them and determine if appropriate follow-up action has been taken.	Concealment

THREAT: No Follow-Up on Unusual Conditions

PROBABLE IMPACT: Loss of Assets, Disclosure, Disruption

RECOMMENDED DETECTIVE CONTROL METHOD: Analysis

No.	Potential Vulnerability	Countermeasure Needed			Suggested Countermeasure	Crime Action Phase
		Yes	No	N/A		
3.	Are items which cannot be identified retained in a suspense account for an extended period of time?				List all items in suspense accounts and determine whether appropriate follow-up action has or is being taken on those items.	Concealment
4.	Will items be deleted from the application without appropriate follow-up action?				Analyze items deleted from the application, by reason for deletion, and if the reasons appear questionable, or the magnitude large, investigate to determine the appropriateness of deleting the items.	Concealment

Fig. 9-6. Continued

THREAT: Repeated Processing of the Same Event

PROBABLE IMPACT: Loss of Assets

RECOMMENDED DETECTIVE CONTROL METHOD: Analysis

No.	Potential Vulnerability	Countermeasure Needed			Suggested Countermeasure	Crime Action Phase
		Yes	No	N/A		
1.	Are identical transactions processed more than once by an application?				For an extended period of time, such as a month or a quarter, sort all transactions and list duplicate transactions for investigation.	Concealment
2.	Will a single transaction for a customer be processed in different ways, but is not an identical transaction? (For example, it may be entered once as a $100 item, and then re-entered as two $50 items.)				Sort transactions over an extended period of time by customer number and order them by source, or cluster the amounts so that an analysis of the listing has a high probability of revealing duplicate processing in the same account.	Concealment
3.	Will a large number of duplicate transactions be entered in such a manner that they are difficult to detect by sorting and analysis?				List large numbers of high-risk transactions, such as credits to an accounts receivable for other than payment, to the same account. Also list variances in the normal type of processing to a particular account between two different timeframes. For example, look at activities, such as returned products, for customers between two quarters or the same quarter within two different years.	Concealment

THREAT: Lack of Follow-Up on Potential Security Violations

PROBABLE IMPACT: Loss of Assets, Destruction of Plant, Destruction of Media, Disclosure, Disruption

RECOMMENDED DETECTIVE CONTROL METHOD: Analysis

No.	Potential Vulnerability	Countermeasure Needed			Suggested Countermeasure	Crime Action Phase
		Yes	No	N/A		
1.	Will repeated attempts to break security occur, and there will be no follow-up on these potential or successful security violations?				List the frequency of invalid attempts by location and determine if the appropriate follow-up action is taken on repeated attempts.	Concealment
2.	Are security violations reported to data processing or security personnel and no follow-up taken on those reported violations?				Periodically review the population of suspected violations of security to determine that appropriate action has been taken on those violations.	Concealment
3.	Are potential violations recorded on a security log or security file, but no follow-up action taken on those violations?				Select a sample of violations recorded on the security log and investigate to determine that appropriate follow-up action has been taken.	Concealment
4.	Is follow-up action taken on security violations, but potential perpetrators are not punished?				Review a representative sample of security violation investigations to ensure that the appropriate action is taken based on the result of those investigations.	Concealment

Fig. 9-6. Continued

THREAT: Lack of Follow-Up on Potential Security Violations

PROBABLE IMPACT: Loss of Assets, Destruction of Plant, Destruction of Media, Disclosure, Disruption

RECOMMENDED DETECTIVE CONTROL METHOD: Analysis

No.	Potential Vulnerability	Countermeasure Needed			Suggested Countermeasure	Crime Action Phase
		Yes	No	N/A		
5.	Is the length of time between the suspected violation and the investigation so long that the investigations are not effective in limiting losses?				Stratify violations by the number of days before investigation is undertaken to determine the promptness of investigations. If not prompt, instigate appropriate action.	Concealment

THREAT: Lack of Management Follow-Up

PROBABLE IMPACT: Loss of Assets, Destruction of Plant, Destruction of Media, Disclosure, Disruption

RECOMMENDED DETECTIVE CONTROL METHOD: Analysis

No.	Potential Vulnerability	Countermeasure Needed			Suggested Countermeasure	Crime Action Phase
		Yes	No	N/A		
1.	Does management receive reports on security violations but fail to take action on those reports?				Periodically select a representative sample of security violation reports sent to management and determine whether or not appropriate action has been taken on those violation reports.	Concealment
2.	Does management fail to take prompt action on the more serious security violations because they do not recognize the seriousness of the violations?				Select a representative sample of reports to ensure that the reports indicate, through a ranking or narrative indication, the seriousness of the report. Determine if management takes appropriate action on serious security violations.	Concealment
3.	Is the length of time for management to take action on security violations so long that it would not prevent major losses?				Stratify the violations sent to management by number of days to take action. If the time span is extensive, recommend that appropriate management action be taken on a timely basis.	Concealment

Fig. 9-6. Continued

THREAT: Control Overrides

PROBABLE IMPACT: Loss of Assets

RECOMMENDED DETECTIVE CONTROL METHOD: Analysis

No.	Potential Vulnerability	Countermeasure Needed			Suggested Countermeasure	Crime Action Phase
		Yes	No	N/A		
1.	Are the overrides of computer controls abused?				Stratify the overrides by frequency and type and investigate apparent flagrant violations of the capability.	Concealment
2.	Are control overrides used for invalid purposes?				For a predetermined period (i.e., a month) sort overrides by the individual responsible for the override area and send them to that individual to confirm the propriety of the use of the overrides.	Concealment
3.	Will specific individuals abuse the override privilege for their own benefit?				Sort overrides by the individual entering the overrides and investigate unusual or flagrant violations of the capability.	Concealment
4.	Will individuals commit a computer crime using the override capability?				List override by timeframe and investigate large frequencies of overrides occurring in a limited timeframe.	Concealment
5.	Does the lack of management concern over the use of overrides lead to their increased misuse?				Develop trends of the use of overrides by individual, by type, and by area to determine whether their use is increasing.	Concealment

THREAT: Key Data Stored in Programs

PROBABLE IMPACT: Loss of Assets

RECOMMENDED DETECTIVE CONTROL METHOD: Analysis

No.	Potential Vulnerability	Countermeasure Needed			Suggested Countermeasure	Crime Action Phase
		Yes	No	N/A		
1.	Is data which poses a high risk to the organization stored in programs under the control of a programmer without management knowledge?				Identify the types of variables included within programs from an analysis of the source master and review that list for potential exposures. Take appropriate action.	Concealment
2.	Are programmers changing variables within their programs for inappropriate purposes?				Identify the high-risk variables and analyze changes to the source master to those variables. Confirm that the changes are authorized.	Concealment
3.	Are key variables in programs erroneously changed?				List from the source master changes to high-risk variables and confirm that they have been correctly changed.	Concealment

Fig. 9-6. Continued

THREAT: Programs Readily Accessible

PROBABLE IMPACT: Loss of Assets

RECOMMENDED DETECTIVE CONTROL METHOD: Analysis

No.	Potential Vulnerability	Countermeasure Needed			Suggested Countermeasure	Crime Action Phase
		Yes	No	N/A		
1.	Due to the ease of access to programs, are they changed by unauthorized individuals?				Review the changes to the source master and determine that those changes were created by authorized individuals.	Concealment
2.	Are object codes changed by unauthorized individuals?				Review, through operating logs, accesses to object programs and verify that those accesses are authorized.	Concealment
3.	Do authorized people make unauthorized changes to programs due to the ease of access?				Review each source code change and trace it back to an improved user change request.	Concealment
4.	Are changes to the source or object code library unidentifable because inadequate records are maintained?				Compare different versions of the source and object code libraries to determine what changes have occurred during the time span between the creation of the two different versions. Investigate changes to key programs to determine that those changes were authorized.	Concealment

THREAT: Unauthorized Modification to the Operating System

PROBABLE IMPACT: Loss of Assets

RECOMMENDED DETECTIVE CONTROL METHOD: Analysis

No.	Potential Vulnerability	Countermeasure Needed			Suggested Countermeasure	Crime Action Phase
		Yes	No	N/A		
1.	Are unauthorized modifications made to the operating system?				List the modifications that have been made to the operating system and verify that they have been properly authorized.	Concealment
2.	Are high-risk modifications made to the operating system?				Analyze the modifications of the operating system by type and list the high-risk types for additional investigation.	Concealment
3.	Are modifications made to the operating system through the unauthorized use of user exits?				List all of the user exit routines added to the operating system and verify that they are all authorized modifications.	Concealment
4.	Are unauthorized routines incorporated into authorized modifications to the operating system?				Identify the changes that have been made to the operating system and, if from the vendor, verify that they are the correct vendor change. If not from the vendor, verify authorization.	Concealment
5.	Do operators modify the operating system during execution?				Review the operator and job accounting log to identify modifications to the operating system and investigate that they are authorized modifications.	Concealment

Fig. 9-6. Continued

THREAT: Unbroken Audit Trail

PROBABLE IMPACT: Loss of Assets

RECOMMENDED DETECTIVE CONTROL METHOD: Analysis

No.	Potential Vulnerability	Countermeasure Needed			Suggested Countermeasure	Crime Action Phase
		Yes	No	N/A		
1.	Is the audit trail adequate to recover operations after a problem?				Conduct a disaster test in which a simulated disaster occurs which will force computer operations to demonstrate whether or not they can recover operations.	Planning
2.	Can the modifications made to a specific version of an operating system be reconstructed?				Starting with an older version of the operating system, determine whether the current version can be reconstructed.	Planning
3.	Can the procedures followed during the generation of an operating system be determined?				Review the operator log and job accounting log to determine whether or not the procedures taken during the generation of an operating system can be documented from those logs.	Planning
4.	Does the operating system activity recorded under the operator log account for all operating system activities?				Verify from the vendor-recorded computer usage that the operating system transactions account for all of that time.	Concealment

THREAT: Unauthorized Processing in a Supervisory Mode

PROBABLE IMPACT: Loss of Assets, Destruction of Media, Disclosure, Disruption

RECOMMENDED DETECTIVE CONTROL METHOD: Analysis

No.	Potential Vulnerability	Countermeasure Needed			Suggested Countermeasure	Crime Action Phase
		Yes	No	N/A		
1.	Is the operating system used for executing privileged operating commands controlled?				Attempt to execute a privileged operating system command from the master terminal to determine whether there are sufficient procedures to stop the use of those facilities. If not, instigate them.	Planning
2.	Are routines entered through user exits that will enable programs to enter the supervisory mode?				Examine the routines using operating system exits to determine whether or not they can enter into the supervisory mode.	Planning
3.	Are supervisory mode commands used for unauthorized purposes?				Identify from operating logs the supervisory commands used, and then sort them by user to determine that that individual is authorized to use those commands.	Concealment
4.	Are files accessed through the supervisory mode that should not be accessed through that mode?				Sort the file usage records from the job accounting tape, by file, and then send that list to the user to confirm that all uses have been authorized.	Concealment

Fig. 9-6. Continued

THREAT: Unauthorized Acts at Remote Terminals

PROBABLE IMPACT: Loss of Assets

RECOMMENDED DETECTIVE CONTROL METHOD: Analysis

No.	Potential Vulnerability	Countermeasure Needed			Suggested Countermeasure	Crime Action Phase
		Yes	No	N/A		
1.	Are users misusing terminals by performing unauthorized acts?				Using communicatons logs, list the activities by resource, and then send those lists to the accountable individual to confirm whether or not the activities are authorized.	Concealment
2.	Do authorized individuals perform unauthorized acts?				Identify potentially dangerous acts and then sort those by user to determine whether that user is authorized to perform those acts.	Concealment
3.	Are terminal users able to circumvent terminal physical controls to perform unauthorized acts?				Put key people in positions where they can observe and analyze use of the terminal to detect obvious unauthorized acts through physical abuses of the terminal.	Concealment

THREAT: Replaying Messages

PROBABLE IMPACT: Loss of Assets

RECOMMENDED DETECTIVE CONTROL METHOD: Analysis

No.	Potential Vulnerability	Countermeasure Needed			Suggested Countermeasure	Crime Action Phase
		Yes	No	N/A		
1.	Are message logs replayed to re-enter some transactions twice?				Messages should be sequentially numbered by terminal so that the replaying of the messages would be immediately identifiable.	Planning
2.	Are messages replayed from a terminal?				Periodically sort messages from terminals to determine whether duplicate messages have been entered.	Concealment
3.	Are messages from one terminal replayed through other terminals?				Periodically sort all messages to determine whether messages have been replayed into the system.	Concealment

10

Preventing computer crime

THE MAJORITY OF THIS BOOK HAS DEALT WITH RESPONDING TO THE threat of computer crime. In the previous chapter we looked at the detection of various forms of computer crime. Now it is time to examine the ways we can prevent our systems from coming under attack. In this chapter we will look at some strategies for preventing computer crime. We will examine internal control methods and ways to perform audits both internally and externally. Next we will look at an overview of the requirements of a security force. We will consider some examples of software designed to increase the security of our systems and look at the supervisor as a tool to watch for computer crimes. Finally we will examine what has been called the single best defense against computer crime.

Prevention strategy

There are two major strategies for dealing with computer crime. The first is to develop a set of countermeasures designed to keep computer crimes from happening. In this instance the company will spend money up front to try to prevent the crimes from taking place.

In the other instance the company does not try to prevent the crime, but rather attempts to detect it shortly after it happens, so as to limit the loss. In that case the company will spend its money on the loss itself and in the detection of that loss.

Both are valid strategies. In this chapter we will concentrate on the former, the prevention of computer crime. In chapter 9 we looked at the detection methodology. It is advised that a company use prevention methods to make it difficult to penetrate their systems and a set of detection tools to identify instances where the prevention tools failed.

Threats that should be prevented

It makes sense to prevent those threats that are most cost effective to prevent, while detecting the others. Some of the more expensive or critical threats include

Large loss threats   This sort of threat has the potential to cause great financial distress for the organization.

Disruptive threats   Threats that could either stop or disrupt the effectiveness of the organization cannot be tolerated (for example, threats that could destroy the computer center or the data necessary to run the system, hence causing an extended period of system unavailability).

High visibility threats   These threats would cause serious damage to the image of the business. They must be prevented to ensure that the business can continue to function as normal. An example of this would be a massive computer embezzlement from a bank.

Habit-forming threats   Although these threats are not large at the outset, they can lead the perpetrator to commit larger crimes if they are not prevented.

Management may dictate that there are other threats which are unacceptable for a specific business. For example, it may be deemed as undesirable for the records of a health clinic to be accessed from outside the system. In that case, the reading of those records would constitute an unacceptable threat and would need to be prevented.

How to commit a computer crime

If a security team is going to prevent computer crime, they first must understand how to commit that crime. It is very helpful if the security force can be divided into two groups, one to act as the perpetrators and the other to act in a defensive role. That way the particular weaknesses of the system can come to light and countermeasures to combat those weaknesses can be developed.

Most computer crimes have a set of common characteristics. Using a data processing analogy, we may say we are looking at the development cycle of a computer crime. This cycle has four parts. Although they are not all unique to computer crime, the actual implementation provides some special insight. The four phases in the commission of a computer crime are planning, execution, concealment, and conversion to more usable forms of assets. We will look at each of these steps in greater detail.

Planning a computer crime

Most computer crimes are not spontaneous events, they are carefully planned, often for extensive periods of time. As an example, one large, international theft of classified data took almost two years to set up. During that time the thieves were acquiring information about the system they wanted to penetrate. The actual theft happened after 23 months of research.

Some of the information computer criminals need to acquire includes:

- Resources controlled by a specific applications program
- Controls on system access and system security
- Ways to enter data into the system
- Program listings and system documentation
- Locations of programs and methods for modifying them
- Locations of the system data
- Where the input data is stored and the format of that storage
- The methodology for error correction and emergency modification of input data or executing programs
- The timing of the runs of specific programs
- How information is moved through the system

The list is extensive. The criminal does not need all of this data to commit a crime; however, the more that is accumulated, the easier the task of committing the crime. Countermeasures should be aimed at restricting access to the kinds of data listed above.

Execution of the crime

Execution of a computer crime differs from the execution of most other crimes. The presence of the perpetrators is not necessary for the crime to be committed. Rather the crime can be committed from long distance over phone lines, or even by a program that commits the actual crime while the perpetrator is not present. There are many different methods for committing computer crime, including:

- Using terminals/communications channels to gain access
- Modifying applications programs or the operating system
- Entering extra or modified transactions to an input file
- Physical removal of programs or data
- Accessing controlled information and the copying of same
- Physical actions such as arson or physical theft of data
- Manipulating the actions of programs or people

Concealment

Once the crime has been committed, the criminal usually tries to remove the traces of the crime. These traces are called tracks and represent the most common method by which criminals are detected. There are several common ways to hide illicit activity, including:

- Representing the crime as an error or omission in an otherwise normal run

- Representing a fraudulent transaction as one of the normal transactions for that run

- Modifying an individual account but manipulating the system totals to reflect normal results

- Misrepresenting a criminal activity as an error or flaw within the system

- Performing the illegal act in concert with an authorized activity

Conversion

Once the target of the theft has been attained, there still remains the problem of converting the assets into a more useful form. If the target was acquisition of data, then that data must be converted into some other form—usually into cash by selling it. If the crime is for revenge, then this step is skipped, for there are no assets to convert to another form. Most computer crimes are motivated by personal gain, so the conversion step exists. There is little the security force can do to increase the difficulty of this step, and it is a phase shared by most crimes involving material. About the only way this step can be utilized to capture computer criminals is to look for patterns outside the norm for that individual. Sudden wealth or a change in attitude are often signals which should be noted.

The selection of countermeasures

There are six steps in the process of selecting countermeasures to be used against computer crime. They are:

1. Identify the potential perpetrators and penetration points. It is essential that you determine who is going to attack your system and from where the attack will come.

2. Determine the magnitude of the risks. This will enable you to put a priority on the threats and deal with the most significant first.

3. Identify the most probable threat. Like the last step, this will enable you to focus your preventive efforts where they will bear the most fruit. It is important to remember that all threats need not be prevented, only those that pose a significant loss.

4. Decide if prevention or detection is the method of choice. As was mentioned earlier, some crimes are better handled through detection of the event rather than the deployment of some preventive process. Other crimes need to be prevented and detection is not an option.

5. If prevention is the treatment of choice, select a method. There are four prevention categories: internal controls, audits, security forces, and surveillance. Later in this chapter we will look at each of these.

6. Select the countermeasure of choice and implement it. Use the information in Fig. 10-1 as an aid in selecting the appropriate countermeasure for any specific threat.

Using this six-step process makes it possible to quickly identify a logically appropriate response to many threats. In addition, by understanding the phases of development of a crime, the appropriate countermeasure can be implemented for each stage.

COMPUTER CRIME THREATS MATRIX
(THEIR PROBABLE IMPACT AND COUNTERMEASURES)

No.	Threat	Probable Impact					Preventive Countermeasures			
		Loss of Assets	Destruction/Plant	Destruction/Media	Disclosure	Disruption	System of Internal Controls	Audits	Security Force	Surveillance
	Data Input Threats									
1.	Undetected, unreasonable, or inconsistent source data	x					x			
2.	Key entry changes not detected	x								x
3.	Misinterpretation of record formats	x								x
4.	Fraudulently adding, deleting or modifying data	x								x
5.	Inserting or deleting transactions	x								x
6.	Modification of personal data	x						x		
7.	Emergency entry of transactions	x					x			
8.	Improper use of error correction procedures	x					x			

Fig. 10-1. Computer crime threats matrix.

Fig. 10-1. Continued

	Misuse By Authorized End-Users									
9.	Sale of privileged information				x				x	
10.	Acquisition and sale of complete list of information				x				x	
11.	Theft of services	x					x			
12.	Destruction or modification not for personal gain		x	x		x				x
13.	Sell information to an unauthorized individual				x				x	
	Uncontrolled System Access									
14.	Theft of data or programs	x			x				x	
15.	Destruction of EDP facilities		x						x	
16.	Unauthorized access to EDP facility	x	x	x	x	x			x	
17.	Unauthorized access through remote terminals	x			x		x			
18.	Unauthorized access through dial-in lines	x			x		x			
19.	Inadvertent revealing of passwords	x			x					x
20.	Piggybacking a terminal	x			x					x
21.	Password not voided when employee terminated	x			x		x			
22.	Unauthorized access	x			x					x
23.	Undetected repeated attempts	x			x		x			
	Ineffective Security Practices									
24.	Poorly defined authorization access	x			x		x			
25.	Incomplete enforcement of security	x	x	x	x	x			x	
26.	No follow-up on unusual conditions	x			x	x	x			
27.	Repeated processing of the same event	x					x			
	Ineffective Security Practices (Continued)									
28.	Careless handling of sensitive data				x					x
29.	Lack of follow-up on potential security violations	x	x	x	x	x		x		
30.	Lack of management follow-up	x	x	x	x	x		x		
	Procedural Errors Within The EDP Facility									
31.	Ignoring operational procedures	x					x			
32.	Operations manager or supervisor circumventing operational controls	x					x			

33.	Lapses of security during reorganization and recovery	x	x		x			x	
34.	Failure to protect files during maintenance		x	x			x		
35.	Inadequate supervision during non-working hour shifts	x	x	x	x				x
36.	Control overrides	x			x				
37.	Inadvertently or intentionally mis-labeling storage media		x	x				x	
38.	Failure to erase sensitive information			x		x			
39.	Output routed to wrong individual			x					x
	Program Errors								
40.	Key data stored in programs	x			x				
41.	Trojan Horse routines	x					x		
42.	Programs readily accessible	x						x	
43.	Program theft	x						x	
44.	Program time bombs		x		x		x		
45.	Ghost program versions	x		x		x			
	Operating System Flow								
46.	Operating system control weakness	x		x		x			
47.	Disable operating system control	x					x		
48.	Failure to SYSGEN controls	x	x	x		x			
49.	Lack of copy protection			x		x			
50.	Unauthorized modification to the operating system	x						x	
51.	Unbroken audit trail	x				x			
52.	On-line system crash protection	x						x	
53.	Unauthorized processing in a supervisory mode	x	x	x	x	x			
	Communication System Failure								
54.	Lack of positive identification	x		x		x			
55.	Unauthorized monitoring			x				x	
56.	Unauthorized acts at remote terminals	x							x
57.	Unauthorized modification of communication software			x		x			
58.	Wire tapping			x				x	

Fig. 10-1. Continued

59.	Unauthorized takeover	x		x						x
60.	Stealing encryption keys	x		x				x		
61.	Spoofing	x				x				
62.	Replaying messages	x				x				

The computer crime threat matrix

There are five areas of concern that must be considered when looking at the impact of computer crime on an organization. Each of those areas is explained below. Figure 10-1 lists a series of computer crimes, the probable impact, and the suggested countermeasure. The areas of concern are:

- Loss of assets. This is very common, simple theft.
- Destruction of the plant. This is less common, and is usually done by terrorists. In this instance the physical plant and machines are destroyed.
- Destruction of data or media. In this attack, either the physical media are destroyed or the data housed on that media are destroyed.
- Disclosures. This is the releasing of information to unauthorized parties. Although the organization has not lost the data, it is now out of control and may constitute a severe hazard.
- Disruption. In this case, the sole purpose for the crime is to cause problems in the system. Most often this form of attack is an accident; but accidental or not, it must be guarded against.

System of internal controls

Many studies have shown that internal controls are the most significant means by which to reduce computer crime. There are two classes of internal controls: general controls and application specific controls. We will look at the way these two types of controls can work together to produce an overall system which may noticeably reduce the risk of computer crime.

Characteristics

All internal control systems should include three characteristics:

Risk identification   The whole purpose of a control system is the reduction of risk. Until some set of risks is identified there is no purpose in developing a set of controls. The data section included later in this chapter lists a substantial number of risks. This list could form the beginning of this type of system.

Controls proportional to the risk   It is tempting to seize on one particular risk factor and build an elaborate control system to circumvent that risk. However, each response to a vulnerability must be appropriate to the magnitude of the risk involved. Highly vulnerable areas need strong controls, but weak risks require minimal control.

Controls must be tested   Internal controls can be tested, evaluated, and retested until they are correct and reliable. An internal control system that has never been tested cannot be said to be the reason the system has not been violated.

Important internal control countermeasures

While there are nearly as many internal control system variations as there are systems, there is a recognized subset which has proven effective. The types of control countermeasures that seem to be effective are listed below.

Access controls   If a criminal cannot get into the system, then no mischief can occur. By the same token, if unauthorized individuals cannot get into a set of files, then they will more than likely not harm those files. It is important, however, to ensure that authorized users can reach the resources they need with a minimum of difficulty.

Accountability   If individuals are responsible for each action they perform, then they are more likely to perform them in the expected manner. On the other hand, if careful accounting is maintained and somebody commits a crime, there is a good chance it will be recorded and traced to the perpetrator. Accountability works best when it is widely publicized.

Audit trails   Just as accountability works to help computer professionals maintain their honesty, audit trailing helps encourage programmers to write honest programs. An audit trail is an account of each activity taken by a program. It can be used to trace a criminal activity and identify which program performed the activity.

Error message follow-up   Most automated systems provide reasonably complete error facilities. When unusual conditions or situations occur, the programs usually generate error or warning messages. In many cases of computer crime, the applications informed the operators that unusual activity was occurring, but the warnings were ignored. It must become policy to investigate any error or warning message.

Anticipation (normal range) controls   Over time, patterns of the normal flow of a program develop. If these patterns are recorded and used as a guide, then abnormal situations may be more easily detected. When a deviation from the norm occurs, it is usually due to an error or other problem. Notification at this time provides the possibility for very rapid response by the control team.

Data validation   Either the software or a preprocessor should always check input data for validity and correctness. If input data passes rigorous checks, it is likely to represent correct processing. It is not enough to ensure that the data is within the correct range. Data must also be cross-checked against other data and have internal validity checks run.

External controls   Controls developed to be used outside the software environment to check the validity of inputs, outputs, and the results of standard processing are very powerful tools. The more controls used to interrogate the system's integrity, the less chance a criminal will attempt to corrupt the system.

Vulnerability countermeasure data

The following is a list of computer crime threats that are effectively reduced using a system of internal controls as the countermeasure.

- Undetected, unreasonable, or inconsistent source data
- Emergency entry of transactions
- Improper use of error correction procedures
- Theft of services
- Unauthorized access through remote terminals
- Unauthorized access through dial-in lines
- Password not voided when an employee is terminated
- Undetected repeated attempts at access
- Poorly defined authorization access
- No follow-up on unusual conditions
- Repeated processing of the same event
- Control overrides
- Failure to erase sensitive information
- Key data stored in programs
- Ghost program versions
- Operating system control weaknesses
- Failure to SYSGEN controls
- Lack of copy protection
- Broken audit trails
- Unauthorized processing in a supervisory mode
- Lack of positive identification
- Unauthorized modification of communication software

Figure 10-2 lists a series of potential vulnerabilities and the suggested type of control which would serve as a countermeasure.

THREAT: Undetected, Unreasonable, or Inconsistent Source Data

PROBABLE IMPACT: Loss of Assets

RECOMMENDED PREVENTIVE CONTROL METHOD: System of Internal Controls

No.	Potential Vulnerability	Countermeasure Needed Yes	No	N/A	Suggested Countermeasure	Crime Action Phase
1.	Has the attributes of the data used in computer systems been defined in sufficient detail so that the reasonableness of the data could be verified?				Develop standardization data documentation forms or acquire and use a data dictionary.	Planning
2.	Have data validation routines been incorporated into the automated systems which are consistent with the fully defined data elements?				Document with the data definition the desirable data validation measures or integrate the data dictionary into the operating environment.	Execution
3.	Are variations noted by the data validation routines investigated on a timely basis?				Require that these error messages contain space to describe the result of any investigation and who performed that investigation. Have supervisors regularly review the timeliness of these actions.	Execution
4.	Has the user of the system defined the reasonableness and consistency of data based on current usage?				Develop a profile of the users of data and then identify, for investigation, any variances from the current norm.	Execution
5.	Are special authorizations required when unusual processing occurs, such as for large orders, withdrawals, etc.?				Determine what level of loss is unacceptable and then implement special authorization controls at that level and above.	Planning

Fig. 10-2. Vulnerability countermeasure Tables No. 1–22.

Fig. 10-2. Continued

THREAT: Emergency Entry of Transactions

PROBABLE IMPACT: Loss of Assets

RECOMMENDED PREVENTIVE CONTROL METHOD: System of Internal Controls

No.	Potential Vulnerability	Countermeasure Needed			Suggested Countermeasure	Crime Action Phase
		Yes	No	N/A		
1.	Have procedures been established on what types of transactions will be entered on an emergency basis?				Develop a listing of the conditions that would warrant entering transactions on other than the normal basis.	Planning
2.	Has a list of individuals who are authorized to enter transactions in the computer system on an emergency basis been defined?				Determine from management who has the authority to enter emergency transactions.	Planning
3.	Are procedures established so that only authorized individuals can enter authorized emergency transactions?				Develop a matrix showing the emergency type transactions and the individuals who can enter them, and then develop procedures to verify that the entry is in conformance with those procedures.	Execution
4.	Is a listing of all emergency transactions that are entered into the system prepared?				Modify computer sytems so that all transactions entered, other than through the normal means, are listed for later review.	Concealment
5.	Does supervision regularly review the reasonableness of emergency transactions?				Establish procedures so that management reviews all emergency transactions.	Concealment

THREAT: Improper Use of Error Correction Procedures

PROBABLE IMPACT: Loss of Assets

RECOMMENDED PREVENTIVE CONTROL METHOD: System of Internal Controls

No.	Potential Vulnerability	Countermeasure Needed			Suggested Countermeasure	Crime Action Phase
		Yes	No	N/A		
1.	Is a record maintained of all errors rejected from the computer system?				Incorporate in computer systems a mechanism which maintains records on transactions rejected from the system.	Planning
2.	Has the responsibility for correction of each type of error been defined?				Determine from management who has the responsibility to correct each type of error detected in the computer system.	Planning
3.	Are the re-entered transactions compared to the original transactions to ensure and evaluate the reasonableness of the correction?				Re-entered information should be processed through the normal system validation routines to verify its reasonableness.	Execution
4.	Does the system maintain a record of accountability for the error correction process?				A history file should be maintained which, among other events, records accountability for error correction.	Execution

Fig. 10-2. Continued

THREAT: Theft of Services

PROBABLE IMPACT: Loss of Assets

RECOMMENDED PREVENTIVE CONTROL METHOD: System of Internal Controls

No.	Potential Vulnerability	Countermeasure Needed			Suggested Countermeasure	Crime Action Phase
		Yes	No	N/A		
1.	Are logs of computer usage maintained?				Acquire a job accounting system, such as IBM's SMF, to record usage of computer resources.	Planning
2.	Are individuals held accountable for their usage?				Use a job numbering system which holds individuals accountable for computer usage.	Planning
3.	Is the use of the computer reconciled to the vendor's internal clock usage?				Reconcile the vendor's clock time to the recorded usage time.	Concealment
4.	Are unusual uses of the computer investigated, for example, excessive time for a single individual or a new individual consuming large amounts of time?				Develop user profiles and check variances from those profiles.	Execution

THREAT: Unauthorized Access Through Remote Terminals

PROBABLE IMPACT: Loss of Assets and Disclosure

RECOMMENDED PREVENTIVE CONTROL METHOD: System of Internal Controls

No.	Potential Vulnerability	Countermeasure Needed			Suggested Countermeasure	Crime Action Phase
		Yes	No	N/A		
1.	Is a system of passwords used at remote terminals?				Require all users of the terminal to be pre-approved and issued passwords.	Planning
2.	Are users limited to predetermined authorized acts?				Obtain from management the type of actions that authorized users can perform on a terminal, and then limit their capabilities to those actions.	Planning
3.	Are logs maintained on remote terminal usage?				Utilize a job accounting log which records terminal usage.	Execution
4.	Are users apprised of who is accessing their resources through remote terminals?				Periodically prepare a listing of individuals using the computer resources (primarily data resources), and then prepare confirmations for users to confirm that only authorized individuals are accessing their resources.	Execution

Fig. 10-2. Continued

THREAT: Unauthorized Access Through Dial-In Lines

PROBABLE IMPACT: Loss of Assets and Disclosure

RECOMMENDED PREVENTIVE CONTROL METHOD: System of Internal Controls

No.	Potential Vulnerability	Countermeasure Needed			Suggested Countermeasure	Crime Action Phase
		Yes	No	N/A		
1.	Can the point of origin of the call-in through dial lines be positively identified?				Disconnect on all dial-in services and call back to the authorized number.	Execution
2.	Are passwords required for the use of dial-up lines?				Design and implement a series of passwords which identify dial-up line users.	Planning
3.	Is a log maintained of the dial-in services?				Create an audit trail which documents what services are provided through dial-in lines.	Concealment
4.	Do the individuals who own resources being accessed through dial-in lines know who is accessing those resources?				Periodically prepare confirmations for the owners of the resources being accessed through dial-in lines asking them to confirm that the users are authorized.	Execution

THREAT: Password Not Voided When Employee Terminated

PROBABLE IMPACT: Loss of Assets and Disclosure

RECOMMENDED PREVENTIVE CONTROL METHOD: System of Internal Controls

No.	Potential Vulnerability	Countermeasure Needed			Suggested Countermeasure	Crime Action Phase
		Yes	No	N/A		
1.	When employees are terminated, are they terminated on the spot from an accessibility to the computer perspective?				At the point where employees are notified of their termination, their passwords should be deleted from the computer system.	Planning
2.	Is the individual responsible for deleting passwords notified promptly when individuals are terminated?				Copies of all termination notices should be sent to the individual responsible for computer passwords prior to the point where their passwords should be terminated.	Planning
3.	Are terminated employees notified that they can no longer use the computer resources?				Include in the termination procedure a step to notify employees that their computer privileges have been terminated.	Planning
4.	Are usage logs regularly reviewed to determine that terminated employees are not using computer resources?				Include a step in the termination procedure that will search backward from the date of termination to list uses by the terminated employee.	Concealment

Fig. 10-2. Continued

THREAT: Undetected Repeated Attempts

PROBABLE IMPACT: Loss of Assets and Disclosure

RECOMMENDED PREVENTIVE CONTROL METHOD: System of Internal Controls

No.	Potential Vulnerability	Countermeasure Needed			Suggested Countermeasure	Crime Action Phase
		Yes	No	N/A		
1.	Has it been determined what is a realistic number of attempts for an authorized user to make?				Propose to management a level of authorized attempts in the range of 3 to 5.	Planning
2.	Are controls established to shut down terminals in which an authorized password has not been entered in a reasonable number of attempts?				Install procedures that shut down terminals after the maximum number of unauthorized attempts and only permit the terminal to be reopened with supervisors present.	Execution
3.	Are logs maintained of the number of unauthorized accesses?				Maintain logs of unauthorized access and investigate usage of those terminals where there is a high frequency of unauthorized access.	Planning
4.	Are procedures such that an individual who has exceeded the maximum number of unauthorized attempts cannot easily go to another or the same terminal after a predetermined lapse of time and again attempt to enter the system?				Assign individuals to specific terminals so that they cannot rove and attempt to access from multiple terminals.	Execution

THREAT: Poorly Defined Authorization Access

PROBABLE IMPACT: Loss of Assets and Disclosure

RECOMMENDED PREVENTIVE CONTROL METHOD: System of Internal Controls

No.	Potential Vulnerability	Countermeasure Needed			Suggested Countermeasure	Crime Action Phase
		Yes	No	N/A		
1.	Are all of the computer resources identified?				Require that an inventory be made and each controllable resource identified.	Planning
2.	Have the owners of each of those resources identified who can access those resources?				Require that owners of the resources identify the individuals authorized to access their resources.	Planning
3.	Have control measures been developed to ensure that only authorized users can access the resources for which they are authorized?				Acquire a security system that can enforce the defined accessibility to resources.	Planning
4.	Are all data processing users, including technicians, covered under the access rules?				Only permit the defined authorized users from accessing the protected resources. All other individuals should be excluded access.	Planning

Fig. 10-2. Continued

THREAT: No Follow-Up on Unusual Conditions

PROBABLE IMPACT: Loss of Assets and Disclosure

RECOMMENDED PREVENTIVE CONTROL METHOD: System of Internal Controls

No.	Potential Vulnerability	Countermeasure Needed			Suggested Countermeasure	Crime Action Phase
		Yes	No	N/A		
1.	Have all conditions warranting follow-up action been identified?				Require owners of computer resources to identify conditions on which they would like to follow up.	Planning
2.	Have procedures been established to identify those unusual conditions and to notify the responsible individuals they have occurred?				Install the appropriate procedures to notify responsible individuals of unusual conditions.	Planning
3.	Do the responsible individuals take the appropriate follow-up action?				Develop logs which require the date of action, who took it, and the results of the action be recorded. Items not followed up should be periodically investigated by management.	Execution
4.	As new problems occur, are they added to the unusual condition follow-up list?				Develop procedures that inform the responsible individuals of new unusual conditions.	Planning

THREAT: Repeated Processing of the Same Event

PROBABLE IMPACT: Loss of Assets

RECOMMENDED PREVENTIVE CONTROL METHOD: System of Internal Controls

No.	Potential Vulnerability	Countermeasure Needed			Suggested Countermeasure	Crime Action Phase
		Yes	No	N/A		
1.	Are all events that have a financial impact uniquely identified?				Uniquely identify all events which will have a financial impact on the organization.	Planning
2.	Where possible, are events such as funds owed to vendors deleted from the system immediately upon payment so that the system would not accept that event if it was re-entered?				Attempt, in systems, to develop a match between the authorization and execution process so that the event, once completed, is eliminated from the system.	Planning
3.	Are events periodically sorted by identifier so that duplicate items will be listed?				Recommend that normal procedures periodically probe for duplicate items.	Execution
4.	Are events periodically sorted by the same accountability source so that the type of claims made can be monitored, for example, processing for a tuition refund twice?				Recommend that an analysis be made by accountability source periodically to review for possible repeat processing.	Execution

Fig. 10-2. Continued

THREAT: Control Overrides

PROBABLE IMPACT: Loss of Assets

RECOMMENDED PREVENTIVE CONTROL METHOD: System of Internal Controls

No.	Potential Vulnerability	Countermeasure Needed			Suggested Countermeasure	Crime Action Phase
		Yes	No	N/A		
1.	Have the users accountable for systems defined which controls can be overridden?				Have users develop an inventory of which controls can be overridden.	Planning
2.	Have the individuals who are authorized to override controls been identified?				Require the users to prepare a list of individuals authorized to override their controls.	Planning
3.	Has a list been prepared of the individuals who have overridden controls, which controls are overridden, and to what extent?				Develop a procedure that lists all control overrides.	Concealment
4.	Are controls sufficient to ensure that only individuals who are authorized override controls for which they are authorized?				Develop control override matrices and enforce them in the application systems.	Execution
5.	Are listings of overrides by individuals authorized to override regularly prepared to identify the extent to which they have used those privileges?				Periodically provide users with listings of all the overrides performed by authorized individuals to ensure the reasonableness of use of those privileges.	Execution

THREAT: Failure to Erase Sensitive Information

PROBABLE IMPACT: Disclosure

RECOMMENDED PREVENTIVE CONTROL METHOD: System of Internal Controls

No.	Potential Vulnerability	Countermeasure Needed			Suggested Countermeasure	Crime Action Phase
		Yes	No	N/A		
1.	Are all sensitive media files identified?				Ask users to develop an inventory of sensitive files and information.	Planning
2.	Are sensitive files marked or monitored in such a way that their location can be monitored?				Require operations to mark or monitor computer files so they are readily identified.	Planning
3.	Are sensitive files erased when they are no longer needed for production purposes?				Provide a process that makes erasing sensitive information easy.	Planning
4.	Is a positive feedback process implemented so that it is known when sensitive files are erased?				Implement a process that sends back to the user, who is accountable for sensitive information, a list of when that information is erased.	Planning
5.	Are sensitive files which are not erased on a timely basis investigated?				Require that investigation be undertaken when a sensitive file is not erased at the appropriate time.	Concealment

Fig. 10-2. Continued

THREAT: Key Data Stored in Programs

PROBABLE IMPACT: Loss of Assets

RECOMMENDED PREVENTIVE CONTROL METHOD: System of Internal Controls

No.	Potential Vulnerability	Countermeasure Needed			Suggested Countermeasure	Crime Action Phase
		Yes	No	N/A		
1.	Has an inventory been made of the variable data stored in programs that have a financial impact, such as tax rates, withholding rates, prices, etc.?				Require that programmers prepare a list of the key financial variables included within computer programs.	Planning
2.	Are users aware of what information is stored in programs and under the control of the computer programmer?				Send users the list of financial variables and computer programs to ensure they want those under the control of the programmers.	Planning
3.	Are users sent positive feedback information when the variables are changed?				Develop a process so that when particular variables are changed in computer programs, the users are aware of those changes.	Execution

THREAT: Ghost Program Versions

PROBABLE IMPACT: Loss of Assets and Disclosure

RECOMMENDED PREVENTIVE CONTROL METHOD: System of Internal Controls

No.	Potential Vulnerability	Countermeasure Needed			Suggested Countermeasure	Crime Action Phase
		Yes	No	N/A		
1.	Can only one version of a program be maintained on the object code master library?				Restrict the object code library to a single version of the same program (unless they have two different execution dates).	Planning
2.	Do job control language changes that call new program versions need to be approved by supervision?				Require that supervision approve the use of all new program versions.	Planning
3.	Is every cataloged program on the source library confirmed as a valid production program?				Periodically review the source code library, system by system, to ensure that each cataloged object code program is proper.	Execution
4.	Is a history maintained of all of the versions created of a single program?				Require an audit trail of changes to a program be recorded and reviewed to ensure that all changes are authorized.	Concealment

Fig. 10-2. Continued

THREAT: Operating System Control Weakness

PROBABLE IMPACT: Loss of Assets and Disclosure

RECOMMENDED PREVENTIVE CONTROL METHOD: System of Internal Controls

No.	Potential Vulnerability	Countermeasure Needed			Suggested Countermeasure	Crime Action Phase
		Yes	No	N/A		
1.	Are the operating system risks identified?				Organize a risk management team to identify operating system risks.	Planning
2.	Are the controls provided by the operating system vendor identified?				Obtain a list from vendor documentation of the available controls.	Planning
3.	Are the controls implemented that can reduce the identified risk?				Require that approval must be obtained before a vendor-provided control is deleted from the operating system.	Planning
4.	Is an assessment of the adequacy of controls in the operating system performed before the system is entered into production?				Require that the operating system controls be evaluated and that additional controls be added where appropriate.	Planning

THREAT: Failure to SYSGEN Controls

PROBABLE IMPACT: Loss of Assets, Media Destruction, and Disclosure

RECOMMENDED PREVENTIVE CONTROL METHOD: System of Internal Controls

No.	Potential Vulnerability	Countermeasure Needed Yes	No	N/A	Suggested Countermeasure	Crime Action Phase
1.	Is the decision on what operating system controls will be utilized made by someone other than the individual who SYSGENS the operating system?				Require that control selection be independent of the individual SYS-GENNING the operating system.	Planning
2.	Are all of the operating system controls identified?				Obtain from the vendor documentation a list of all operating system controls.	Planning
3.	Does an independent person review the generated operating system to ensure that it encompasses all the specified controls?				Require an independent group to make a positive identification of the generated operating system controls.	Execution
4.	Is the generated operating system free of generation error and warning messages?				The independent group that reviews the inclusion of controls should also ensure there are no generation errors or warning messages.	Execution

Fig. 10-2. Continued

THREAT: Lack of Copy Protection

PROBABLE IMPACT: Disclosure

RECOMMENDED PREVENTIVE CONTROL METHOD: System of Internal Controls

No.	Potential Vulnerability	Countermeasure Needed			Suggested Countermeasure	Crime Action Phase
		Yes	No	N/A		
1.	Are records maintained when computer files are copied?				Records should be maintained on all sensitive computer files when they are copied.	Planning
2.	Are copies of computer file subject to the same security procedures as the original?				Require that the same security protection be applied to copies of files as to the original.	Planning
3.	Does a list of the disposition of computer files include both copies and originals?				Require that all of the processes that apply to original files also apply to copies of those files.	Planning

THREAT: Unbroken Audit Trail

PROBABLE IMPACT: Loss of Assets

RECOMMENDED PREVENTIVE CONTROL METHOD: System of Internal Controls

No.	Potential Vulnerability	Countermeasure Needed			Suggested Countermeasure	Crime Action Phase
		Yes	No	N/A		
1.	Is the audit trail for applications defined?				System specifications should include audit trail specifications.	Planning
2.	Does the audit trail satisfy legal, audit, and record retention requirements?				Have the audit trail reviewed by the auditors, legal department, and record retention people to ensure that it satisfies their requirements.	Planning
3.	Must all changes to the audit trail be approved?				Changes to the audit trail, especially deletions, should be approved by the users and other interested parties.	Execution
4.	As enhancements are made to computer systems, are those requirements incorporated into the audit trail?				Require that procedures installing changes to computer systems consider the impact on audit trails.	Planning

Fig. 10-2. Continued

THREAT: Unauthorized Processing in a Supervisory Mode

PROBABLE IMPACT: Loss of Assets, Destruction of Media, and Disclosure and Disruption

RECOMMENDED PREVENTIVE CONTROL METHOD: System of Internal Controls

No.	Potential Vulnerability	Countermeasure Needed			Suggested Countermeasure	Action Phase
		Yes	No	N/A		
1.	Are all supervisory mode capabilities identified?				Request that the technical personnel develop a list of supervisory mode facilities.	Planning
2.	Are the individuals authorized to process in a supervisory mode identified?				Request that management develop a list of people who can use the supervisory mode facilities.	Planning
3.	Are logs maintained on who uses the supervisory facilites, when, and on which resources?				Include the supervisory mode processing within the operations audit trail.	Concealment
4.	Are supervisory mode operations restricted to a limited number of terminals?				Restrict supervisory mode operations to a limited number of terminals, especially those where the use of the terminal could be monitored by supervision.	Execution
5.	Are lists periodically prepared indicating which individuals used which supervisory mode capabilities?				Periodically prepare a list of uses of supervisory mode capabilities so that the individuals using them are accountable for their acts.	Execution

THREAT: Lack of Positive Identification

PROBABLE IMPACT: Loss of Assets and Disclosure

RECOMMENDED PREVENTIVE CONTROL METHOD: System of Internal Controls

No.	Potential Vulnerability	Countermeasure Needed			Suggested Countermeasure	Action Phase
		Yes	No	N/A		
1.	Are all users of communication facilities required to identify themselves prior to using those facilities?				Require an identification process so that only authorized users can use communication facilities.	Planning
2.	Are users restricted to certain terminals and processes?				Where practical, users should be restricted to certain terminals, hours, and processes to provide a higher probability that only authorized individuals use communication facilities.	Planning
3.	Does the identification vary by the degree of protection needed for the resources being accessed?				Develop multiple levels of identification so the degree of positive identification increases in proportion to the need to protect the assets being accessed.	Planning
4.	If a positive identification cannot be made, are procedures taken to terminate communication with that party?				Develop procedures that cut off communication with parties who cannot be positively identified.	Planning

Fig. 10-2. Continued

THREAT: Unauthorized Modification of Communication Software

PROBABLE IMPACT: Disclosure

RECOMMENDED PREVENTIVE CONTROL METHOD: System of Internal Controls

No.	Potential Vulnerability	Countermeasure Needed			Suggested Countermeasure	Action Phase
		Yes	No	N/A		
1.	Must all modification to communication software be approved?				Apply the same change control procedures to communication software as other application systems.	Planning
2.	Are changes to communication software be restricted to those provided by the software vendor?				Restrict software changes to those provided by the software vendor.	Planning
3.	Is an audit trail of changes to the communication system software prepared and reviewed by management?				Require that an audit trail of change to the communication system be made and that it be regularly reviewed by management.	Concealment

Internal/external audit

Auditing represents a wide range of activities that can be used to prevent and detect computer crime. One of its strongest deterrent factors is the knowledge that it will be undertaken. The more widely publicized an audit is, the more likely it is that it will prevent some illegal activity from occurring.

Auditing as a countermeasure

Auditing refers to an independent appraisal of some part of a computer system by an outside group. The scope of the audits can be as wide as the management is willing to pay for.

When a computer crime audit is conducted, the auditors may be able to prevent computer crime in one of two ways. First, they can install procedures and programs that facilitate the capture of incorrect computer users. Second, they can prevent the crime merely through the reputation of auditors as professionals who catch computer criminals.

The responsibility for the prevention of computer crime must rest squarely on the shoulders of management. They must take an active role to support the efforts of the auditors. Inconveniences caused by the audit software or procedures will be accepted by the staff when it is apparent that the audit has management's support. Without management's active support, many audit functions would perform at less than ideal levels.

The following section lists a series of activities that have proven to deter computer crime. This list is not complete, for there are untold numbers of computer crimes that were never committed because of the presence of a strong audit environment. Significantly important audit activities include

Promoting a strong audit image   The fact that there are auditors working will probably decrease the incidence of some forms of crime. The stronger the image, the better it works to prevent crime. Some techniques that can improve the image of auditing include:

- Make the results of the audit very visible. The more visible the results, the more the deterrent factor.
- Widely publicize the audit findings (good or bad). As employees become aware of the power of the audit software, its deterrent value increases.
- Make the auditors and their programs easily available to anyone who wants to increase the quality of their code.

Performing surprise audits   Varying the interval or timing of some audits may significantly increase their usefulness. If a criminal has only a couple of hours warning in which to cover his/her tracks, it is likely that the audit will uncover the crime. By the same token, if it is known that unannounced audits are the norm, then their deterrent value is significant.

Using EDP audit specialists If this type of professional is available, seek out information on current types of auditing and the crimes which lend themselves to detection through audit.

Working with systems development to build in audits The best time to install audit software in an application is during the design phase. At that point, it is easy to build in code that will perform range checking and other data validation activities. In addition to the overt enhancements, there is usually a positive change in the attitudes of the staff toward building self-auditing programs.

Helping to define risks The auditors experience and background are usually helpful in performing risk analysis.

Performing special reviews When a new form of computer crime is found, the auditors should run checks on the system to ensure that it is clean. At the same time, the auditors must evaluate their company's exposure to this sort of attack.

Figure 10-3 examines a series of computer crime threats and the way the auditing function can be used to eliminate those threats.

Security force

In the context of this book, the security force represents the investigative arm of the organization. Security needs vary as much as business and physical plants vary. In some installations the physical safety of the personnel and equipment are of greatest concern. In other organizations it is the safety of the data which occupies the largest portion of the security officer's work load. In this section we will look at security as it pertains to the prevention of computer crimes.

Security force as a prevention to computer crime

In the context of data processing, the security force has moved from a policelike organization to one that more closely resembles the FBI. Rather than being armed defenders of territory, the modern security force uses many sophisticated tools to protect computers, the data on those computers, and the people who use those computers.

The modern security force is normally of greatest value in the following areas:

- Identifying potential criminal threats
- Understanding how computer crime is committed
- Providing the first line of defense against criminal actions directed at the computer
- Finding, interrogating, and dealing with certain criminals
- Investigating the possibility of computer crime activity

THREAT: Modification of Personal Data

PROBABLE IMPACT: Loss of Assets

RECOMMENDED PREVENTIVE CONTROL METHOD: Auditing

No.	Potential Vulnerability	Countermeasure Needed			Suggested Countermeasure	Crime Action Phase
		Yes	No	N/A		
1.	Are individuals permitted to enter transactions affecting themselves personally; for example, can payroll clerks enter their own payroll information?				Include within system, controls that prevent employees from entering data and accessing their own personal accounts.	Planning
2.	Are regular listings prepared showing activity in employee accounts that might be accessible by those employees?				Include in systems the provision to provide special listings showing the activity in employee accounts.	Execution
3.	Do audits include evaluation of activity of employee accounts?				The audit program should include a provision to audit employee accounts, and this concept should be widely publicized in the organization.	Execution
4.	Are warning messages produced if funds are directed to an employee's account from other than normal business activities?				Develop procedures that will produce warning messages for special transactions, such as bank debits and credits, which move funds into employee accounts.	Execution
5.	Do auditors investigate the organization's vulnerability when new computer crime methods are identified?				Review the professional literature for new computer crime threats; and if they could be utilized by employees, investigate the organization's vulnerability in those areas.	Planning

Fig. 10-3. Vulnerability countermeasure Tables No. 23–33.

Fig. 10-3. Continued

THREAT: Lack of Follow-Up on Potential Security Violations

PROBABLE IMPACT: Loss of Assets, Destruction in Plant, Destruction of Media, Disclosure, and Disruption

RECOMMENDED PREVENTIVE CONTROL METHOD: Auditing

No.	Potential Vulnerability	Countermeasure Needed			Suggested Countermeasure	Crime Action Phase
		Yes	No	N/A		
1.	Are special forms or other means used to identify security violations?				Recommend the development of a security violation reporting system.	Planning
2.	Are all noted security violations directed to a member of senior management?				Recommend that a copy of all security violation instances be forwarded to a member of senior management.	Planning
3.	Has a formal investigative procedure been developed to investigate each security violation?				Recommend that a formal procedure be developed which will ensure that all security violations are investigated.	Execution
4.	Do auditors periodically review the follow-up procedure to ensure that it is functioning properly?				Include within the audit program a provision to periodically review the follow-up on security violations for completeness.	Planning

THREAT: Lack of Management Follow-Up

PROBABLE IMPACT: Loss of Assets, Destruction in Plant, Destruction of Media, Disclosure, and Disruption

RECOMMENDED PREVENTIVE CONTROL METHOD: Auditing

No.	Potential Vulnerability	Countermeasure Needed			Suggested Countermeasure	Crime Action Phase
		Yes	No	N/A		
1.	Has senior management developed a computer crime policy?				Recommend that senior management address the area of computer crime and develop an organization policy on computer crime.	Planning
2.	Are security violation recommendations sent to senior management for their information?				Recommend that copies of security violation reports and their recommendations be sent to senior management.	Execution
3.	Is management advised if no action is taken on security violation recommendations within a reasonable period of time?				Recommend that a procedure be established which will involve senior management in security violation recommendations if operations management does not take action within a stated period of time.	Execution
4.	Does management become involved in security violations when operating management does not take appropriate action?				Periodically review the security violation reports to determine that, when appropriate action is not taken within a reasonable period of time, senior management becomes involved.	Execution

Fig. 10-3. Continued

THREAT: Ignoring Operational Procedures

PROBABLE IMPACT: Loss of Assets

RECOMMENDED PREVENTIVE CONTROL METHOD: Auditing

No.	Potential Vulnerability	Countermeasure Needed			Suggested Countermeasure	Crime Action Phase
		Yes	No	N/A		
1.	Are the error-correction procedures within the EDP facility identified?				Ensure that the error procedures within the EDP facility are readily identifiable.	Planning
2.	Are methods established to ensure that the operating procedures in the EDP facility are properly executed?				Ensure that, as operating procedures are developed and/or installed, there is appropriate feedback information to confirm when these procedures have been properly performed.	Planning
3.	Is EDP facility management notified when operating procedures are not performed as specified?				Ensure that the systems provide reports to management when normal operating procedures are not performed.	Execution
4.	Does management take appropriate action when EDP facility operating procedures are not performed?				Periodically review to ensure that management takes appropriate action when procedures are not performed.	Execution

THREAT: Operations Manager or Supervisor Circumventing Operational Controls

PROBABLE IMPACT: Loss of Assets

RECOMMENDED PREVENTIVE CONTROL METHOD: Auditing

No.	Potential Vulnerability	Countermeasure Needed			Suggested Countermeasure	Crime Action Phase
		Yes	No	N/A		
1.	Are procedures installed within the systems that provide feedback information when controls are circumvented?				Recommend that warning messages be issued when key controls are circumvented in EDP systems.	Planning
2.	Do the warning messages advising that controls are circumvented go to someone other than the individual having the opportunity to circumvent the controls?				Recommend that warning message be sent to an independent group for investigation.	Execution
3.	Are system override messages promptly investigated?				Periodically review to ensure that control override situations are promptly investigated.	Execution
4.	Are lists of control overrides periodically prepared showing the extent of overrides by each individual capable of performing the override?				Require accountability for conducting an override, and then periodically have lists prepared which show the frequency of override, by individual.	Execution

Fig. 10-3. Continued

THREAT: Failure to Protect Files During Maintenance

PROBABLE IMPACT: Destruction of Media and Disclosure

RECOMMENDED PREVENTIVE CONTROL METHOD: Auditing

No.	Potential Vulnerability	Countermeasure Needed			Suggested Countermeasure	Crime Action Phase
		Yes	No	N/A		
1.	Are computer files removed from the computer before vendor personnel are permitted to perform maintenance (if possible)?				Recommend that procedures be established to remove files from the computer prior to the performance of vendor maintenance.	Planning
2.	Can vendor personnel gain access to computer files over communication lines installed for vendor maintenance (e.g., IBM's project RETAIN)?				Recommend that computer files be removed from the computer before vendor communication lines are activiated for maintenance.	Execution
3.	Are company employees present when vendor maintenance occurs?				Recommend that vendor maintenance activities be monitored by key employees.	Execution
4.	Are vendor personnel included in the organization's access security systems?				Include vendor personnel in the access security systems and restrict them to those functions necessary to perform their job.	Planning
5.	Are lists periodically prepared showing those activities performed by vendor personnel relating to computer files?				Periodically review the functions performed by vendor personnel to ensure they are all appropriate functions.	Execution

THREAT: Trojan Horse Routines

PROBABLE IMPACT: Loss of Assets

RECOMMENDED PREVENTIVE CONTROL METHOD: Auditing

No.	Potential Vulnerability	Countermeasure Needed			Suggested Countermeasure	Crime Action Phase
		Yes	No	N/A		
1.	Are the changes made to programs (by programmers) reviewed by supervisory personnel?				Recommend that new lines of source code entered into computer programs be reviewed by supervisory personnel.	Planning
2.	Are programs inspected by an independent party after they are developed?				Recommend that programs be inspected by an independent party to ensure that they conform to specifications.	Execution
3.	Is the execution of programs periodically monitored to detect unused source code?				Recommend that programs be periodically analyzed by program optimizer routines designed to detect blocks of unused source code.	Execution
4.	Are unused blocks of source code investigated to determine the function performed by that source code?				Recommend that blocks of unused source code be investigated by independent parties to determine the objective and need for that source code.	Execution

Fig. 10-3. Continued

THREAT: Program Time Bombs

PROBABLE IMPACT: Destruction of Media and Disruption

RECOMMENDED PREVENTIVE CONTROL METHOD: Auditing

No.	Potential Vulnerability	Countermeasure Needed			Suggested Countermeasure	Crime Action Phase
		Yes	No	N/A		
1.	Are instances where processing is disrupted and media is destroyed investigated to determine whether or not they were caused by sabotage?				Recommend that investigations be conducted in cases of serious disruption and loss of key files to determine whether or not sabotage has occurred.	Execution
2.	Are the changes made by programmers to programs reviewed by supervisory personnel?				Recommend that new lines of source code entered into computer programs be reviewed by supervisory personnel.	Planning

THREAT: Disable Operating System Control

PROBABLE IMPACT: Loss of Assets

RECOMMENDED PREVENTIVE CONTROL METHOD: Auditing

No.	Potential Vulnerability	Countermeasure Needed			Suggested Countermeasure	Crime Action Phase
		Yes	No	N/A		
1.	Are the operating system controls documented?				Recommend that the controls included within the operating system be documented.	Planning
2.	Does the operating system provide feedback to indicate whether or not the controls have been executed?				Utilize, wherever practical, feedback mechanisms that provide positive indication that controls have been executed.	Planning
3.	Are logs maintained of operating system commands that could be used to disable operating system controls?				Recommend that logs be maintained and regularly reviewed of those commands which could be used to disable operating system controls.	Execution
4.	Must management approval be obtained to disable an operating system control?				Recommend that controls can only be disabled after management approval has been obtained.	Planning
5.	Are instances where controls are disabled investigated to determine that the purpose is reasonable and that it does not expose the organization to large risks?				Ensure that the disabling of controls is reasonable and that it does not subject the organization to high risk.	Planning

Fig. 10-3. Continued

THREAT: Spoofing

PROBABLE IMPACT: Loss of Assets

RECOMMENDED PREVENTIVE CONTROL METHOD: Auditing

No.	Potential Vulnerability	Countermeasure Needed			Suggested Countermeasure	Crime Action Phase
		Yes	No	N/A		
1.	Are computer users instructed to shut down terminal operations after they have completed their work?				Explain to users the spoofing risk of piggybacking on their operations if they leave a terminal without closing down their processing, even though they are told the terminal is not operating correctly.	Planning
2.	Are terminal programs terminated after a reasonable period of inactivity (this is necessary because a program can simulate the security systems and "spoof" an individual into believing they are interacting with the security system when, in fact, they are interacting with an application spoofing program)?				Install a procedure that shuts down a terminal after "X" minutes of no activity from an application program operated at that terminal.	Planning
3.	Are data processing personnel and users trained to challenge the identification and authority of a requestor before providing that individual with requested information or capabilities?				Install a procedure that requires positive identification before an act or capability occurs to avoid being "spoofed" into thinking an individual has appropriate authority.	Planning

THREAT: Spoofing

PROBABLE IMPACT: Loss of Assets

RECOMMENDED PREVENTIVE CONTROL METHOD: Auditing

No.	Potential Vulnerability	Countermeasure Needed			Suggested Countermeasure	Crime Action Phase
		Yes	No	N/A		
4.	Are data processing professionals trained not to provide confidential information over the telephone or through the mail until they have assured themselves that the request is properly authorized?				Implement a procedure that prohibits individuals from providing information to unknown individuals over the telephone or through the mail without supervisory approval, regardless of the organization that individual purports to represent.	Planning
5.	Are employees instructed to report instances to supervision where they believe they have been "spoofed?"				Inform personnel involved with data processing that they should report attempted spoofing to data processing supervision.	Execution

Fig. 10-3. Continued

THREAT: Replaying Messages

PROBABLE IMPACT: Loss of Assets

RECOMMENDED PREVENTIVE CONTROL METHOD: Auditing

No.	Potential Vulnerability	Countermeasure Needed			Suggested Countermeasure	Crime Action Phase
		Yes	No	N/A		
1.	Are computer messages sequentially numbered to identify the re-entry of a message?				Implement a process that numbers data processing messages and checks the sequence of those numbers.	Planning
2.	Are messages in the same timeframe compared to determine whether they are a replay of an existing message?				Develop a routine that will compare a computer message to other messages entered from the same terminal and/or individual during a predetermined previous timeframe.	Execution
3.	Are messages periodically sorted in order to identify duplicates?				Periodically sort messages to determine whether or not duplicates are processed.	Execution
4.	Are messages periodically sorted, by source, to identify the re-entry of transactions?				Request that messages be periodically sorted, by source, to determine whether the same individual or location is replaying messages.	Execution

In large organizations there may be two security forces, one responsible for the physical plant and the other responsible for the protection of the data processing and software systems.

Security countermeasures

Security countermeasures ought be implemented by those in the organization who are responsible for the physical security of the facility as well as the security of the software. There is a tremendous difference between the security required to keep the casual user from playing with the system and that required to protect data from a sophisticated industrial or foreign spy. This is why the maxim "regardless of your preventive security, always maintain your ability to detect active crime" is important.

The other caution is to beware of placing too much trust in devices. High-tech cameras and motion detectors can be easily defeated by trained agents. By itself, high tech is not sufficient protection. The following are some of the ways security measures might be effective.

Posted guards   The mere presence of a guard may have an inhibiting effect on potential criminals.

Secure areas   Creating areas with limited access through a cipher lock or utilizing some form of badge will increase the security at minimal impact to the valid users.

Sensors   These devices can find a person in a room of chairs and tables like a conference room. In most cases, they are used after hours to detect entry to restricted areas.

Cameras   High-resolution cameras can be used to determine who is using a specific terminal, what is being done on the terminal, and what the results are. In addition, they can be used to record who went into and out of secure areas.

TV monitors and cameras   These tools can provide constant, direct monitoring of sensitive areas. The new portable models make it possible to take clandestine video nearly anywhere.

Posted warnings   This old, yet effective and inexpensive method of marking areas is still useful today. Prosecution must follow violation to show that the signs mean business.

Security software   This form of software will be discussed in the next section. Essentially, it consists of a set of programs which will intercept most, if not all, attacks on the system.

Figure 10-4 lists a series of vulnerable areas and the response by the security force to dispose with that threat.

THREAT: Sale of Privileged Information

PROBABLE IMPACT: Disclosure

RECOMMENDED PREVENTIVE CONTROL METHOD: Security Force

No.	Potential Vulnerability	Countermeasure Needed			Suggested Countermeasure	Crime Action Phase
		Yes	No	N/A		
1.	Is an inventory maintained of information considered privileged?				Recommend that an inventory of privileged information be maintained.	Planning
2.	Is bait information included in the privileged information?				Recommend that bait records be included within groups of privileged information. (A bait record is information contained within the privileged information that will identify the group of information from which it was taken. For example, the security officer may put his name on a privileged file but use a special middle initial. Therefore, if any information ever arrives at that individual with that name, the security officer knows that the file has been compromised.)	Execution
3.	Is the privileged information provided security measures equivalent to the value of that information?				The type of security provided for information should be directly related to the value of that information to the organization.	Planning
4.	Are end-users restricted to those pieces of information which they need for their job and no more?				Install a level of security that restricts users' access to privileged information to those pieces needed to do their job.	Planning

THREAT: Acquisition and Sale of Complete List of Information

PROBABLE IMPACT: Disclosure

RECOMMENDED PREVENTIVE CONTROL METHOD: Security Force

No.	Potential Vulnerability	Countermeasure Needed			Suggested Countermeasure	Crime Action Phase
		Yes	No	N/A		
1.	Does the organization maintain an inventory of information lists that require protection?				Recommend that an inventory be made of lists of information that require protection.	Planning
2.	Do each of the lists of information include bait records?				Bait records should be placed on all lists of information requiring protection so that the compromise of that information can be readily identifiable.	Concealment
3.	Are individuals prohibited from removing tape files and other media from the computer room and the organization's property?				Tag computer media with a magnetic device that will trip an alarm system should the media be removed from the computer center.	Execution

Fig. 10-4. Vulnerability countermeasure Tables No. 34–49.

Fig. 10-4. Continued

THREAT: Sell Information to an Unauthorized Individual

PROBABLE IMPACT: Disclosure

RECOMMENDED PREVENTIVE CONTROL METHOD: Security Force

No.	Potential Vulnerability	Countermeasure Needed			Suggested Countermeasure	Crime Action Phase
		Yes	No	N/A		
1.	Has an inventory been made of information that has a high market value?				Conduct an inventory to identify information that has a high market value.	Planning
2.	Do the highly marketable pieces of information require more security than is given for the file in which they are stored?				Ensure that each computer file or resource receives a degree of protection which is consistent with the security due for the most valuable information within the file.	Planning
3.	Do individuals having access to the file in which that marketable information is contained have a need to use that highly marketable information?				Eliminate highly marketable information from files for which most users having access to the file do not need.	Planning
4.	When the highly marketable information is not in use, is it stored in a secure location?				Maintain secure locations to store valuable information when it is not in use.	Planning

THREAT: Theft of Data or Programs

PROBABLE IMPACT: Loss of Assets and Disclosure

RECOMMENDED PREVENTIVE CONTROL METHOD: Security Force

No.	Potential Vulnerability	Countermeasure Needed			Suggested Countermeasure	Crime Action Phase
		Yes	No	N/A		
1.	Have programs been evaluated to indicate their value to other organizations?				Develop a rating system which will indicate the value of each program or other data to other organizations.	Planning
2.	Are program listings controlled information, and thus accounted for?				Develop a procedure for numbering program listings and then account for those listings.	Planning
3.	Are program listings destroyed when they are no longer needed?				Recommend that program listings and other listings of data be shredded when they are no longer needed.	Planning
4.	Are individuals prohibited from using photocopy machines personally?				Recommend that photocopy machines be under the custody of a clerical person and that this person account for what is being photocopied.	Planning
5.	Do computer programs and other secure data indicate that they are the property of the organization for which they were developed?				Include on each program, or have each key person sign, a statement which formally recognizes that the programs and data are property of the organization for which they were developed.	Planning

Fig. 10-4. Continued

THREAT: Destruction of EDP Facilities

PROBABLE IMPACT: Destruction of Plant

RECOMMENDED PREVENTIVE CONTROL METHOD: Security Force

No.	Potential Vulnerability	Countermeasure Needed			Suggested Countermeasure	Crime Action Phase
		Yes	No	N/A		
1.	Is access to the computer facility restricted to those requiring access?				Restrict access to the computer room to those having a need to access the computer room.	Planning
2.	Are all visitors to the computer facility escorted at all times?				Recommend that visitors be escorted for the entire time they are in the computer facility.	Planning
3.	Are EDP facilities monitored during nonworking hours?				Use monitors, sensors, cameras, or patrolling guards to ensure that unauthorized individuals are not in the computer facilities during nonworking hours.	Execution
4.	Are keys to the computer room tightly controlled?				Control the issuance of keys to the computer center.	Planning
5.	Are locks and other entry devices to the computer facilities changed periodically?				Periodically change the access control devices to the computer center.	Planning
6.	Are security violators reprimanded or prosecuted by management?				Recommend that first-time violators be reprimanded or prosecuted depending upon the act being performed.	Execution

THREAT: Unauthorized Access to EDP Facility

PROBABLE IMPACT: Loss of Assets, Destruction in Plant, Destruction of Media, Disclosure, and Disruption

RECOMMENDED PREVENTIVE CONTROL METHOD: Security Force

No.	Potential Vulnerability	Countermeasure Needed			Suggested Countermeasure	Crime Action Phase
		Yes	No	N/A		
1.	Is an automatic security system, or guard, posted at the entrance of the facility to prevent unauthorized access?				Post a guard or receptionist outside the EDP facility to verify credentials of individuals entering, or provide them with electronic passes to enter the EDP facility.	Planning
2.	Is the EDP facility securely locked during nonworking hours?				Ensure that the EDP facilities cannot be entered routinely during non-working hours.	Planning
3.	Will an alarm be sounded if unauthorized individuals access the EDP facility during nonworking hours?				Use sensors, roving guards, or equivalent means to detect unauthorized access during nonworking hours.	Execution
4.	Are individuals permitted to remove assets from the EDP facility without approval or search?				Develop a system of passes needed to remove any package from the EDP facility, and use guards to search briefcases or other means of removing facilities.	Execution
5.	Are unescorted visitors in the EDP facility challenged during working hours?				Put the responsibility on supervisory personnel to challenge unescorted visitors in the EDP facility during working hours.	Planning

Fig. 10-4. Continued

THREAT: Incomplete Enforcement of Security

PROBABLE IMPACT: Loss of Assets, Destruction in Plant, Destruction of Media, Disclosure, and Disruption

RECOMMENDED PREVENTIVE CONTROL METHOD: Security Force

No.	Potential Vulnerability	Countermeasure Needed			Suggested Countermeasure	Crime Action Phase
		Yes	No	N/A		
1.	Has the level of desired security for the EDP resources been defined?				Recommend that the resources be individually identified, and then the level of security for each resource be defined.	Planning
2.	Are security measures consistent with the desired level of security?				Install security countermeasures that are consistent with the desires of management for security.	Planning
3.	Does management reprimand or prosecute security violators?				Request that management back security forces in reprimanding or prosecuting security violators.	Planning
4.	Do the security countermeasures have mechanisms to record when security is not enforced?				Build security countermeasures in such a manner that they record when security is not properly applied.	Planning
5.	Does someone regularly review security to ensure that the approved security measures are implemented?				Implement a procedure for management to receive reports of instances where security is not enforced and take action on those violations.	Planning
6.	Are data processing personnel trained to enforce security procedures?				Include in DP personnel job descriptions a responsibility to enforce security measures.	Planning

THREAT: Lapses of Security During Reorganization and Recovery

PROBABLE IMPACT: Loss of Assets, Destruction of Media, and Disruption

RECOMMENDED PREVENTIVE CONTROL METHOD: Security Force

No.	Potential Vulnerability	Countermeasure Needed			Suggested Countermeasure	Crime Action Phase
		Yes	No	N/A		
1.	Is the security software in operation during the reorganization and recovery process?				Do not permit reorganization recovery to occur unless security software is in operation.	Planning
2.	Are data processing personnel prohibited from entering or deleting production transactions during the reorganization recovery process?				Ensure that record counts are maintained before and after reorganization and recovery, to ensure that all of the records are accounted for.	Execution
3.	If security software cannot be operational during recovery are other equivalent security means in force?				Develop alternate security measures to be in force when the primary security mechanisms are not operational.	Planning

Fig. 10-4. Continued

THREAT: Inadvertently or Intentionally Mislabeling Storage Media

PROBABLE IMPACT: Destruction of Media, Disclosure of Media

RECOMMENDED PREVENTIVE CONTROL METHOD: Security Force

No.	Potential Vulnerability	Countermeasure Needed			Suggested Countermeasure	Crime Action Phase
		Yes	No	N/A		
1.	Is the security media labeled by someone independent of the project team?				Assign the responsibility of labeling storage media to a data librarian.	Planning
2.	Are computer files labeled both internally and externally?				Develop procedures that would prohibit a computer file from being used if both the internal and external label were not consistent.	Planning
3.	Are instances of labeling problems reported to operations supervision?				Develop procedures that require all labeling variances to be reported immediately to supervision.	Execution
4.	Are storage media labels uniquely identified, such as prenumbered labels, and are the labels controlled?				Use a special type label or prenumbered label, so that only officially sanctioned labels can be used on storage media.	Execution

THREAT: Programs Readily Accessible

PROBABLE IMPACT: Loss of Assets

RECOMMENDED PREVENTIVE CONTROL METHOD: Security Force

No.	Potential Vulnerability	Countermeasure Needed			Suggested Countermeasure	Crime Action Phase
		Yes	No	N/A		
1.	Do programmers have unrestricted access to the object code library?				Restrict access to the object code library so that supervisory approval must be obtained to add to, modify, or delete programs on the object code library.	Planning
2.	Is programmer access restricted to the source code library?				Access to the source code library should be restricted to situations where the programmer has been authorized to change a source code.	Planning
3.	Do supervisors review added, deleted, and changed source code prior to permitting the creation of a new object code program?				Require supervisors to ensure that changed source code is reasonable based upon the program change requests.	Execution
4.	Do the program libraries produce a history of changes to both source and object code libraries?				Develop procedures that prepare and maintain a history of changes to both object and source code.	Planning

Fig. 10-4. Continued

THREAT: Program Theft

PROBABLE IMPACT: Loss of Assets

RECOMMENDED PREVENTIVE CONTROL METHOD: Security Force

No.	Potential Vulnerability	Countermeasure Needed			Suggested Countermeasure	Crime Action Phase
		Yes	No	N/A		
1.	Are programmers informed that programs are the property of their employer?				Have programmers sign statements indicating they recognize that programs are the property of their employer.	Planning
2.	Are all program listings controlled and stored under the custody of the organization?				Create a documentation center and require that documentation be stored there during nonworking hours.	Planning
3.	Are all program listings and documentation obtained from individuals before they are terminated from the organization?				All program documentation should be confiscated before a programmer is informed of termination. If the individual terminates, program documentation should be confiscated immediately.	Execution
4.	Are programmers prohibited from obtaining copies of the programs on electronic media?				Prohibit the removal of electronic media from the computer center.	Execution

THREAT: Unauthorized Modification of the Operating System

PROBABLE IMPACT: Loss of Assets

RECOMMENDED PREVENTIVE CONTROL METHOD: Security Force

No.	Potential Vulnerability	Countermeasure Needed			Suggested Countermeasure	Crime Action Phase
		Yes	No	N/A		
1.	Are all modifications to the operating system approved by management?				Implement a procedure that requires approval prior to modifying the operating system.	Planning
2.	Must all changes to the operating system originate from the operating system vendor?				Develop a policy that permits only vendor-initiated changes to the operating system.	Planning
3.	Is an audit trail maintained of changes made to the operating system?				Maintain an audit trail of operating system changes and verify that those changes have been authorized.	Planning
4.	Are control copies of the operating system maintained?				Maintain control copies of the operating system and periodically compare them to the production version so that all changes between the two versions can be verified.	Planning

Fig. 10-4. Continued

THREAT: On-Line System Crash Protection

PROBABLE IMPACT: Loss of Assets

RECOMMENDED PREVENTIVE CONTROL METHOD: Security Force

No.	Potential Vulnerability	Countermeasure Needed			Suggested Countermeasure	Crime Action Phase
		Yes	No	N/A		
1.	Are all terminals removed from system operation after a crash?				Terminal users should be required to reopen terminals after a system crash.	Execution
2.	Do all on-line messages have sequential number protection?				Require that terminal messages be sequentially numbered so that all messages can be accounted for after a system crash.	Execution
3.	Does supervision oversee the recovery of an on-line system after it has crashed?				Require supervision to be present during the recovery of an on-line system.	Execution
4.	Are standardized recovery procedures established for on-line systems?				Develop and follow standardized recovery procedures.	Planning
5.	Are all on-line crashes investigated for unauthorized acts either causing the crash or after the crash?				Require that a report be prepared as to the cause and events surrounding an on-line system crash.	Planning

THREAT: Unauthorized Monitoring

PROBABLE IMPACT: Disclosure

RECOMMENDED PREVENTIVE CONTROL METHOD: Security Force

No.	Potential Vulnerability	Countermeasure Needed			Suggested Countermeasure	Crime Action Phase
		Yes	No	N/A		
1.	Is confidential information scrambled or processed through cryptography before transmission over communication lines?				Develop procedures so that confidential information will not be sent in the clear over communication lines.	Planning
2.	Is key information routed over different lines or transmitted at different times to make monitoring more difficult?				Vary the method or time of transmission of key information.	Planning
3.	Is highly secretive processing performed in locations that are not penetrable by electronic gear?				Highly secretive processing should be performed in locations and transmitted by a means that minimizes electronic eavesdropping.	Planning

Fig. 10-4. Continued

THREAT: Wire Tapping

PROBABLE IMPACT: Disclosure

RECOMMENDED PREVENTIVE CONTROL METHOD: Security Force

No.	Potential Vulnerability	Countermeasure Needed			Suggested Countermeasure	Crime Action Phase
		Yes	No	N/A		
1.	Are all communication lines under the control of the organization and/or common carriers?				Use communication lines under the custody of the organization or common carriers.	Planning
2.	Is electronic gear used to identify wire taps?				Connect electronic evaluation gear to communication lines to identify potential wire taps.	Execution
3.	Are all the lines and connection boxes properly secured?				Enclose the wire and terminal boxes in such a manner that they are difficult to access.	Planning

THREAT: Stealing Encryption Keys

PROBABLE IMPACT: Loss of Assets and Disclosure

RECOMMENDED PREVENTIVE CONTROL METHOD: Security Force

No.	Potential Vulnerability	Countermeasure Needed			Suggested Countermeasure	Crime Action Phase
		Yes	No	N/A		
1.	Are encryption keys maintained in a secure location?				Place encryption keys in a secure location.	Planning
2.	Is a security officer responsible as custodian for the security keys?				Store security keys under the custody of a security individual when not in use.	Planning
3.	Are encryption programs and/or keys adequately protected between production uses?				If software security encryption keys are used, the encryption programs (if used) should be erased after usage and the key maintained under the custody of a security person or subject to special computer security.	Planning
4.	Are encryption keys changed periodically?				Encryption keys should be changed periodically.	Planning

Security software

Many software and system vendors have attempted to build programs that provide some defense against the abuse and misuse of computers. These programs range from the early password protection on files through more modern and much more sophisticated software that protects against a variety of different forms of attack. This market is rapidly growing because of the proliferation of damaging software, such as viruses. Along with this methodology for protecting systems, we must consider ways to prevent the theft of software. Theft is usually prevented by using special software called copy protection code.

Simple protection schemes

One of the most direct protection mechanisms is restricting physical access to areas or equipment. In the early days of computing, only operators were allowed near the computers. All jobs were submitted using cards, and paper printouts were returned to the user. There was little possibility of an unauthorized person getting close to a computer. The only requirement for protection then involved the files stored on the computer. Many different protection strategems evolved, but they had one common thread. They usually restricted access to the various functions of the data file. On some systems there were different passwords for reading, writing, deleting, and running the contents of the file. On other systems, like Digital Equipment Corporation's VMS series, these functions were controlled by special codes granted when the user's account is created.

As the use of computers increased, the need to determine whether a user was authorized also evolved. At first, the operators knew all the authorized users. Later it became important to validate a user before granting access to the system. A logical extension of the file protection password was the access password. This prevented a user from signing onto or using a computer unless the proper password was entered along with a unique identification number. Authorization to use a computer has become more sophisticated in recent years, and remains one of the prime problems for computer security.

Preventing unauthorized phone access

When computers were tied to modems, a whole new avenue of potential attack was opened. At first it seemed that the same protection schemes used to prevent unauthorized access via terminal would work for phone access. With the proliferation of microcomputers however, simple password protection became insufficient for users demanding tight security. One of the most recent trends is the callback package. The procedure used for this combination of software and hardware is as follows: The user phones the computer and enters his special identification and password. The computer hangs up, places a call to that user at a predetermined number, and grants access. This prevents anybody from using the password/identification pair from anywhere but the authorized phone. It is predicted that, in the future, a particular microcomputer with special identification at a predefined number will be necessary to access highly secure computers.

Protecting systems against an attack via snuffware

In chapter 6 we looked in depth at virus detection and protection programs available for both families of microcomputers (DOS and Apple). Similar programs exist for large computers. The threat is reduced on the mainframe computer because there has been systems software incorporated to prevent one user from harming another by accidental access. Vendors, like Computer Associates International of Chicago, provide software which greatly enhances the security of large computers. In addition, increased tracking and auditing software on many classes of machine will enhance the detection of attacks.

Protecting software from theft

Software piracy is by many accounts the largest class of computer crime in the world. If the economic impact of this type of crime were carefully calculated it would undoubtedly outweigh all other forms of crime combined. Copy protection began when software vendors realized that a significant number of programs were being copied and potential income was being lost. Early protection schemes involved simple encoding of the data on the diskettes. Then came the schemes which wrote the data in strange ways on the diskettes. Finally, this form of protection evolved into the destruction of the diskette in a specific location, usually using a laser to burn a hole in the diskette.

Other forms of protection involve using what is called a key disk. In this method of protection a special diskette is required, usually in a specific disk drive, before the software will run. This type of protection is popular with game programmers. Sometimes special information is required from a user manual or some other documentation along with the key disk.

A third class of copy protection involves a hardware key. This device is usually inserted into either a printer or other communications port. If the software cannot find the key, it will not run. This type of protection is usually intended to prevent the simultaneous use of more than one copy of a single program.

All of these copy protection schemes have the goal of preventing the user community from stealing software from the developers. There are some problems with this type of protection. The most significant is that the federal government will no longer buy any software that has copy protection included. Many vendors have dropped their protection in order to maintain access to the government market. Games are the most frequently copied programs, and they have no federal market so protection is still common on games. User management should be aware of this class of crime because many large developers, such as Lotus and Aldus, are becoming much more aggressive in prosecuting software pirates.

Software security requirements in the future

It seems only logical that the future will see computer crime as a significant terrorist tool. Already China has been plagued with a pervasive computer virus which may have been released as a terrorist act in response to their recent political troubles. As the computer criminal becomes more sophisticated and as more and more of our business evolves to a dependence on computers, the finesse of protection programs must also evolve. We can expect that artificial intelligence programs will be determining the allowable access and activity of each user. In that environment the user will be protected, the system will be protected, and the data will be protected. Protected that is, as long as the artificial intelligence program remains uncorrupted.

Considerations for user access

With all this talk of computer crime and harmful access, it is very tempting to create an environment that is overly safe. Any protection method, however, must take into account that the principle reason we use computers is to make our lives less complex. Any protection scheme must minimize the difficulties for the users or it fails the most significant test. Remember that any protection method that protects the system from legitimate users, or prevents legitimate users from performing necessary tasks, fails as a workable tool. Do not sacrifice the usefulness of your system for security. A balance must be struck between a system that is safe for the user to use and one that is friendly and open enough to enable legitimate users to perform their duties.

Supervisory surveillance

One important defense against employee wrongdoing is the supervisory staff. Supervisors review and monitor the work performed by subordinates. Supervision should be incorporated as an important, positive force to detect and prevent data processing crime. This section describes the role of the first-line supervisor in the prevention of computer crime. It also includes those countermeasures which can best be accomplished by supervisory surveillance.

First-line supervision and its crime-prevention role

First, it is necessary to point out that the role of first-line supervisors should not be redefined as that of the police. Most first-line managers have more than enough to do without adding crime busting to their tasks. But those who supervise have a unique opportunity to monitor computer processes and the people who perform them, and to detect the potential for crime. Through their attitude and example, they can help create an honest and open environment where integrity is important. When a computer crime occurs, part of the change that must be made involves the supervision of the criminal's area. If the supervisor should have found the probem before it occurred, then part of the blame rests squarely on the supervisor.

Ways first-line supervision can prevent computer crime

Some of the most effective ways for first-line supervision to foster an anti-computer-crime environment include:

- Detecting and reprimanding employees for minor policy violations
- Detecting breaches of control functions or security procedures
- Counseling employees on the importance of integrity within their function
- Creating an environment in which computer crime is difficult to perform, both from the point of view of the employee's peers and because of careful monitoring
- Monitoring and reviewing the work of subordinates to help them avoid improprieties and accidents
- Counseling employees as friends regarding the harm computer crime can do, and how the cost of that crime can be tied directly to their rate of pay

Countermeasures tied to supervisory surveillance

In the normal performance of their duty, supervisory personnel are the basic countermeasures against employee initiated computer crime. Although it is not necessary to induce paranoia in supervisors, they do need to be increasingly aware of the processes of computer crime and the signs of its occurrence. The following list is a partial description of those countermeasures for which the first-line supervisor is responsible.

Continuous observation   A supervisor is in a good position to observe the actions of subordinates. This is a function of the supervisory role. An educated supervisor can look for evidence of computer crime as part of the normal supervisory role. Examples of suspicious or noteworthy behavior include:

- Regular violation of security procedures
- Frequent attempted violation of protection schemes
- Taking sensitive material home

- Significant changes in spending habits
- Dissatisfaction with job or employer
- Strong feelings of resentment about promotion or raise, either your own or other employees

Any of these signs could signal problems with an employee. The first-line supervisor is in an ideal position to detect and intercept these sorts of feelings.

Review of work   The supervisor is normally required to review the work of subordinates. This review provides an excellent opportunity to look for signs of potential accidents or intentional wrongdoing. Once subordinates realize that their work will be reviewed, they will most likely make greater efforts to conform to the rules and regulations of the organization. It is important to recognize good and careful work so as to encourage it. This review process must be viewed as an opportunity for praise rather than a time of error correction.

Approval of critical activities   In some cases it may be advisable to submit the plans for critical tasks for supervisory approval before they are undertaken. For example, it may be wise to have a supervisor review the list of files to be deleted before a major cleanup program is run.

Sampling (spot checking)   Because it is not usually possible to review all the work performed under one supervisor, some sort of sampling model is usually used. This model frequently uses random spot checks of one or more subordinates' work as a representation of the whole. When subordinates are aware that their work could be checked at any time, and if the review is positive, they will most likely carefully follow the rules at all times.

Surveillance by supervisors is one of the most cost effective of the security measures available to reduce computer crime. If the supervisor fosters an environment where integrity and ethical conduct are the norm, and where employees are rewarded for proper behavior, computer crime should decrease. By function as well as by example, the first-line supervisor provides the primary detection and deterrent opportunity in most organizations (see Fig. 10-5).

The best defense against computer crime

Throughout this book we have considered various aspects of computer crime—from the use of a computer to commit crimes to crimes against computers in the form of piracy and virus attack. However, one important countermeasure that has been referenced only in passing is that of an ethical user community. Many of the crimes we have discussed would not necessarily take place if the individuals who committed them had been properly educated in the ethics of data processing.

The best defense we can have against computer crime is to educate our fellow computer professionals, our employees, and most importantly the generation of programmers currently in school. With ethical programmers, or at least programmers who are aware of their professional responsibility, we can reduce the incidence of computer crime. For example, many people still believe that when they purchase a software package they buy the rights to that package. They are unaware that all they are buying is the right to use that software, not the right to copy it for their friends. They are not committing the crime of software piracy because they choose to commit a crime, they are acting in a criminal manner from ignorance of what is right.

This is our challenge, to educate the user population and the programming community so they can make informed choices. It makes a world of difference if a hacker, knowing it is illegal, breaks into a system, or if a hacker, thinking it is no big deal, breaks into the same system. We cannot afford to have naive users damaging systems through unknowing behavior. We cannot afford to have security violations happen because a user did not know they were not supposed to peruse the system.

One partial answer to these problems is for programmers to develop a professional, ethical stance and promote it. This will not solve all computer crime, for there will always be individuals who choose to be less than ethical, but it will reduce the incidence of crime by accident and default. As the computer community becomes more important, and as computers become more and more a part of our lives, the need for ethical programming and use becomes more urgent.

THREAT: Key Entry Changes Not Detected

PROBABLE IMPACT: Loss of Assets

RECOMMENDED PREVENTIVE CONTROL METHOD: Supervisory Surveillance

No.	Potential Vulnerability	Countermeasure Needed			Suggested Countermeasure	Crime Action Phase
		Yes	No	N/A		
1.	Do the individuals preparing the source documents have the opportunity to see what information was entered into the computer?				Provide lists of entered transactions to the originator to verify that they have been entered correctly.	Execution
2.	Are key-entered items verified using the original source document?				When key validation occurs, it should use the original source document.	Planning
3.	Are key entry operators monitored by their supervisor?				Supervisors should spot check the work of key entry operators to ensure that it is entered correctly.	Planning
4.	Are data entry problems traced back to the source of those problems?				Key entry operators should be held accountable for their work by tracing problems back to the operator who entered the data.	Planning

THREAT: Misinterpretation of Record Formats

PROBABLE IMPACT: Loss of Assets

RECOMMENDED PREVENTIVE CONTROL METHOD: Supervisory Surveillance

No.	Potential Vulnerability	Countermeasure Needed			Suggested Countermeasure	Crime Action Phase
		Yes	No	N/A		
1.	Do supervisors monitor their subordinates to ensure they understand the record formats?				Supervisors should provide adequate instruction on how to interpret record formats.	Planning
2.	Are users of record formats held accountable for the uses of those formats?				All data processing acts should indicate who is accountable for those acts. Supervisors should trace problems associated with misinterpretation of record formats back to the individual accountable.	Execution
3.	When record formats are changed, are subordinates appropriately notified?				Supervisors should instruct subordinates on changes to record formats and how they affect their job.	Planning

Fig. 10-5. Vulnerability countermeasure Tables No. 50–62.

Fig. 10-5. Continued

THREAT: Fraudulently Adding, Deleting, or Modifying Data

PROBABLE IMPACT: Loss of Assets

RECOMMENDED PREVENTIVE CONTROL METHOD: Supervisory Surveillance

No.	Potential Vulnerability	Countermeasure Needed			Suggested Countermeasure	Crime Action Phase
		Yes	No	N/A		
1.	Can each computer transaction be traced to the originator and entry of that data?				Record accountability for the origination and entry of all data.	Planning
2.	Is the work of data input personnel periodically spot checked to ensure the correctness of entered data?				Supervisors should periodically spot check the work of their subordinates to ensure it is entered correctly.	Execution
3.	Is input data subject to reasonableness data validation edits?				Supervisors should incorporate reasonability checks into the data validation routines.	Execution
4.	Are batch totals maintained on transactions so that transactions cannot be added or deleted without detection?				Supervisors should verify that batch totals are correct.	Execution
5.	Do supervisors require approval to override system controls?				Transactions that override normal system controls should be approved by supervisors prior to entry.	Execution

THREAT: Inserting or Deleting Transactions

PROBABLE IMPACT: Loss of Assets

RECOMMENDED PREVENTIVE CONTROL METHOD: Supervisory Surveillance

No.	Potential Vulnerability	Countermeasure Needed			Suggested Countermeasure	Crime Action Phase
		Yes	No	N/A		
1.	Are counts maintained of the number of authorized transactions entered into the computer system?				Supervisors should verify through control totals that the appropriate number of transactions have been entered.	Execution
2.	Do supervisors monitor the types of transactions entered with an awareness that subordinates may enter unauthorized transactions or delete authorized transactions?				Supervisors should continuously or randomly review entered transactions for correctness.	Execution
3.	Are questionable transactions investigated by supervision?				Data validation routines should identify questionable transactions for follow-up by supervisors.	Execution

Fig. 10-5. Continued

THREAT: Destruction or Modification Not For Personal Gain

PROBABLE IMPACT: Destruction of Plant, Destruction of Media, and Disruption

RECOMMENDED PREVENTIVE CONTROL METHOD: Supervisory Surveillance

No.	Potential Vulnerability	Countermeasure Needed			Suggested Countermeasure	Crime Action Phase
		Yes	No	N/A		
1.	Are disgruntled employees closely monitored by supervision?				Disgruntled employees should be identified and subjected to closer monitoring by supervision.	Execution
2.	Are unusual conditions or damage investigated by supervision?				Supervisors should be alert that what appears to be a routine problem may, in fact, be sabotage.	Execution
3.	Are records maintained on unusual modification and destruction?				Supervisors should look for a pattern of problems occurring in the presence of a single subordinate.	Execution
4.	Are individuals permitted to be in the computer room without a supervisor or second person present?				Procedures should prohibit a single individual from working alone in the computer center.	Planning
5.	Are backup copies released without supervisory approval?				Subordinates should not have the opportunity to get both the original and backup copies of computer media.	Execution

THREAT: Inadvertent Revealing of Passwords

PROBABLE IMPACT: Loss of Assets and Disclosure

RECOMMENDED PREVENTIVE CONTROL METHOD: Supervisory Surveillance

No.	Potential Vulnerability	Countermeasure Needed			Suggested Countermeasure	Crime Action Phase
		Yes	No	N/A		
1.	Are passwords taped to terminals?				Supervisors should ensure that passwords are not written on or in close proximity to terminals.	Planning
2.	Do subordinates write passwords on key cards used for access or identification or in other easy-to-acquire locations?				Supervisors should be alert to the improper recording of passwords which may make gaining access easy.	Planning
3.	Do employees give their password to other employees?				Supervisors should be alert to conditions in which one employee gives his/her password to another employee.	Execution
4.	Are employees subject to severe reprimand or dismissal for revealing their passwords?				Supervisors should create a stringent policy against revealing passwords and then enforce that policy.	Planning
5.	Are compromised passwords immediately deleted?				When supervisors become aware that passwords have been compromised, they should immediately delete or change the passwords.	Execution

Fig. 10-5. Continued

THREAT: Piggybacking a Terminal

PROBABLE IMPACT: Loss of Assets and Disclosure

RECOMMENDED PREVENTIVE CONTROL METHOD: Supervisory Surveillance

No.	Potential Vulnerability	Countermeasure Needed			Suggested Countermeasure	Crime Action Phase
		Yes	No	N/A		
1.	Are subordinates instructed to shut down a terminal before leaving?				Supervisors should monitor subordinate action to ensure they shut down terminals before leaving them.	Planning
2.	Are terminals automatically shut down after "X" minutes of inactivity?				Procedures should be installed to shut down a terminal after "X" minutes of inactivity.	Planning
3.	Do supervisors monitor the use of terminals to prevent piggybacking?				Potential piggybacking of terminals should be immediately investigated by supervisors.	Execution
4.	Do supervisors periodically visit unattended terminals to ensure they are not open?				Supervisors should be instructed to look for terminals which might be susceptible to piggybacking.	Planning

THREAT: Unauthorized Access

PROBABLE IMPACT: Loss of Assets and Disclosure

RECOMMENDED PREVENTIVE CONTROL METHOD: Supervisory Surveillance

No.	Potential Vulnerability	Countermeasure Needed			Suggested Countermeasure	Crime Action Phase
		Yes	No	N/A		
1.	Do supervisors know which subordinate has access to which computer resources?				Supervisors should maintain records of subordinates' authorities.	Planning
2.	Are unauthorized accesses or access attempts in the general proximity of a supervisor's work station given to that supervisor for investigation?				Supervisors should be held accountable for overseeing access on hardware in close proximity to their work station.	Execution
3.	Do supervisors monitor the type of transactions that are occurring on computer devices in close proximity to their work station?				Supervisors should periodically review the work of their subordinates on computer facilities.	Planning

Fig. 10-5. Continued

THREAT: Careless Handling of Sensitive Data

PROBABLE IMPACT: Disclosure

RECOMMENDED PREVENTIVE CONTROL METHOD: Supervisory Surveillance

No.	Potential Vulnerability	Countermeasure Needed			Suggested Countermeasure	Crime Action Phase
		Yes	No	N/A		
1.	Is sensitive data stored in open locations?				Supervisors should continually look for sensitive data in easy-to-access locations.	Planning
2.	Is sensitive data stored at a subordinate's work station during nonworking hours?				Supervisors should periodically review the work stations of their subordinates to ensure that sensitive data is not left unattended during nonworking hours.	Execution
3.	Is sensitive data discarded intact?				Supervisors should periodically review trash receptacles to ensure that sensitive data is not left unattended during nonworking hours.	Execution
4.	Is sensitive data properly identified?				Supervisors should monitor employee work to ensure that they properly label and identify sensitive data.	Planning
5.	Are supervisors informed as to what sensitive data is in the possession of their subordinates?				Supervisors should maintain a log of sensitive data stored or in use in their work area.	Planning

THREAT: Inadequate Supervision During Nonworking Hour Shifts

PROBABLE IMPACT: Loss of Assets, Destruction of Media, Disclosure, and Disruption

RECOMMENDED PREVENTIVE CONTROL METHOD: Supervisory Surveillance

No.	Potential Vulnerability	Countermeasure Needed			Suggested Countermeasure	Crime Action Phase
		Yes	No	N/A		
1.	Are subordinates allowed to work alone during nonworking hours?				Supervisors should require subordinates to indicate when they will be at their work station during nonworking hours so appropriate supervision can be made during those times.	Planning
2.	Do subordinates have a logical reason to be at their work station during nonworking hours?				Records should be maintained of who is at their work station during nonworking hours so that the purpose for the work can be determined.	Execution
3.	Is extensive nonpaid overtime investigated?				When employess spend extensive time at their work station during nonworking hours, the purposes for this work should be investigated.	Execution
4.	Are copy machines or copy devices operational without supervision?				Copy devices should be locked when they are not supervised.	Execution

Fig. 10-5. Continued

THREAT: Output Routed to Wrong Individual

PROBABLE IMPACT: Disclosure

RECOMMENDED PREVENTIVE CONTROL METHOD: Supervisory Surveillance

No.	Potential Vulnerability	Countermeasure Needed			Suggested Countermeasure	Crime Action Phase
		Yes	No	N/A		
1.	Is the recipient of output reports indicated on the report?				Procedures should be invoked to ensure that the name of the recipient appears on the first page of all reports.	Planning
2.	Are sensitive reports left unattended?				Reports containing sensitive information should either be locked or in someone's possession at all times.	Planning
3.	Are recipients of reports instructed to call operations if reports do not arrive at the expected time?				Supervisors should instruct recipients of reports to call operations if the reports do not arrive when expected.	Execution
4.	Are recipients receiving the wrong report instructed to call supervision and report the incident?				Supervisors should investigate and take appropriate action when a report is delivered to the wrong individual.	Execution

THREAT: Unauthorized Acts at Remote Terminals

PROBABLE IMPACT: Loss of Assets

RECOMMENDED PREVENTIVE CONTROL METHOD: Supervisory Surveillance

No.	Potential Vulnerability	Countermeasure Needed			Suggested Countermeasure	Crime Action Phase
		Yes	No	N/A		
1.	Do supervisors monitor the acts performed at terminals in close proximity to their work station?				Supervisors should understand what acts should be performed at terminals in close proximity to their work station and then verify that only those authorized acts are performed.	Execution
2.	Do supervisors challenge users of terminals they do not know?				Supervisors should be instructed to challenge an individual's right to use a terminal unless they know that individual.	Execution
3.	Does the audit trail of terminal activities indicate at which terminal acts occur?				Supervisors should be informed of questionable acts performed at terminals in close proximity to their work station so that supervisors can be alert to identifying those conditions as they occur.	Planning
4.	Does the system predetermine what acts are authorized at each terminal?				Terminals should be restricted to certain acts, and if other acts are attempted, they should be denied.	Planning

Fig. 10-5. Continued

THREAT: Unauthorized Takeover

PROBABLE IMPACT: Loss of Assets and Disclosure

RECOMMENDED PREVENTIVE CONTROL METHOD: Supervisory Surveillance

No.	Potential Vulnerability	Countermeasure Needed			Suggested Countermeasure	Crime Action Phase
		Yes	No	N/A		
1.	Are subordinates allowed to bring their own processing equipment to their work station?				Supervisors should not permit subordinates to bring electronic processing equipment (other than hand-held calculators) to their work station.	Planning
2.	Do supervisors prevent subordinates from hooking electronic equipment into communication capabilities?				Organization communication facilities should be restricted to organizational equipment.	Planning
3.	As part of their responsibility, do supervisors maintain logs on work that occurs?				Supervisors should maintain logs of computer processing in order to monitor both time usage and functions performed.	Execution
4.	Is the amount of computer usage charged to a supervisor reconciled to manually maintained records in order to verify the correctness of those charges?				Supervisors should maintain sufficient records so that they can substantiate the accuracy and time charges, and investigate differences.	Execution

Index